DRAMA IN REAL LIFE®

Reader's Digest Paperbacks

Informative. . . . .Entertaining. . . . .Essential. . . . .

Berkley, one of America's leading paperback publishers,
is proud to present this special series of the best-loved
articles, stories and features from America's most trusted
magazine. Each is a one-volume library on a popular and
important subject. And each is selected, edited and endorsed
by the Editors of Reader's Digest themselves! Watch for
these others . . .

THE LIVING WORLD OF NATURE
UNFORGETTABLE CHARACTERS
WORD POWER

Berkley/Reader's Digest Books

THE EDITORS OF *READER'S DIGEST*

DRAMA IN REAL LIFE®

A BERKLEY/READER'S DIGEST BOOK
published by
BERKLEY BOOKS, NEW YORK

DRAMA IN REAL LIFE®

A Berkley/Reader's Digest Book, published by arrangement with Reader's Digest Press

PRINTING HISTORY
Berkley/Reader's Digest edition/November 1980

ISBN: 0-425-04723-7

A Berkley Book® TM 757,375
PRINTED IN THE UNITED STATES OF AMERICA

Acknowledgments

Grateful acknowledgment is made to the following organizations and individuals for permission to reprint material from the indicated sources:

The Atlantic Monthly (December 1976) for "Notes While Being Hijacked" by Richard Brockman, copyright © 1976 by The Atlantic Monthly Co.; *Argosy* (March 1971) for "One of the Comrades is Missing" by Ken Agnew, copyright © 1971 by Popular Publications, Inc.; *Gourmet* (December 1978) for "An Evening at the Waldorf" by Jean and Bud Ince, copyright © 1978 by Gourmet, Inc.; Mrs. June Mellies Reno and Mr. Jhan Robbins for "I Hit and Ran"; *The Washington Post Potomac* (February 26, 1967) for "Abortion: One Girl's Story" by Vivian Yudkin, copyright © 1967 by The Washington Post Co.; Elsevier-Dutton Publishing Co., Inc. for "A Bullet From Nowhere" adapted from CHIEF!: CLASSIC CASES FROM THE FILES OF THE CHIEF OF DETECTIVES by Albert A. Seedman and Peter Hellman, copyright © 1974 by Albert A. Seedman and Peter Hellman. Reprinted by permission of the publisher, E. P. Dutton; *Yankee Magazine* (November 1976) for "If We Stay Here, We'll Die . . ." by Franklin R. Jones, copyright © 1976 by Yankee, Inc.; *New York Magazine* (September 27, 1976) for "I Catch a Burglar" by John Berendt, copyright © 1976 by NYM Corp. Mr. Fulton Oursler, Jr. for "The Undelivered Letter" and "A Will of Her Own" by Fulton Oursler; *Medical Economics* (November 1, 1976) for "Rescue From a Fanatic Cult" by Charles H. Edwards, M.D., copyright © 1976 by Medical Economics Co.; *Family Weekly* (September 29, 1959) for "Ordeal in the Desert" by Evan Wylie, copyright © 1959 by Family Weekly; *Guideposts* (January 1966) for "Could You Have Loved As Much?" by Bob Considine, copyright © 1966 by Guideposts Associates, Inc.; *Des Moines Sunday Register* (November 13, 1949) for "Teen-Agers' Rendezvous with Death" by George Mills, copyright © 1980, Des Moines Register & Tribune Co.; Macmillan Publishing Co., Inc. for "The Milk Run" condensed from TALES OF THE SOUTH PACIFIC by James A. Michener. Used by permission of Mac-

Contents

"A Man Don't Know What He Can Do"

by Elise Miller Davis

Just before midnight Roy Gaby, driving for a Houston, Texas, trucking company, ran out of gasoline while returning from Waco in a heavy 14-wheel truck-trailer. From a house nearby he telephoned his wife, "SOS, honey, I'm out of gas." Mrs. Gaby sighed, bundled up the baby and set out to the rescue in the family car. It was February 18, 1952.

On the way home Mrs. Gaby drove ahead of Roy. About ten miles from Houston a speeding car, with an apparently drunken driver who never stopped, darted out of a side road, forcing Mrs. Gaby's car off the highway on the right. In the rear-view mirror she caught a glimpse of Roy's truck swerving to avoid a collision. Then she heard a crash.

The engine had smashed into a mammoth oak tree, the trailer had piled up on the cab and Roy was trapped in the twisted debris.

A passing motorist rushed into the village of Fairbanks and notified Deputy Sheriff Don Henry.

Henry decided to try "untelescoping" the wreck. "We attached a wrecker to the front of the mashed-in engine, hoping to pull it straight enough to get Gaby out. But the idea didn't work. We added the power of a truck at the front of the wrecker. Finally, two more trucks were attached to the rear, and they pulled in the opposite direction. But still, no soap."

Small flames appeared beneath the truck, and there was no extinguisher at hand. Halting passing drivers, Henry set helpers

1

to working frantically at the crumpled doors with hammers and crowbars. The twisted doors refused to budge. Henry crawled onto the hood of the cab and turned his flashlight on the victim. The steering wheel was crushed against Gaby's waist and his feet were pinned between twisted brake and clutch pedals. Tiny flames were licking at his feet.

"I'm an accident investigator," Henry told me later, "and I've seen a lot of terrible sights. But I've never seen one more terrible and I've never felt more helpless. I looked at Mrs. Gaby and the baby, then back at the poor guy in the burning cab, and I felt like praying for a miracle."

At that moment, a husky black man appeared out of the darkness.

"Can I help?" he asked quietly. Henry shook his head. Nobody could help if three trucks and a wrecker couldn't budge that cab, and by the time cutting torchers and fire apparatus arrived it was going to be just too bad. The stranger calmly walked over to the cab, put his hands on the door and *wrenched it off!*

Speechless, the crowd watched him reach in the cab and tear out the burning floor mat. Then he put out the flames around Gaby's legs—with his bare hands.

"It was just about then that I caught a glimpse of the big fellow's face," said one of the witnesses. "At first I thought he was in a trance. Then I saw that set expression for what it was—cold, calculated fury. I'd seen it before—at Pearl Harbor, on Okinawa. I remember thinking: *Why, that guy's not calm, he's enraged.* It was just as if he despised fire."

Swiftly, almost as if rehearsed, the black man worked on, poking large arms into the truck cab. "He straightened that steering wheel like it was tin," the driver of the wrecker said. "With his left hand on the brake pedal and his right on the clutch, he all but uprooted the whole works to free Gaby's feet."

But the crucial job wasn't done. The victim still lay encased in what witnesses called "a squashed sardine can over a bonfire."

Patiently, then stubbornly, the big man struggled to squeeze in beside Gaby. The space was too tiny. Stepping back from the cab, he hesitated fleetingly. The flames were growing. He glared at them, slumped to a squatting position and began pushing into the cab, fighting crazily. At long last he was in far enough to rest his feet firmly on the floorboard. He started rising slowly. His muscles bulged in the half-light and the sleeves of his shirt tore.

"My God, he's trying to push up the top!" a woman's voice called.

Neck and shoulders against the caved-in cab roof, he pushed. Hard.

"We actually heard the metal give," reported a farmer who had come to the scene. Discussing the rescue afterwards, Deputy Henry shook his head, still baffled. "And he held that top up until we could pull Gaby out."

In the excitement of attending Gaby, no one thought to thank the stranger or even ask his name. Later, at the hospital with Gaby, Deputy Henry told newsmen: "The mysterious Samson disappeared as quietly as he'd come. If I hadn't witnessed it I'd never believe a lone man could do a job we couldn't do with three trucks and a wrecker."

"I wish I knew his name," put in Mrs. Gaby. "He was a giant."

No giant, 33-year-old Charles Dennis Jones was in fact six-feet-two inches tall and weighted 220 pounds. He'd been out to nearby Hempstead to change tires on a disabled truck when he came upon the accident. By morning the whole city of Houston was wondering about his identity. Newspapers throughout the country carried the story. But Jones didn't tell even his wife about his experience. His boss, C. C. Myers, became suspicious, however, when he noticed the big fellow walk away from a group of employes who were discussing the amazing rescue. Remembering the mission he'd sent Jones on the night before, Myers grabbed a photograph from company files and headed for the sheriff's office. "Yes, that's him," agreed Deputy Henry.

And Myers knew immediately how Charlie Jones found the strength to lick that fire.

One December night 14 months before, Jones had come home to the three-room house where he lived with his wife, Mildred, and their five small children. Under one arm he carried a tiny pine tree and a single string of Christmas lights.

They'd had a lot of bad luck that year. Only two months before both his mother and Mildred's had died within a week, leaving grief, doctor bills, funeral expenses. But Evelyn Carol, his eight-year-old first-born, wanted some *real* Christmas-tree lights and he had them. He'd manage. He was healthy and husky and could stand a 16-hour day. Double work meant double pay. And they had a roof over their heads. Paid for.

Mildred left for church, where she was singing that evening. Jones tucked in the children. As he undressed, he wondered if he should risk leaving the tree lights on. He decided he would. Evelyn Carol wanted to surprise her mother and he'd promised. He fell asleep.

Mildred's pillow was still untouched when Jones awoke, sure he was having a nightmare. There was a burning in his nostrils, a crackling sound in his ears. He heard a child's cry: "Daddy!" Instantly he was on his feet, awake in a world on fire, pushing through choking waves of smoke, grabbing small bodies until he counted five, finding his way to the open window, pitching the children out.

People gathered. And Mildred came running through the darkness, crying his name. Then Jones heard a man's voice, maybe his own: "No, no—Evelyn Carol, come back, come back!" A child's answer: "But I must get my Christmas lights!" And like a fleeting spirit Evelyn Carol in a little white nightgown ran back toward the flames.

Later a neighbor told how the men couldn't hold Jones. How he'd raced after his child but hadn't reached her because just as he neared the dwelling its last remains exploded. How the blast had thrown Jones to the ground unconscious, and he'd been dragged out of danger.

The next morning, for the first time in ten years, Charles Dennis Jones failed to report to work at Robertson Transport. Everybody there had heard. When a man loses a child and his home, has four children to support and another one on the way, what can other men do?

Before nine o'clock a paper was circulating—from workshops to offices to yards. By noon it bore the names of 84 Robertson employees, and was sealed in an envelope and delivered to Charlie Jones. In the envelope Jones found $765.50.

The following day friends at Hughes Tool Co., where Mildred had formerly worked, sent in $80. By mail, from strangers, came $16. There were countless offers: Can you use a refrigerator? An army cot? A boy's coat, size 6? It seemed everyone had united to help the Jones family. And before long Charlie began to work on a new home. He figured that before the new baby came he'd have his family back under their own roof.

You could understand why he always would hate fire.

Reading a newspaper account of Jones's heroic rescue, R. A. Childers, a Houston businessman, wrote the papers, saying he would give $400 to start a fund providing an annual college scholarship for a black high school graduate. The rescue had taken place during Brotherhood Week. "Could anything be more characteristic of brotherhood than the fact that Jones walked away without waiting for thanks?" Childers asked.

And so it came about in the new house Charlie and Mildred and their children had built with their own hands that they received a group of citizens who informed them of the proposed Charles D. Jones Endowment Fund. Jones heard the committee's proposal in his faded blue overalls, eyes glazed by unshed tears. His wife stood beside him, his children huddled near. He didn't say a word.

Finally, Childers broke the silence. Somehow Charlie must give a statement to the press. There was the mystery he might yet clear up. How in the name of heaven had he managed to wrench off a steel door, beat out flames with his hands, raise with his own back the crushed-in top of a driver's cab?

Charlie Jones looked at Childers and at the hushed group around him. He cleared his throat and said, simply:

"A man don't know what he can do until another man is hurting."

Notes While Being Hijacked

by Richard Brockman

On September 10, 1976, five terrorists hijacked a Trans-World Airlines jetliner between New York and Chicago. Dr. Richard Brockman, a psychiatric resident at Columbia Presbyterian Medical Center in New York, was one of the passengers. During the ordeal, he wrote this account of his experience.

New York. LaGuardia. 6:45 p.m. Flight 355 for Chicago and Tucson. Long lines at the airport. Finally my ticket. Through security quickly. Aisle seat. Takeoff.

Have a drink. A blonde, about 23, keeps going back to the restrooms. Pretty. Good figure. Walks quickly, eyes straight.

"Ah . . . ladies and gentlemen, this is the captain speaking. Please don't be alarmed. This plane has been taken over by hijackers. We are now flying to Montreal, as they have demanded. Stay calm. Just do what they say, and they assure me no one will be hurt."

The blonde again. She goes to a large bearded man at the rear of the aisle, talks, then walks up front to a slender, oily-skinned man with beard and dark glasses. My first thought— it's all a game. But the man up front—a Palestinian? Damn. I have no religion. Or do I? I am a Jew. I am part of it.

The captain again: "Please stay calm. These people are armed. They threaten to blow us up if we do not obey them."

I introduce myself to the man beside me. Married, he tells me, two sons. President of a small manufacturing plant. We talk.

6

* * *

Montreal. Raining on a dark runway. Blonde drifts down the aisle smiling, uttering absurdities. "Do you have to use the bathroom? Thirsty? Can I get you something?" Blue eyes shining, hair turned up at the end. As if she hijacked the plane so she could play hostess. The oily-skinned one walks the aisle. Two sticks of dynamite taped to his chest, detonator in his hand.

The big one with the beard walks by. He's wearing a suit, right hand in the pocket bulging a gun. I take out a pen. I am ready to write my will.

"This is the captain speaking. We are going to Gander, Newfoundland. The hijackers have not told me of any further plans. The plane has been refueled, and we will be taking off within the next five minutes."

The jets roar, the plane moves. So far I have seen four hijackers: the blonde; the oily-skinned one—now in the cockpit; one in a black-leather jacket, sitting in the stewardess chair facing us, with a black pot in his lap, wired and fused; and last, the big one standing at the back of the plane like a simple shepherd. My seatmate tells me another one is sitting in the back cradling another bomb. Five altogether.

At 30,000 feet, everyone is calmer. The blonde and the shepherd tell us we'll be all right. Oily Skin emerges from the cockpit and walks down the aisle. Stops three or four seats in front of me. "We are going to give you papers to read. We have no intention of killing anybody. All we want is for our declaration to be published in the American press. We want the world to recognize the injustices against our people in Croatia."

Croatia! I knew they were not Irish, but I had feared they might be Palestinian.

Gander seems deserted. Hijackers move back and forth in the aisle, conferring. Finally the blonde says: "We are going to let 30 people off the plane here."

Twenty-five are picked on the usual basis: age, sex, infirmity. Another announcement from the blonde: "Do any of you feel you need to get off because of illness or other problems?" Several people raise their hands. A woman going to Chicago to get married. She can go. A husband and wife who are scared. No. A young man on his way to Chicago for an operation; he can go.

The hijackers have trouble finding the last few people to release. A priest is on board; asked if he wants to leave, he says he wants to stay. A middle-aged businessman is asked; he suggests they let the women leave first. Finally, 35 are chosen and begin to file out. I ask a man to call my home and tell them I am still alive.

We leave Gander past midnight. The sparse dots of light disappear, and we are over the ocean. It begins to settle in: I have been hijacked. Fall asleep.

The sun comes up over the ocean. Have I been awake the whole time, or asleep since the beginning? Stone cliffs from the sea. We land in Iceland, remain at the far end of the long runway. I can see figures in squad cars parked in the distance.

"Everybody stay where you are. Don't leave your seat." We stay for an hour or two or three. I grow more passive, more tired, more hungry. What time is it? Nine o'clock.

Finally we move. We are headed for Paris. We discuss how to behave: Treat the hijackers in a courteous manner, do what they say, don't ask too many questions—and try not to trip the one holding the bomb. The last instruction is the one I have the most difficulty with. I don't want to let them get away with it. I don't want to be led around the world like a good lamb and at the end of it all, when I expect to be freed, be gutted and hanged. How long are the knives in the galley? Can we kill all five of them at once? Are they crazy enough to blow us up in flight?

The hijackers circulate among the passengers. Someone discusses Croatia with the blonde. I can't believe it when the passenger challenges her political arguments. People are forgetting who they are. We enter French airspace. A French fighter plane escorts us now. "Pull the shade," the one in black leather screams as he hurries from window to window. The plane is silent except for its engines slowing us down into Paris. The ground comes quickly.

The plane taxis for at least ten minutes. Somehow I know that Paris is the end. Nothing happens for hours. The hijackers are no longer friendly, no longer smile.

Silence is finally broken. "This is the captain speaking. We have landed in Paris at Charles de Gaulle Airport. We are in radio contact with the authorities in France. I have confidence that the world understands the seriousness of our condition, and will agree to the demands of the hijackers. Please remain calm and do as you are told."

I go to the toilet up front and stand for a minute by the cockpit. The captain to Oily Skin: "Look, it's the French. Don't you understand, they are creating the problems. They weren't even going to let us land in Paris. They wanted us to fly to Rheims. A military base. They were just going to surround us with tanks and say, 'Surrender or we'll blow you up.' I had to tell them, 'Look, I have no choice. The hijackers tell me to land in Paris, and I have no choice.' And finally the French say okay."

I go back to my seat, and the priest goes to the cockpit. "My fellow passengers, my friends"—they've got him on the loudspeaker—"the negotiations are not going well. We must pray." (No, Father, I am not ready to pray.) "I know that not all of you are Catholics" (I am a Jew, Father), "but we must all of us come to terms with our God as best we know how. Ask him for forgiveness for our sins." (I have not sinned, damn it, I have not sinned.)

I don't believe what is happening. Write. Write to the people I love: It is becoming more and more likely that I won't be alive tomorrow. I am terrified. But I want to talk to you one last time. I love you all dearly. Please live your lives as happily as you can. You know I love you and you know how much I wanted to live. And be sad. But get over it, please. Don't mourn me.

I walk toward the cockpit, talk to a stewardess. The captain is on the radio: "Mr. Ambassador, you have lived your whole life for this moment. Now get it done, Mr. Ambassador." His voice is cracking.

Oily Skin storms out of the cockpit. "Everyone up. All of you. To the back of the plane. Get moving." We are pushed into a tighter and tighter bunch, 50 of us. "We have been good to you. We have been fair. And what happens? Nothing. Now it is time. If they don't meet our demands, we will blow you all up. Do you understand? They were supposed to have published our declaration in the papers, and they didn't. They do it for the PLO, but not for us. Well, we will show them. They better do it. Or you will pay for it. All of you."

My thoughts burn in my head, dry up, and die. There is no chance as far as I can see.

Three people are chosen to leave the plane: a passenger, the blonde, the copilot. There is hope. Negotiations are going better. They herd us again. But this time I am not worried. Even if they kill me, I am too tired to feel any difference.

The oily one emerges from the cockpit. Smiling. It is over. "Do not worry, my friends." Friends! If I had enough strength, I would spit. "Do not worry, my friends. They have granted our demands. You will be released." He smiles at us as if we have shared some joint cause, some union of purpose. Am I supposed to thank you? He smiles at me. I look away; he still has the dynamite taped to him. They tell us to sit down.

We are all relieved. I see smiles. Some tears. Some of the passengers thank the hijackers. For what? One of the passengers puts his arm around the shepherd. "You know, Petar"—the shepherd's name is Petar—"have you thought about going back to New York with us? You would get a fairer trial in America than from the French." What is he saying? Do I hear right? The lamb asking the wolf to share a meal?

The hijackers confer once again. Break up. The oily one back to the cockpit. Emerges. Smiling. "You see, my friends, we wanted the world to understand our cause, a cause of oppressed people. Now the world knows. I do not care what happens to me. They can kill me. Put me in jail for life. I don't care. The message is sent; I have done my work for my people.

"You are free to go now. You see, my friends, there is no dynamite. You see"—he unstraps the sticks from his chest, removes the black tape, pulls off a piece—"you see. Just clay, my friends. We never intended to hurt you. And the pots"— he removes the tape and opens one of the pots. "Just clay, my friends."

I close my eyes. Nothing is real. No one is threatened. I am six years old back in Brooklyn: It is cops and robbers. They had no guns. No dynamite. No danger. I must have been dreaming. Time to wake up. It is 8 a.m. in Paris. *Bonjour.*

"This is the captain speaking. We have all been through an incredible experience. But it is over for us. No one is hurt. However, it is not over for the hijackers. Their ordeal is just beginning. They have a cause. They are brave, committed people. Like the people who helped to shape our country. They are trying to do the same for theirs. I think we should give them a hand."

I look around. The hijackers are smiling. The audience is applauding. Stop clapping, you fools. Let me out of here.

I am on a runway, bag in hand. Other passengers are around me. The air feels good. Green grass beside the runway. Wind in my face. No press. No curious onlookers. A bus stops several hundred yards away. We walk to it. Get on. It drives us off the runway, past busloads of cops. Up to the hotel, then scores of pressmen, cameras, questions. Say nothing.

I find my seatmate in the lobby. We touch, hold on. Good to see you alive. Join me for breakfast? I am not sure who asks. Sit down at the counter. I order ham and eggs for both of us. The coffee smells good.

We Delivered Our Own Baby

by Gerald J. Miller
AS TOLD TO VIVIAN CADDEN

It all started, it will always seem to me, with the window screens. On ambition and secondhand furniture, we had moved into a house in Garrett Park, Md., in November, five months after Marge and I got married. We were trying to get the house fixed up before the baby came, and we thought we had plenty of time. The baby wasn't due before the end of March, 1959.

That night—it was February 15—Marge and I decided to sleep upstairs, since the window screens we'd finished painting were piled in our downstairs bedroom.

Somewhere around five in the morning Marge started to roam between the bed and the bathroom. I remember wishing sleepily that she would stop this dizzy round—up and clicking the light on, opening and closing doors, running the water and shutting it off, then back into bed. After one of these trips I mumbled, "What's the matter?"

"Nothing," she said. "I'm just restless and fidgety."

At 5:30 the lights switched on again, and Marge announced that as long as she couldn't sleep she was going downstairs to make some coffee. I struggled out of bed and followed her. "I keep feeling as if I have an upset stomach," she told me.

"I'm going to call the doctor," I said.

"At five-thirty in the morning?" she asked. "Don't be ridiculous."

She put the coffee on, then suddenly headed for the bath-

12

room again. "Maybe you *had* better call the doctor," she said
over her shoulder.

Marge had been to the doctor for her regular visit just a few
days before, and everything was in order. She is not the fragile,
complaining type. If she was making noises now, I thought,
we'd better find out what was wrong.

I dialed the doctor's exchange, and in a few minutes he
called back. In a patient, tired voice he said he thought he had
better speak to Marge. She explained her discomfort to him.

"Contractions?" he wanted to know.

"No, not contractions," Marge said. "There isn't really any
pain. I just feel very warm and the baby feels very heavy."

The doctor said, "Why don't you come on in to Georgetown
Hospital and we'll check you over?"

Marge told me to get her clothes from upstairs and a suitcase, which I did. I got my trousers on and gave Marge a hand
stepping into her dress because she seemed shaken and uncertain. In a moment she let the dress slip to the floor and fled
back to the bathroom. I heard her gasp, and when I flung the
door open she was propping herself up on the washstand and
there were tears in her eyes.

"It was a pain, Jerry—and I can *feel* the baby. I'm so hot
all over."

I wanted to lift her and carry her, but she waved me off
and said, "Jerry, call the doctor back!"

I called the doctor's exchange again. Then somehow, in a
wild frenzy, waiting for the phone to ring back, I took the
sweeper out of the closet and vigorously vacuumed the rug.
I'll never know why. Just before the phone rang, Marge called
from the downstairs bedroom, "It's too late."

Then the doctor was on the phone. "Get the rescue squad
to bring her to the hospital," he said. (The rescue squad is the
ambulance and emergency service run by the fire department.)

I dialed the operator and asked her to send the rescue squad.
Then I ran to the bedroom.

Marge was lying uncovered on the bed. Our Irish setter was
curled up by the pile of screens on the floor, motionless but
whining in sympathy. As I came through the door Marge was
tossing and murmuring, "I'm so hot, so hot," and then she
stiffened and gasped, "Jerry, the baby's coming!"

I saw him—the top of his head.

I ran to the closet and pulled out an armful of towels and

spread them under Marge as best I could. Then I ran to the bathroom and wet a washcloth and held it on her forehead. "Jerry, say a prayer that the baby will live," she cried.

I *was* praying—dear God, how I was praying! Marge said, "You'll have to help me, Jerry."

The head came out and then the shoulders, and the cord was wrapped around one shoulder. I pushed the cord aside without thinking, just feeling that it was in the way and might strangle him. I was pleading, "What should I do? What should I do?" and spreading more towels—and suddenly the baby was there.

His face was up. His ears were folded forward, two flaps against his head. His eyes were closed and he had no eyebrows or eyelashes. He was bluish white and covered with sticky fluid, and he lay deathly still on the towel. I had a moment of sickening fear and panic. And then I lifted the baby in my right hand and held him upside down. He opened his mouth and cried and moved his arms, and I knew I was crying too.

Marge could see, as I held him up, that it was a boy. But we had known all along that it would be.

I laid the baby down and vaguely thought: There are things I must do. But I was paralyzed with fascination. The baby was so small and he had no fingernails or toenails—just the slightest rim and indentation where they would be. One of his ears had unfolded and I gently turned the other one back. His head was perfectly formed. He was my son and he was beautiful. I think I would have just knelt there absorbing this wonder if Marge, urgent and insistent, had not brought me back to my senses.

"Wipe his face, Jerry," she said.

I could not take my eyes off him, but I shuffled toward the bureau and managed to pull some tissues from the top drawer. Marge said, "No! Take the gloves." I found them—a pair of long white cotton gloves. With Marge giving directions I turned one glove inside out and wiped out the baby's mouth and his nose and his eyes.

Then I thought about the cord. I didn't know whether I had much time—whether I could wait or must tie it quickly. I took the shoelaces out of my shoes and laid them on the bed, then looked around for scissors. There must be a dozen pairs of scissors in our house but I could find only one, the pinking shears.

Back at the bedside, I looked at the baby and at the shoelaces and at the pinking shears in my hand and I couldn't bring myself to do anything, although Marge was encouraging me.

At this point the doorbell rang. It was the rescue squad, two men in black slickers and shiny white firemen's helmets. In their first-aid kit was a pair of clamps that looked like candle snuffers. The older fireman clamped the cord in two places and with fine, old-fashioned courtesy handed me a splendid pair of straight scissors with which to cut the cord. I found a fresh towel, wrapped the baby in it. Both the firemen offered to take him but I said, "No!" and Marge turned her head to look at me and smiled—her first smile since she had come down to put the coffee on just an hour before.

The firemen lifted Marge onto a tremendous aluminum stretcher and carried her out to the ambulance. As far as I was concerned, riding in the ambulance with the baby kicking and wiggling in my arms, the emergency was over.

At ten minutes past seven that morning Marge was sitting up in a hospital bed eating cereal and poached eggs, the baby was in an incubator and the doctor had pronounced them both fine. At longlast I was where a father belongs—in a hospital corridor with all the doors closed against me. Only later would the thought of all the unknown dangers, the mistakes I could have made or perhaps did make, hit me and make me break out in a sweat. At that moment I was living on elation. I had actually delivered our own baby, and I was the proudest man in the world!

Attacked by a Killer Shark!

by Rodney Fox

Kay looked quite miserable standing there as I said good-by at 6:30 that Sunday morning. She was expecting our first child, and the doctor had told her firmly: don't go.

I wish now the doctor's advice had applied to me as well. Two hours later, however, found me standing on the cliff at Aldinga Beach—34 miles south of our home in Adelaide, South Australia. This was why I had set out so early. Now I had time to study carefully the dark patterns of bottom growth on the coral reef that shelves to seaward under the incoming blue-green swells.

Aldinga reef is a watery paradise, a teeming sea jungle, a happy hunting ground for underwater spearfishermen like myself. Forty of us—each in black rubber suit and flippers, glass-windowed face mask, snorkel, lead-weighted belt and spearfishing gun—were waiting for the referee's nine-o'clock whistle to announce that the annual South Australian Skin-Diving and Spearfishing Championship competition had begun. Each of us would have five hours to bring in to the judges the biggest bag, reckoned both by total weight and by number of different species of fish.

My own chances looked good. I had taken the 1961-62 championship and I had been runner-up the next season. I had promised Kay that this competition in December 1963 would be my last. I meant to clinch the title and then retire in glory, diving thenceforth only for fun, when Kay and I both might want to. I was 23 and, after months of training, at the peak of form. We were "free divers," you understand, with no artificial breathing aids. I had trained myself to dive safely to 100 feet and to hold my breath for more than a minute without discomfort. At the nine-o'clock whistle blast we waded into the surf.

Each man towed behind him, by a light line tied to his lead-weight belt, a buoyant, hollow fish float. We would load our fish into these floats immediately on spearing them. This would minimize the amount of fresh blood released in the water. Blood might attract from out beyond the reef the big hunting fish—the always hungry and curious great predatory sharks that prowl the deeper water off the South Australian coast. Lesser sharks—like the bronze whaler and gray nurse—are familiar to skin divers and have not proved aggressive. Fortunately the dread white hunter, or "white death" sharks, caught by professional fisherman in the open ocean, are rarely seen by skin divers. But as a precaution two high-powered patrol boats crisscrossed our hunting area keeping a wary lookout.

The weather was bright and hot. An offshore breeze flattened the green wave tops, but it roiled the water on the reef. Visibility under the surface would be poor. This makes it difficult for spearfishermen. In murky water a diver often gets too close to a fish before he realizes it's there; thus he scares it away before he can get set for a shot.

By 12:30, when I towed to shore a heavy catch of parrot fish, snapper, snook, boarfish and magpie perch, I could see from the other piles that I must be well up in the competition. I had 60 pounds of fish on shore, comprising 14 species. It was now 12:35, and the contest closed at two. As fish naturally grew scarcer in the inshore areas I had ranged out to three quarters of a mile for bigger and better game. On my last swim-in from the "dropoff" section of the reef, where it plunges from 25-foot to 60-foot depth, I had spotted quite a few large fish near a big, triangular-shaped rock which I felt sure I could find again.

Two of these fish were dusky morwongs—or "strongfish," as we Australian skin divers usually call them. Either of these would be large enough to tip the scales in my favor; then one more fish of another variety would sew things up for me, I decided. I swam out to the spot I'd picked, then rested face down, breathing through my snorkel as I studied through my face glass the best approach to the two fish sheltering behind the rock. After several deep breaths I held one, swallowed to lock it in, upended and dived.

Swimming down and forward so as not to "spook" them, I rounded the large rock and thrilled to see my quarry. Not 30 feet away the larger dusky morwong, a beauty of at least 20 pounds, was browsing in a clump of brown weed.

I glided forward, hoping for a close-in shot. I stretched both hands out in front of me, my left for balance, my right holding the gun, which was loaded with a stainless-steel shaft and barb. I drifted easily over the short weed and should have lined up for a perfect head-and-gill shot, but...

How can I describe the sudden silence? It was a perceptible *hush*, even in that quiet world, a motionlessness that was somehow communicable deep below the surface of the sea. Then something huge hit me with tremendous force on my left side and heaved me through the water. I was dumbfounded.

Now the "thing" was pushing me through the water with wild speed. I felt a bewildering sensation of nausea. The pressure on my back and chest was immense. A queer "cushiony" feeling ran down my right side, as if my insides on my left were being squeezed over to my right side. I had lost my face mask and I could not see in the blur. My speargun was knocked violently out of my hand.

The pressure on my body seemed actually to be choking me. I did not understand what was happening. I tried to shake myself loose but found that my body was clamped as if in a vise. With awful revulsion my mind came into focus, and I realized my predicament: *a shark had me in his jaws.*

I could not see the creature but it had to be a huge one. Its teeth had closed around my chest and back, with my left shoulder forced into its throat. I was being thrust face down ahead of it as we raced through the water.

Although dazed with the horror, I still felt no pain. In fact, there was no sharp feeling at all except for the crushing pressure on my back and chest. I stretched my arms out behind and groped for the monster's head, hoping to gouge its eyes.

Suddenly, miraculously, the pressure was gone from my chest. The creature had relaxed its jaws. I thrust backward to push myself away—but my right arm went straight into the shark's mouth.

Now I felt pain such as I had never imagined. Blinding bursts of agony made every part of my body scream in torment.

As I wrenched my arm loose from the shark's jagged teeth, all-encompassing waves of pain swept through me. But I had succeeded in freeing myself.

I thrashed and kicked my way to the surface, thudding repeatedly into the shark's body. Finally my head pushed above water and I gulped great gasps of air.

I knew the shark would come up for me. A fin brushed my flippers and then my knees suddenly touched its rough side. I grabbed with both arms, wrapping my legs and arms around the monster, hoping wildly that this maneuver would keep me out of his jaws. Somehow I gulped a great breath.

We went down deep again—I scraped the rocks on the bottom. Now I was shaken violently from side to side. I pushed away with all my remaining strength. I had to get back to the surface.

Once again I could breathe. But all around, the water was crimson with blood—my blood. The shark breached the surface a few feet away and turned over on its side. Its hideous body was like a great rolling tree trunk, but rust-colored, with huge pectoral fins. The great conical head belonged unmistakably to a white hunter. Here was the white death itself!

It began moving toward me. Indescribable terror surged through my body. One tiny fragment of the ultimate horror was the fact that this fearful monster, this scavenger of the sea, was my master. I was alone in its domain; here the shark made the rules. I was no longer an Adelaide insurance salesman. I was simply a squirming something-to-eat, to be forgotten even before it was digested.

I knew the shark was attacking again and that I would die in agony when it struck. I could only wait. I breathed a hurried little prayer for Kay and the baby.

Then, unbelievingly, I saw the creature veer away just before it reached me, the slanted dorsal fin curving off, just above the surface! Then my fish float began moving rapidly across the water.

The slack line tightened at my belt, and I was being pulled forward and under the water again. At the last instant the shark had snatched the float instead of me and had fouled itself somehow in the line. I tried to release my weight-belt to which the line was attached, but my arms would not obey. We were moving very fast now and had traveled under water 30 or 40 feet, my left hand still fumbling helplessly at the release catch.

Surely I'm not going to drown now rushed through my mind. Then the final miracle occurred: the line parted suddenly and I was free once more. They tell me that all I could scream when my head reached the surface was: "Shark!... Shark!" It was enough.

Now there were voices, familiar noises, then the boatful of friends I'd been praying would come. I gave up trying to move and relied on them to help me. In this new world of people, somebody kept saying, "Hang on, mate, it's over. Hang on." Over and over. I think without that voice out there I would have died.

The men in the patrol boat were horrified at the extent of my injuries. My right hand and arm were so badly slashed that the bones lay bare in several places. My chest, back, left shoulder and side were deeply gashed. Great pieces of flesh had been torn aside, exposing the rib cage, lungs and upper stomach.

Police manning the highway intersections for 34 miles got our ambulance through in record time. The surgeons at Royal Adelaide Hospital were scrubbed and ready, the operating table felt warm and cozy, the huge silver light overhead grew dimmer... until late that night or early next morning I opened my eyes and saw Kay alongside my bed.

I said, "It hurts," and she was crying. The doctor walked over and said, "He'll make it now."

Today my lungs work well, although my chest is still stiff. My right hand isn't a pretty sight, but I can use it. My chest, back, abdomen and shoulder are badly scarred.

God knows I didn't want to, but Kay realized right from the start that I had to go skin diving again. A man's only half a man if fear ties him up. Five months after I recovered, I returned to the sea to leave my fears where I had found them.

But my skin diving is different nowadays. I've got my confidence back, but with it came prudence. You can't count on getting through a second round with a shark; anyhow, there are plenty of risks you have to take in this world without going out of your way to add needless ones.

So now I stay away from competition, and leave the murky water to the daredevils who've never felt a shark's jaws around their chest.

A Message From Beyond

by Wilma Yeo

It was a chance meeting and a strange one—the strangest I have ever experienced. Though it may sound unbelievable, this account of what happened on that late summer afternoon in Indiana is absolutely true. The other person involved will vouch for it.

My husband and our 15-year-old twin daughters had remained at home in Kansas City, Mo., while I went with a group of friends to the annual writers' conference at Indiana University in Bloomington. I had misgivings about leaving my family for eight days, even though they assured me over and over they were looking forward to a chance to run things themselves—"with Mom out of the way."

I didn't give much thought to the uneasiness I felt because I am always an unwilling traveler, homesick for familiar surroundings. I was certain that once I became involved in the conference workshops and lectures my uneasiness would disappear.

We were quartered in the Indiana Memorial Union, a building big enough to provide both meeting rooms and housing for the 125 conferees. We were all writers who had been admitted on the merits of previously submitted manuscripts. These manuscripts had been judged by workshop leaders, who would then set up an individual consultation for each of the writers. We neophytes looked forward eagerly to these half-hour private conferences with well-established, often famous, authors.

The manuscript I had sent was my first juvenile novel.

Although I had already sold one picture book, I was nonetheless quivering with expectancy as the time drew near for my person-to-person consultation with the juvenile-workshop leader. It was scheduled for five o'clock that first day, in her room on the third floor.

My last workshop ended at three. Feeling restless, I went up to my second-floor room, changed clothes and rearranged the stack of books, notebooks and paraphernalia typically carried by all conference members. I chalked up my feeling of nerves to the forthcoming interview. Though I usually enjoy being alone, I now felt an increasing need to be with other people.

In hope of finding some of my friends, I went down to the main lobby, where writers gathered to talk shop. No one I knew was there, so I introduced myself to another woman and talked with her until five minutes before five. Then I told her I was off to my conference, and headed for the stairway.

When I found the correct room, I knocked rather timidly. I felt awed by the prestigious accomplishments of the author within. What would she say about my writing? The door opened so quickly I had the fleeting thought her hand may have been on the knob.

I introduced myself and noticed that she looked distressed. I decided she had had a trying day; workshop leaders are constantly besieged by lesser-known writers seeking advice.

"You are on time," she said. I glanced at my watch. It was exactly five o'clock. She motioned me toward one of the two comfortable chairs in the room. I took it, aware that she was no more at ease than I.

She did not sit down, but paced about as if trying to escape something. She moved toward the desk and picked up the manuscript I had mailed in earlier. Then she dropped it as if it were too weighty to hold.

Her next words left me even more puzzled. "I don't know what to say to you!"

My expectations plunged, but I gave an embarrassed laugh and said, "Well, if it's that bad, I can take it. I have other—"

"It's not that," she interrupted. "It's very hard to speak to you." She backed away a step. "Perhaps another time." Her face had grown pale and she made a futile attempt at a smile.

I could only assume she was ill. "Can I help you?" I asked.

"I don't know," she said in a weak voice. She repeated, "I really don't know what to say to you."

It *must* be my manuscript that has upset her, I thought. It must be very bad, and she's struggling against a charitable nature to be honest and tell me so.

Yet I *knew* it wasn't that bad. I was totally perplexed. I had talked earlier with another writer who had already received her critique from this same leader. Though the criticism had been fairly severe, the neophyte writer had reported no such experience as this.

"Please don't worry about it," I found myself begging. "I've had lots of rejections. I can take—"

"Oh, please," she stopped me. "Let me talk with you another time."

"Of course," I said—rather stiffly, I'm afraid. By now I was so upset that I felt I must look as miserable as she did.

I murmured good-by and hurried from her room with my stomach churning. Going down the steps, I searched for a face-saving way to explain this disheartening experience to my friends, who I knew were eager to hear the outcome of my consultation. When I reached the door to my room, I dropped my armload of notebooks to the floor and went down on my knees to search through my large, cluttered bag for the room key. Before I found it, I heard footsteps on the stair and looked up.

It was the workshop leader. Her eyes widened as she saw me kneeling there. "Then it's you, not me," was her strange remark. She fled down the next flight of steps.

Once inside my room I decided to stay there and skip dinner, in order to avoid seeing anyone for a while. Immediately after the meal there was to be an all-member, all-staff meeting. By that time I would surely have pulled my chaotic thoughts together.

But later, in the auditorium, my cheeks were still burning at the thought of having to describe the episode. I was glad when I didn't see anyone I knew as I sat down.

The program had barely begun when someone touched me gently on the shoulder. It was a man from my group. His face was serious, but I assumed he was signaling me to join the other writers from Kansas City. I felt a little irritated, as I still wanted to nurse my misery alone.

I was surprised when he led me all the way out of the auditorium, and even more surprised to see my other friends awaiting me there.

From their expressions, I knew immediately something was terribly wrong. They told me, as gently as it is possible to tell anyone shocking news, that my husband was dead. He had been killed in a plane crash. I couldn't comprehend. Plane crash? Surely he had gone to his office that day!

It turned out he had had unexpected business to attend to in Texas, and had flown there on the company jet. During the return trip, the pilot had to make a crash landing in Arkansas. My husband was the only one killed. *It had happened at five o'clock.*

The next traumatic weeks are not a part of this story. And I did not think again of the conference or of my writing for a long time. Then, perhaps two months later, I received a letter. It was from the workshop leader. She expressed her sympathy, then wrote: *I feel I must tell you what happened to me that day at the Indiana conference. The minute you walked into my room I was almost overpowered by a sense of impending tragedy. The feeling grew stronger by the second, and I could not break through it—could not even speak through it.*

The same all-encompassing premonition of disaster had come to me one other time in my life. It was many years ago, when my own husband was killed in an accident at sea. I did not know if the unseen presence you seemed to bring into the room foretold tragedy again for me, or if it was for you. But I recognized it. I knew it was there for one of us.

I was frantic with the thought that something might have happened to someone in my family. As soon as you left, I started down the steps to the main desk to ask if there had been a message for me. When I reached the second floor and saw you kneeling in front of your door, I knew: My premonition— call it what you will—was for you.

I went on down to the desk anyway and called my home. Everything there was all right. Later, I heard what had happened to your husband. I felt I should write to you and explain.

I did not answer the woman's letter. I could not. What was there to say? Though the episode happened ten years ago, I can still see her frightened face, hear her stammering for a way to explain the unexplainable.

The manuscript that brought us together has since been published by Simon and Schuster, and I am again happily married. Time does indeed wear away the sawtooth edges of sudden death. But even time does not explain the phenomena that sometimes accompany it.

"Where There Is Love"

by Aletha Jane Lindstrom

We got him with the other animals when we bought the farm. Not that we wanted the black, shaggy mongrel. We had our hearts set on a collie—a pup we could train for the farm and as a companion for five-year-old Tim. But when the former owners failed to return for their dog, we resigned ourselves to keeping him. Temporarily, we thought.

"If we ignore him, maybe he'll just take off," I said to Carl, my schoolteacher husband. He didn't. In fact, the big beast apparently considered the farm *his* responsibility. Each dawn he inspected the animals and the farm buildings. Then he made a complete circuit of the entire 80 acres. That finished, he bounded across the sloping fields to slip beneath the fence for a visit with old Mr. Jolliff, who lived near a brook at the farm's edge.

The big dog—we learned from Mr. Jolliff that his name was Inky—was pensive and aloof those first weeks. Grieving for his former master, Inky asked no affection, and we offered none. Except Tim, who sat by the hour on the back steps, talking softly to the unresponsive animal. Then, one morning, Inky crept close and laid his head in the boy's lap. And before we knew it he had become Tim's second shadow.

All that summer boy and dog romped through fields and roamed the woods, discovering fox dens and groundhog burrows. Each day they brought back treasures to share. "Mom, we're home!" Tim would shout, holding the screen door wide for Inky. "Come see what we've got!" He'd dig deep in his jeans and spread the contents on the kitchen table: a pheasant's feather; wilted buttercups with petals like wet paint; stones from the brook that magically regained their colors when he licked them.

September arrived all too soon, bringing with it school for Carl and Tim, and lonely days for Inky and me. Previously, I'd paid little attention to the dog. Now he went with me to the mailbox, to the chicken coop, and down the lane when I visited Mr. Jolliff.

"Why didn't they come back for Inky?" I asked Mr. Jolliff one afternoon.

"And shut him up in a city apartment?" Mr. Jolliff replied. "Inky's a farm dog; he'd die in the city. Besides, you're lucky to have him."

Lucky? I thought ruefully of holes dug in the lawn, of freshly washed sheets ripped from the clothesline. I thought, too, of litter dumped on the back porch: old bones, discarded boots, long-dead rodents. And beer cans! Each morning on his way home from Mr. Jolliff's, Inky retrieved one can from the roadside and placed it neatly on the doorstep. He was noisy, too, challenging each truck and tractor on the road with loud barks that brought me running.

Still, I had to admit Inky was a good farm dog. We learned this in early spring when his insistent barking alerted us to a ewe, about to lamb, lying on her broad back in a furrow, unable to rise. Without Inky's warning she'd have died. And he had an uncanny way of knowing when roving dogs threatened the flock, or when a sheep went astray.

One morning, instead of a beer can Inky placed a starving gray kitten on the doorstep. He hovered anxiously while the fluffy mite lapped her fill of warm milk. Then he carried her to his blanket in the barn, licked her thoroughly and settled down beside her while she slept. From that day on she shared his bed.

But Inky's deepest affection was reserved for Tim. Each afternoon when the school bus lumbered down the road, Inky ran joyously to meet it. For Inky—and for Tim—this was the high point of the day.

One mid-October day when I had been in town, Tim rode home with me after school. He was instantly alarmed when Inky wasn't waiting for us by the driveway.

"Don't worry, Tim," I said. "Inky always expects you on the bus, and we're early. Maybe he's back by the woods."

Tim ran down the lane, calling and calling. While I waited for him to return, I looked around the yard. Its emptiness was eerie.

Suddenly I, too, was alarmed. With Tim close behind me, I ran down to the barn. We pushed the heavy doors apart and searched the dim coolness. Nothing. Then, as we were about to leave, a faint whimper came from the far corner of a horse stall. There we found him, swaying slightly on three legs, his pain-dulled eyes pleading for help. Even in the half-light I could see that one back leg hung limp, the bone partially severed. With a little moan, Tim ran to Inky and buried his face in the dog's neck.

By the time the vet arrived, Carl was home. We placed the dog on his blanket and gently lifted him into the pet ambulance. Inky whimpered, and Tim started to cry.

"Don't worry, son," the vet said. "He's got a good chance." But his eyes told a different story.

It was Tim's bedtime, so I took him upstairs and heard his prayers. He finished and looked up. "Will Inky be home tomorrow?"

"Not tomorrow, Tim. He's hurt pretty bad."

"You tell me doctors make people well. Doesn't that mean dogs, too?"

I looked out across the fields flooded with amber light. How do you tell a little boy his dog must either die, or be a cripple? "Yes, Tim," I said at last. "I guess that means dogs, too." I tucked in his blanket and went downstairs.

Carl had finished chores and was getting ready for a meeting at school. I tossed a sweater over my shoulders. "I'm going down to Mr. Jolliff's" I said. "Maybe he'll know what happened."

I found the old man sitting at his kitchen table in the fading light. He drew up another chair and poured coffee. "Tim in bed?" he asked. "I miss him now he's in school. Thank goodness Inky still comes to see me. Though come to think of it, he didn't show up this morning. I sort of worried about him."

Somehow I couldn't talk about the dog. Instead, I asked, "Do you know if anyone was cutting weeds around here today?"

"Seems to me I heard a tractor down along the brook this

morning," Mr. Jolliff replied. "Why?" He looked at me. "Did something happen to Inky?"

"Yes," I said, and the words were tight in my throat. "His back leg's nearly cut off. The vet came for him. . . ." I wanted to say more, but couldn't. "It's growing dark," I finally murmured. "I'd better be getting home."

Mr. Jolliff followed me into the yard. "About Inky," he said hesitantly. "If he lives, I'd give him a chance. He'll still have you folks and Tim, the farm and the animals. Everything he loves. Life's pretty precious . . . especially where there's love."

"Yes," I said, "but if he loses a leg, will love make up for being a cripple?"

He said something I didn't catch. But when I turned to him, he'd removed his glasses and was rubbing the back of his stiff old hand across his eyes.

By the time I reached our yard the sun was gone, leaving the world to the magic of cool, thin silver and shadow. I walked down by the barn and stood with my arms on the top fence rail. Beyond the lane the horses were moving toward the woods, grazing as they went. I watched until they vanished like phantoms in the moonlit mist brimming the meadow. Then I dropped my head to my arms and let the tears come.

I cried because Inky had been so gentle with the animals, and because he loved Tim so much and Tim loved him. But mostly I cried because I hadn't really wanted him; not until now, when this terrible thing happened. Why do we so seldom know how much we love something until we are faced with its loss?

Inky's paw couldn't be saved. Too vividly, I recalled how Inky had raced across fields and meadows, swift and free as a cloud shadow. I listened skeptically as the vet tried to reassure us: "He's young and strong. He'll get along on three legs."

Tim took the news with surprising calmness. "It's all right," he said. "Just so Inky comes home."

"But those long jaunts the two of you take may tire him now," I cautioned.

"He's always waited for me. I'll wait for him. Besides, we're never in much of a hurry."

The vet called a few days later. "You'd better come for

your dog. He's homesick." I went immediately, and was shocked at the change in Inky. The light was gone from his eyes. His tail hung limp and tattered, and the stump of his leg was swathed in a stained bandage. He hobbled over and pressed wearily against my leg. A shudder went through the hot, thin body and he sighed—a long, deep sigh filled with all the misery and loneliness of the past few days.

At the farm, I helped Inky from the car. The gray kitten came tumbling through the leaves, but Inky seemed unaware of her. He looked first to the sheep, grazing in the pasture; then beyond the fields of green winter wheat to the autumn woods where the horses, dappled with sunlight, moved among the trees. My heart ached as I realized how great must have been his longing for this place. At last, he limped to the barn and slipped between the heavy doors.

While his wound healed, Inky stayed in the barn, coming out only in the evenings. When the low sun slanted across the fields and the horses came up for water, we'd see him standing by the trough. After the horses returned to pasture, he disappeared into the barn.

Throughout those days, the sick feeling never left me. *You are a coward to let him live,* I told myself. *Afraid of hurting yourself, of hurting Tim.* But in my heart I wasn't sure. We so seldom know the real reasons for the things we do, or fail to do.

About a week after bringing Inky home, I was in the yard raking leaves. When I'd finished under the maple, I sat on the steps to rest. It was a perfect Indian summer day; our country road was a tunnel of gold, and sumac ran like a low flame along the south pasture. Reluctantly, I reached for the rake.

Then, with a flurry of leaves, Inky was beside me. I knelt and stroked the fur so smooth and shiny again. He moved, and I was achingly aware of the useless limb. "I'm so sorry, Inky," I said, putting my arms around his neck and pressing my head against his.

Sitting awkwardly, he placed his paw on my knee and looked up at me with soft, intelligent eyes. Then he pricked his ears and turned to listen. In an instant, he was off to meet the school bus. He ran with an ungainly, one-sided lope—but he ran with joy.

Tim jumped from the high step and caught the dog in his arms. "Oh, Inky! Inky!" he cried. Inky licked Tim's face and twisted and squirmed with delight. They remained there for a time, oblivious to anything but the ecstasy of being together again.

Watching them, I knew we'd been right to let the dog live. Most of us, God's creatures, are maimed to some extent either physically or emotionally, yet few of us want to die. What was it Mr. Jolliff had said?

"Life's pretty precious . . . especially when there's love."

"Beth's Been Kidnapped!"

by Donald Robinson

On Thanksgiving weekend in 1976, Elizabeth (Beth) Ferringer was visiting her parents at their isolated home near State College, Pa. Because of his job, her husband Michael had returned home early to Brookville, 81 miles away, so he was not there when, on Sunday evening, 23-year-old Beth's harsh ordeal began.

Nor was her father there. That evening, after a pleasant family dinner, Don Meyer had kissed his wife Susan and daughter Beth good-night, and left for the Autoport, a motel-restaurant he owned in town. At 11:10 p.m., Susan Meyer was chatting on the telephone. Suddenly the line went dead and the lights went out.

As the two women groped their way to the master bedroom for a kerosene lamp, there was a sound of shattering glass, then footsteps. Terrified, Beth and her mother pushed a chair against the bedroom door. Abruptly, the door was kicked in. A brawny man wearing a monster mask stood in the splintered entrance holding a pistol. Another masked gunman loomed behind him.

The men moved quickly. Forcing Susan Meyer to lie face-down on the floor, they tied her hands behind her back with nylon rope. "Don't call the police," they warned as they led Beth away, "or you'll never see your daughter alive again."

The kidnappers pulled a pillowcase over Beth's head, then forced her into the back of her mother's Oldsmobile and drove off.

Soon after she heard the kidnappers leave, Susan Meyer managed to wriggle out of her bonds. She jumped into Beth's car and drove madly to the home of the nearest neighbor, nearly a half mile away. At 12:15 a.m. Don Meyer was told he had an urgent call from his wife.

"Beth's been kidnapped!" Susan sobbed. "They said they'll kill her if you call the police."

Meyer was stunned. He paced the floor, weighing alternatives. Then he decided there was only one thing to do.

Senior resident agent Tom Dolan, who headed the FBI office in State College, was asleep when the phone rang at 12:30 a.m., November 29. But the frantic voice of his friend Don Meyer pulled him from his slumber. *My God*, Dolan thought, *Don's girl. I thought it only happened to strangers.*

The agent's first step was to request a telephone company "trap"—which can trace a call in seconds by computer—on Meyer's Autoport phone. Then he notified FBI divisional headquarters in Philadelphia. Neil Welch, special agent in charge, ordered 50 of his best agents to the scene. In 30 minutes he was on the road himself, driving the 195 miles to State College in sleet and snow.

At 2:25 a.m., Meyer's office phone rang. A male voice said in falsetto, "Do exactly what I say, or you'll never see your daughter alive again."

"What do you want?" Meyer asked.

"One hundred and fifty thousand dollars," the caller declared.

"Let me talk to Beth," Meyer begged.

"Impossible," the caller snapped, and hung up.

The call was traced to a phone booth on the outskirts of town.

An armed surveillance team was sent to watch the booth. But the only person to use it was a city policeman making a routine call to headquarters. Meanwhile, other FBI agents were converging on State College from their offices in Philadelphia, Harrisburg, Williamsport, Allentown and Scranton.

After a seemingly interminable drive, the Oldsmobile came to a stop. Beth was led into a musty building and down some stairs. A heavy chain was brutally cinched about her waist, it was attached to an overhead heating duct so tightly that she could scarcely move without pain. Near her feet were a roll of toilet paper, a jar of peanut butter, a moldy loaf of bread and a container of water.

"If everything goes our way," one of the men said, "we'll be back tonight."

Welch arrived at State College early Monday morning and began working out assignments. He posted agents to cover every major intersection, then told Ed Creasy, a 33-year-old FBI pilot, to go out to University Park Airport and rent a plane suitable for tailing. Creasy got a single-engined Cessna 150 with two seats.

The next call from the kidnappers came at 8:40 a.m. "Write this down," the falsetto voice told Meyer. "We want $25,000 in ten-dollar bills; $50,000 in twenties; $25,000 in fifties; and $50,000 in one hundreds. Put the money in an attaché case. We want used bills with no consecutive serial numbers." The caller also dirrected Don to install a citizens band (CB) radio in his car.

Minutes later, the telephone company rang back. The trap had traced the call to a pay phone in the HUB—the Hetzel Union Building—on the Penn State campus. It was a clever choice by the kidnappers, for they could easily get in and out of this crowded student center without attracting attention.

As daylight penetrated the blackness of the cellar, Beth managed to remove the pillowcase from her head and saw an unused furnace and a partly empty coal bin. She could also see what had been making the scurrying noises through the night: small rodents scampered about her feet. Her teeth chattered from the numbing cold, her feet ached. She could hear cows mooing somewhere outside, but no human voices.

At 12:45 p.m. the voice on the phone asked, "Do you have the money?"

"It took too long getting the CB," Don Meyer replied. "As soon as we're finished with this call, I'll go to the bank. Let me speak to Beth."

"No," the voice said. "I'll call you at 4 p.m."

The trap traced the call to another pay phone at the HUB. Welch now made one of the most crucial decisions of the case. He gambled that the kidnappers would make their next call from the HUB as well, and drew his plans accordingly.

While Meyer drove to the Peoples National Bank to put up his house and business as security for a $150,000 loan, Welch selected ten agents who could pass as students or young instructors. Special agent Dave Richter was in charge of the squad. Tall and blond, he looked ten years younger than his 33 years.

Singly and in pairs, the casually attired FBI men sauntered over to the HUB, where eight phone booths stood near the front entrance. Richter sent agents into the first, third, sixth and seventh booths. An agent would be in the next booth no matter which one the kidnapper chose.

Shortly after 4 p.m. a stocky man strode into the HUB and went straight into the vacant booth next to Richter. As the agent pretended to make his own call, his heart jumped. The man in the next booth was speaking in a falsetto voice.

"Go to the parking lot of the Bald Eagle Restaurant in Milesburg," the man instructed (Milesburg is 13 miles north of State College). "Turn on your overhead light and switch your CB to Channel 7."

Richter excitedly phoned the command post. "I have the guy. He's speaking to Don Meyer now. I'm going to tail him."

The man hung up, then walked casually to a brown late-model Pontiac in the HUB parking lot. By bizarre coincidence, it was parked next to Richter's car.

The Pontiac was registered to the Two Wheels Cycle Shop in State College. "Hold on!" exclaimed Ernest Neil, a local FBI man. "That's Gary Young's place." Gary R. Young, the 33-year-old owner of the motorcycle shop, and his 23-year-old brother, Kent, who worked for him, were not unknown to the police: they were awaiting sentencing on a recent conviction of aggravated assault and recklessly endangering another person.

The safe course for Welch would have been to pick up Gary Young and hope he talked. But Beth Ferringer's life was in danger. Welch decided to go through with the ransom payoff and hope Gary would lead them to his captive.

Daylight was fading. The kidnappers should be returning soon. Suddenly she heard a loud crash. "They've come back," she thought. But the noise had been caused by winds that blew in the boards covering a broken window. The inside temperature dropped, leaving Beth numb with cold, but she refused to give up hope.

* * *

Don Meyer drove to Milesburg, parked at the Bald Eagle and turned on his overhead light. The CB in the station wagon sounded: "Dome Light, do you read me?" Meyer said he did, and was ordered to drive to the Nittany Mall shopping center. As he drove, he switched off the overhead light—and the CB barked, "Turn that light back on." Meyer realized with a start that the kidnappers' car was right behind him. The light would keep him from glimpsing any faces.

As Meyer turned into Nittany Mall, the CB ordered: "Go back toward State College." The directions then came like machine-gun fire. Turn right on Puddintown Road. Take a left on Houserville Road. Proceed to Airport Road. The kidnappers were zigzagging, trying to shake off any followers. They didn't succeed. The surveillance squad—six unmarked cars, alternating as the tail—was on target.

Following orders, Meyer turned onto a narrow road that ran into the woods. It turned to dirt and meandered into a desolate, snow-covered cornfield. The kidnappers' car was nowhere in sight, but the voice on the CB crackled: "Leave the case."

Meyer opened the door and placed the attaché case in the middle of the road. Then he headed back toward State College.

The most critical time in any kidnapping is after the ransom has been dropped off. If the kidnappers suspect that the police are closing in, they may abandon the loot and kill the victim. Welch gambled again. He called off the surveillance squad and left it to Ed Creasy to follow the car from above.

In the meantime, agents Joseph McQuillan and Austin Hamilton, only three-eights of a mile from the scene, were ordered to cut through the heavy woods to a spot where they could observe the pickup. Their eye-witness testimony would be important to any prosecution. Almost a half hour passed. Then the Pontiac pulled up alongside the attaché case. Gary Young reached out, picked up the case and drove off.

At 6:30 p.m. Don Meyer returned to the Autoport. Suddenly, everything seemed to collapse. Gary Young telephoned in a wild rage. He'd spotted the plane. "You blew it! You got airplane surveillance on us," he screamed.

"What the hell are you talking about?" Meyer yelled back.

"There isn't any plane. You have the money. Please, tell me where Beth is!"

Gary subsided. "I'll call you in an hour," he said.

The kidnappers didn't call in an hour. Nor in two hours. "Please, God," Meyer prayed. "Let them call."

The Young brothers drove back to the motorcycle shop, stayed a while and drove out again. By 9 p.m. the FBI plane had been airborne more than four hours. It landed at 9:15 p.m., with two-tenths of a gallon of gas left in the tank.

Before they came down, Creasy signaled the auto-surveillance squad to resume the tail by flashing his lights—lights that Gary Young spotted. Panicked, Young phoned the airport. By sheer good luck, Creasy answered. When Young demanded to know if any policemen were flying, he answered, "Nope, just a student pilot with an instructor."

"But this plane kept turning its lights on and off," Young insisted.

Creasy reacted coolly: "The student probably grabbed the wrong buttons in the dark. Happens all the time."

Young fell for it. At 10 p.m. he telephoned the Autoport and told Don where to find Beth. "Take a hacksaw with you," he said.

As Welch ordered his surveillance teams to move in on the kidnappers—"But no arrests yet"—Beth's parents, her husband Mike and her father-in-law raced to free her. A string of FBI cars tore after them, and they all screeched to a halt near an abandoned farm house 23 miles from State College.

Ernest Neil and a state trooper broke down the cellar door and found Beth shivering on the dirt floor. The water the kidnappers had left her was frozen solid; the temperature was only two degrees above zero. *A few more hours,* Welch thought, *and she would have frozen to death.*

In tears, Beth grabbed Mike. Then her father and father-in-law were hugging her. In the cold outside, Beth's mother waited anxiously. Welch had refused to let her in. He didn't know what they would find.

An FBI agent sawed off Beth's chains. She had no feeling in her legs and could barely walk. Don and Mike quickly bundled her into the warm car. Soon Beth was safely back in her parents' home. The ordeal was over.

* * *

Gary Young was driving alone when FBI agents forced his car off the road and, guns drawn, arrested him. Five other agents hit Kent's apartment, and seized him in his bedroom. The next morning FBI agents found the ransom money hidden in an olive-drab laundry bag under six inches of insulation in Gary Young's attic.

To the FBI's deep regret, the kidnappers could not be prosecuted under federal law—which provides for life imprisonment—since neither brother crossed state lines in the commission of the crime. Both Youngs were sentenced to terms in the Pennsylvania State Correctional Institution. Gary received a ten-to-twenty-year sentence, Kent eight to twenty years.

Search for a Stranger

by Gordon S. Livingston, M.D.

The highly emotional events of that summer were triggered by the most prosaic of questions: a cousin I was visiting asked me how my work was going. I am a child psychiatrist in Columbia, Md., and I answered his question by telling him about a recent conference where I had headed a workshop on behavior difficulties in adopted children. It concluded that such children may experience a disproportionate number of emotional problems requiring professional help.

"One of the factors," I said, "may be the child's burden of 'dual identity,' made worse by the secrecy surrounding the adoption process. In all states but four, courts and social agencies are permitted to seal the records. When an adopted child tries to find out the truth and comes upon all this secrecy, he often concludes there is something shameful about him."

"But why do they need to know they're adopted?" my cousin asked.

"It's a very difficult secret to keep, and if a child learns of it from sources other than his parents, there can be psychological damage. Better that he knows the truth from the beginning." I cited case histories. And, as the father of four, I spoke of efforts to be truthful to Michael, our youngest, who is adopted.

My cousin shook his head in disbelief. "What would you do if you yourself were adopted?"

"Search for my natural parents," I said promptly.

"Well, start looking," he said.

At first I thought he was joking. When it became evident that he was not, it was as though some unseen fist had struck a blow to the pit of my stomach. I tried to compose myself, forcing deep, even breathing.

"You all right?" my cousin asked.

"I'm fine," I assured him. I was far from fine. I felt I had lost an important part of my identity. All the basic facts about myself that I had taken for granted were suddenly stripped away. If I was not Scotch-Irish, as I had supposed, what nationality was I? Raised as an only child, did I actually have brothers and sisters? Who were my natural parents? The alienation the adopted can feel when not prepared for the truth, and the need for a biologic identity, were no longer theories, abstractions: they were real problems—they were mine!

When I confronted my adoptive father late that night in 1976—Mother had died the year before—he looked crushed. "We never told you," he said, "because we were afraid you'd want to meet your real parents and we might lose you."

I put my hand on his arm. "You and Mom *are* my real parents. You loved me and raised me . . . and I love you. Nothing can change that."

He gave me a grateful though tremulous smile and said, "Well, if you feel you must search for them I'll help you all I can."

My birth cerfiticate listed me as being born in Memphis, Tenn., on June 30, 1938. Dad thought the birth date was correct but could not remember the name of the Memphis agency that had arranged the adoption. He and Mother lived in Detroit at the time and had gone to Memphis with friends named Martin who had also adopted a child. It was a thin lead, but after a dozen phone calls I traced the Martins to California and learned from them the agency was the Tennessee Children's Home Society.

There was no phone listing for such an agency, so I wrote to the Tennessee Department of Public Welfare and asked permission to see the records of the Tennessee Children's Home Society. The reply was brief: "The Tennessee adoption law prohibits the reopening of closed adoption records except upon an order from the court in which the adoption was granted."

I arranged with colleagues to care for my patients during my absence, then drove to the Laurel, Md., airport where I hangared my single-engine Cessna airplane. After takeoff I set a course toward Memphis 800 miles west-southwest. As I watched the highways and farms and rivers and cities stretch to the horizon, I realized how remote the chance was of finding my mother. In that vast land I sought a single person whose face I would not recognize, whose name I did not know.

There was no record of the Tennessee Children's Home Society in the Memphis city hall. I went to a local newspaper and asked to see their back issues. I almost wished I hadn't— for I discovered that in the fall of 1950, the Home had been put out of business by court order! The front-page story revealed the director had been selling children for high fees and pocketing the money. She had marketed the babies of unwed mothers, prostitutes, mental patients. I stared hard at the paper. In which of these categories was I?

The next day I engaged a local lawyer to help in the search. Twenty-four hours later he telephoned. "I found you in the Bureau of Vital Statistics," he said. "Your birth name was Donald Alfred Cardell. The sealed records are in the Memphis courthouse. We can try to get a look at them tomorrow." For the rest of that day and a good deal of the night I repeated the name over and over.

The next morning we had a stroke of luck—my lawyer knew the courthouse clerk and when he casually asked for the record of the adoption proceedings, an envelope was delivered to us. With trembling hands I removed a legal document and spread it before us. It was an adoption decree, headed "Probate Court of Shelby County, 17th day of August, 1940." My mother's name was Ann Simmons Cardell. Nothing about my father. The document stated that "The child is destitute and helpless," that "the father has abandoned the child." This could only mean that I was illegitimate. I felt a rush of sympathy for that unwanted child of so many years ago.

"I'd like a copy of my adoption decree," I said to the lawyer. The clerk, suddenly realizing my identity, grabbed the paper out of my hands. "Only the judge can give you permission to see this," she said sharply. But I had seen enough.

Armed with the name, my lawyer made the rounds of the hospitals and finally found a listing of my mother's admission. She was a schoolteacher from Mississippi.

Again I was in the air, heading south toward Jackson, the capital of Mississippi.

When I landed, I hired a car and asked directions to the Department of Education. But though I was given complete access to the files, at the end of a long day's work I had found no Ann Cardell in the listings of teachers. Discouraged, I started to leave the dusty stacks when I noticed an old filing case marked "Academic Records." I opened it and found yellowed manila folders, one of which carried the neatly lettered words, Ann Simmons Cardell. It revealed that my mother had received a master's degree in education in 1952, and gave the name of the college where she had earned it.

From a phone booth I called the college's alumni office and asked if Ann Cardell's address was on their current alumni-letter mailing list. "I'm sorry, sir, but the last correspondence this office had from Miss Cardell was over ten years ago. From Natchez. She may be deceased."

Back at the airport I filed my flight plan for Natchez.

The phone book at the Natchez airport showed six Cardells, none of them Ann. The first one listed was Alfred Cardell, Jr. When he answered the phone I said, "My mother knew an Ann Cardell back in college. I promised her that if I ever came to Natchez I'd look her up. Did you ever know an Ann Cardell?"

"She's my aunt," he replied. "She lives in Savannah."

"I'd appreciate her address," I said, as calmly as I could. "I just may be in Savannah sometime soon."

It was seven in the evening when I landed in Savannah, parked the Cessna and stepped into a phone booth. The phone rang twice. "Hello?"

"Ann Cardell?" I asked.

"Yes."

"Miss Cardell, my name is Gordon Livingston. I've thought a good deal about how to put this, but I haven't come up with any way but simply to say it. I'm your son. I've come a long way. I would very much like to meet you."

There was a pause before she answered, in a southern accent which unaccountably surprised me. "Yes," she said. "There are many things I would like to talk to you about."

When I arrived at the address I found an apartment on a well-groomed street. In response to my knock, the door opened and there stood an attractive and dignified woman in her 60s. From behind glasses she looked at me cautiously. She was a stranger. "Please come in," she said.

Coffee had been made and when I accepted a cup I heard

the china make a tinkling sound in her trembling hands. After some awkward amenities, I said that I would like to know about her and my father. She began to speak in a low, guarded voice. She had been born in 1912 to a farm family in Mississippi. By frugal living her parents were able to send her to college. She taught first and third grades in Mississippi for some 20 years, then retired to take a job as an administrator in the school system of a neighboring state.

When she began to speak of my birth her voice was full of emotion. "Back in those days, in a small southern community, the disgrace of being pregnant and unmarried . . . it was more than I could face . . . more than I could ask my family to face." She continued in a monotone. "It was during my first year of teaching. Your father was older, 28, a most handsome man, a marvelous dancer. He was the only man I ever loved . . . before or since. When I learned I was pregnant I begged him to marry me and give my baby a clear name. He said we'd have to think about things. I never saw him again. I went to Memphis to have my baby and no one back home ever knew anything about it. Three years ago I read that he . . . your father . . . died of cancer."

That was the end of the story, the end of my search. It was not an unusual story in many ways—a one-sided love affair, a young woman bereft and with child. But this was our story, hers and mine, and across the years I could feel the shame and confusion of that young schoolteacher as she faced the decision which would separate her from me.

Her feelings of remorse were deep. "It's been the bitter regret of my life that I lost my baby because of my own cowardice," she said. "But I had my own way of keeping track of your development as a child. I knew that in 1944 you would be six years old and in the first grade. I could hardly wait for my own class of '44. When I gave I.Q. tests I hoped the brightest one was you; when I comforted a defeated child I feared that he might be you."

A remembering smile touched her face. "You did everything at top speed that year. You were aggressive, yet vulnerable and easily wounded by a harsh word. I learned that you needed an atmosphere of tolerance and love. I tried to give it to you by giving it to all those children.

"It was an illusion, of course, but I half believed it, and when it came time for me to say good-by to that class in the spring, I felt sick with guilt. It was as if I were abandoning you the second time.

"Then, during the following winter, there came the news that the third-grade teacher was retiring. I immediately petitioned the school board for a transfer to that grade and it was granted. I would again be your teacher, this time when you were eight.

"That year, as I watched you mature, I was proud that you were becoming your own man but also hurt that the ties between us were loosening. By the end of that year, I was determined to put you out of my mind, for I knew I was being very selfish. Still, I always wanted my child back. As I grew older, I prayed that I would one day meet him as a man . . . so I could ask his forgiveness."

My throat tightened and tears stung my eyes. Forgive her? The very idea that I should judge her was outrageous. I stood woodenly, immobilized by my emotions. She made the first move. Slowly, humbly, she held out her arms. For the first time in 37 years I touched my mother and she touched me.

Day of the 100 Tornadoes

by Joseph P. Blank

At 3:55 p.m. on that terrible Wednesday, April 3, 1974, the National Weather Service station at Louisville clicked out a teleprinter bulletin for Meade County, Ky.: TORNADOES REPORTED NEAR HARDINSBURG AND THREE MILES NORTHWEST OF IRVINGTON AROUND 3:45 P.M. MOVING NORTHEAST ABOUT 50 M.P.H. THE TORNADO WARNING IS IN EFFECT.

The "tornadoes" were, in fact, a single twister spotted by several observers. Moving in a gentle arc, the tornado bypassed Hardinsburg and Irvington, then, scudding low and fast, raced for the heart of Brandenburg, the county seat. Relatively few people in this old, quiet town of 1700, 32 miles west of Louisville, heard the Weather Service warning repeated over radio and television. Some saw the terrifying cloud approaching from a distance; others were startled by its train-like sound when it was only minutes away.

At 4:10, the twister smashed through town with a shrieking roar, tearing apart nearly 40 percent of the homes and businesses, hammering furniture into sticks, squashing cars like grapes. Thirty-one people died; over 200 were injured.

The Brandenburg tornado was one of 100 or more that erupted from widespread storms on that gray, rainy afternoon and evening—an attack that ranks as the most devastating known single-day onslaught of tornadoes in history. It blasted parts of 11 states in the Midwest and South, and jabbed as far north as Windsor, Ont. Whirling at velocities between 100 and

300 m.p.h., the unbelievable winds killed 329 men, women and children, injured more than 4000 and affected nearly 24,000 families. The bill for damage would eventually exceed $700 million.

That there were tornadoes that Wednesday came as no surprise. Meteorologists at the Severe Storms Forecast Center in Kansas City noted early Tuesday that a low-pressure system with cool air behind it was forming over the central Rockies and moving eastward. At the same time, a mass of warm, moist air was rolling northeastward from the Gulf of Mexico. The warm air, moving clockwise, came in low and pushed itself up against the cold air, moving counterclockwise. Heat from the warm air was sucked aloft, creating massive turbulence that roiled to altitudes of 60,000 feet.

By Wednesday, the Kansas City Center was issuing tornado "watches," which meant "stay alert, tornadoes probable." During the afternoon, isolated streams of turbulent air began spinning themselves at ever increasing speed into tornadoes, and by midafternoon weather stations were teleprinting "warnings" based on actual visual sightings or strong radar indications of tornadoes at specific localities.

In Brandenburg, Leck Craycroft, 53, had just returned with his mother-in-law from shopping and was putting the bags of groceries on the kitchen table when he heard a noise like a train. He grabbed his mother-in-law by the arm and pulled her toward the basement steps. When they were halfway down the steps the house blew apart. Still upright, Craycroft was transported along the ground and through the debris like a small boy being carried along by his armpits. He realized he was no longer holding his mother-in-law's arm.

Cut, bruised, his head bleeding, he fell to the ground about 100 yards from his house. He looked around through pelting rain. Green Street, with its houses, trees, lawns, cars and utility poles, was gone. He figured out where his house had been and wended his way through the rubble to look for his mother-in-law.

Nothing was left of his home but the hole where the basement had been. The tornado had torn away the basement cinderblock walls and removed steel lolly posts from the concrete floor. His car was smashed into scrap metal. His mother-in-law was dead, concealed by debris.

Craycroft saw adults and children wandering around in a daze. He thought about his wife, and began walking the three quarters of a mile to the Rural Electric Coöperative Corp., where she worked.

Making his way into the business district, he saw that Brandenburg had been ravaged. Dead and injured were laid out in open areas. Buildings were gutted. Rescuers were pulling apart wreckage to reach survivors. Leck found his wife unharmed in the basement of the RECC building. "Ona, your mom's gone," he said. "I held on to her as long as I could. She's gone. Everything's gone!" They went into the street and saw Leck's sister-in-law, Eleanor Craycroft, among the dead. She had been having her hair done in Alta Dugan's beauty salon. Alta Dugan was also dead.

While Brandenburg was suffering its convulsion, storm centers were spitting out tornadoes over a broad range to the south, east and north. They ripped through parts of Tennessee, Georgia, Alabama, Virginia, West Virginia, North Carolina, Illinois, Indiana, Ohio and Michigan. At Resaca, Ga., the twister was announced by a bombardment of hailstones the size of golf balls. Rescuers found nine-year-old Randall Goble, his face cut and his body badly bruised, staggering 300 yards from his home. He thought he had awakened from a nightmare and asked for his mommy and daddy. But there was no one to comfort him. Searchers had already found the bodies of his parents and two sisters, and neither his rescuers nor the nurses at Gordon County Hospital could tell Randall that he was the only survivor in his family.

In Alabama, the town of Guin was virtually leveled. Twenty-three died there—one of every 100 residents. The Huntsville area was viciously slashed by six tornadoes that left 14 dead. One destroyed the Christian Fellowship Church, where among the debris, a Bible was found blown open to Psalms. Pastor William Cowley picked it up and read, "For we are consumed by thine anger and by thy wrath are we troubled."

In Michigan, a whirlwind skirted Detroit and flicked at Windsor, Ont., lifting most of the roof from a curling rink, smashing down one wall and propelling cinder blocks and players down the ice. Eight players died and 25 were injured.

Rochester, Ind., had five minutes' notice before residents

saw a large black cloud that crackled with lightning moving sinuously along the ground. Swelling and contracting like a living monster, the cloud killed six, injured 77, wiped out 300 homes and damaged 109. At Monticello, Ind., a tornado bombed out much of the business district. It roared down Lake Freeman, lifted four sections of the Penn Central railroad bridge off concrete pilings, blew them 40 feet through the air and dropped them into the lake. Each section weighed 115 tons.

Across the Ohio River from Brandenburg a series of tornadoes made perfect northeast runs to Xenia, Ohio. The unfortunate communities in this 200-mile-long swath looked as if they had been saturation-bombed. Outside Hanover, Ind., Sylvia Humes saw "three funnels about 15 feet from the ground. They sounded like a big blender. The biggest was chomping a house trailer to bits. I got into the closet. I was numb. I just waited for death. Then it got above me and I heard a deep roar with a sucking sound. It seemed like the house was breathing, with the walls of the closet going in and out, in and out." The tornado was high enough over the Humeses' house to cause only minor damage.

But the same twister pirouetted to earth in Hanover itself, destroying or damaging nearly 80 percent of the 600 homes, wrecking the three public schools and the administration building, and causing $10 million in damages to Hanover College. It also picked up a house, turned it around and set it down without injuring the three occupants.

Then the same tornado charged up the Ohio River, raising columns of water and churning trees and debris about like a gigantic washing machine. It made a swift pass at a power plant, twisting thousands of feet of pipe like so much soft spaghetti, then battered the residential north side of Madison, a town of 13,000. Larry O'Connell heard the tornado warning at his plant, and immediately telephoned his wife to shelter herself and their four children under the bed in the master bedroom. After putting down the phone, his wife decided to seek safety in a closet instead.

After the tornado passed, O'Connell drove home and found it wrecked. The master bedroom and its contents had vanished. O'Connell stood stunned, petrified. Then he heard his name called. It was his wife, trailed by the four children, running toward him from a neighbor's house. In a second the family were kissing and hugging each other. O'Connell will build back: "We started from scratch 15 years ago; I guess we can start again."

From Madison the same tornado skipped to the rural village of Bear Branch, Ind., a community of some 200 families. Halbert Walston glanced out a window, saw the black cloud with the glint of objects whirling in it and yelled to his wife, Alice, "Good Lord! Look here!" Then the cloud seemed on them and Walston yelled, "Everybody into the bathroom!" Mrs. Walston and the four children darted into the bathroom. Walston made a flying leap to get through the door but he never touched the floor. The tornado blasted out the bathroom wall, shot him through it and blew his family into the back yard. Walston was airborne for some 40 feet. As he fell on his back he saw his five-year-old daughter, Amy, fly over an apple tree about 75 feet from the house. The wind gently lowered her to earth. then dropped a piece of tin over her.

Mrs. Walston staggered around, lacerated, bruised, blood covering her head, her face swelling. She heard Amy whimpering and found her under the tin, her arm hanging crookedly from her shoulder. Sixteen-year-old Bonetta had a brain concussion and her sister, Dolly, 13, was sitting silently in a daze. Michael, 15, lay staring at the sky, his arm partially severed at the elbow, his nose smashed.

Mrs. Walston knelt by her husband. His ankle and five ribs were broken, his lung was punctured and his arm was badly cut and bleeding. "Halbert," his wife said, "Michael's arm is about off." He slowly rolled over and painfully crawled to his son. He jammed a thumb against the artery in his son's bicep to stop the hemorrhage, then turned to his wife. "Mom," he said, "you don't look too good, but you're the only one that can get help."

Mrs. Walston picked up Amy and, followed by the two older girls, started down the road. She fell, walked, fell, walked. After a quarter-mile, they encountered a neighbor who took Amy and hurried away to find help.

Walston kept his thumb pressed against his son's artery for the hour that it took rescuers to reach them, and in doing so saved the boy's life. At the hospital in Lawrenceburg, Walston had frightful nightmares. He saw his children picked up by the tornado and he reached out in vain to save them. He awoke with a terrified shout.

In the Ohio city of Xenia, population 27,000, radio and TV stations gave residents a good 15 minutes' warning. At 4:35 in the afternoon, anyone looking toward the southwest could see the deadly black cloud, broad on top and narrowing as it reached earth, bearing down on the city.

In general, Xenians aware of the tornado acted correctly. Many remembered to open a few windows (when the low-pressure core of a tornado passes over a tightly closed building, the higher interior atmospheric pressure blows out windows and walls). They fled to basements. In houses, schools and shopping centers without basements, they curled up in interior hallways, closets or bathrooms.

The Xenia tornado was extraordinary for its ferocity. Nearly 50 percent of the city was destroyed or severly damaged, 34 people were killed and more than 1600 were injured. As night approached, chilly and rainy, men and women wandered in a daze through the rubble. Some telephones still functioned deep in the debris; they would ring—unanswered—throughout the night. Homeless dogs whined plaintively. A woman found a neighbor's dead child and let out a great wail of anguish. In a shelter hastily organized in a school, the elderly sat mute, not wanting to eat or sleep, not wanting to start over again.

But within an hour of the disaster, Xenia, as well as other badly hit cities and communities, did start again. Doctors, nurses and other staffers at Greene Memorial Hospital worked around the clock—most without knowing the fate of their own families—and treated almost 600 patients. Between 5:30 p.m. and 8 a.m., Dr. Edward Call, chief of surgery, worked on nine life-and-death cases. Outside, the roar of the tornado was supplanted by the roar of chain saws as volunteers worked through the night to clear the streets of fallen trees. Trucks and bulldozers inched their way through the city. Other trucks with food, clothing and bedding came in along highways.

Representatives of federal, private and church relief agencies were telephoning for airline reservations or driving that very night to the stricken city. Individuals as far east as Mount Kisco, N.Y., as far south as Dallas, and as far west as Seattle, left their jobs and homes and made for Xenia by plane, car and truck to contribute their muscle, their hearts and their wallets.

Xenia had been shattered; its people stunned and shocked. But it was not left to its despair. Hundreds wanted to share and alleviate it.

One of the Comrades Is Missing

by Ken Agnew
AS TOLD TO KENNETH
SCHAEFER

It was now or never for Karl Bley. I put my single-engine airplane into a steep turn and race directly at the East German ship. My low pass was the signal for the 24-year-old machinist from behind the Iron Curtain to jump overboard.

Misgivings filled my mind. The Atlantic Ocean seven miles off the Florida Keys is hostile water at best and, this day-after-Thanksgiving, 1970, choppy swells were waiting to welcome his desperate leap to freedom. If he escaped the powerful suction of the ship's propeller, he would have to take his chances with the sharks until the rescue boat reached him.

Come to that—was Karl Bley even on board the ship? If he was, would he jump—or would he lose his nerve at the sight of that 40-foot drop into the churning wake?

Escape had been Karl Bley's dream since the night two years before, when—aboard the same East German cruise ship-freighter, the M.S. *Völkerfreundschaft*—he had sailed past the glittering lights of Miami. A thousand miles to the northwest in Villa Park, Ill., lived his older brother, Eric. Eric Bley had made it out of East Germany in 1955, followed a year later by his fiancée, Marlis. The two were now naturalized U.S. citizens and outspokenly grateful to their adopted land. Eric had founded a successful machine-building firm in a suburb of Chicago.

For 15 years the brothers had corresponded regularly. (They had worked out a code to get their messages past the ever-watchful East German censors.) Immediately after his 1968 trip to Havana, Karl wrote Eric that if he ever got that close to America again, "I'm going to jump and swim for it." It was no idle boast. Eric knew the hunger his brother felt. He had felt it himself.

He also knew that the chance was slim of swimming the seven miles from ship to shore. So there had been desperation on both sides of the Iron Curtain. It was at this point—two months before—that I was pulled into the affair.

Eric had come to the Florida Keys, south of Miami, looking for help in the escape plan that he and his brother had plotted. On Duck Key, he saw a sleek charter boat, the *Pequod,* belonging to my longtime friend, Capt. Bob Lowe. Fast, in prime condition, *Pequod* was the perfect boat to overtake the *Völkerfreundschaft* when it ran by the Florida coast at 18 knots. Eric found Lowe, who listened in silence to his scheme.

"You want to lay a rescue vessel alongside that ship just when your brother is ready to jump?" Lowe demanded.

Eric nodded.

"It's going to need air-ground coordinating. And a definite signal to your brother that all's set before he makes the leap."

Needing a pilot, Lowe brought Bley to see me. It was Lowe who sold me; I could tell that he liked what he saw in the man. Before he'd finished, I was as hooked as Bob by the desperate determination of a man fighting for his brother's life.

Eric had almost everything we needed to know about the *Völkerfreundschaft*, thanks to an advertising brochure Karl had sent. Passengers would board at the Baltic seaport of Rostock, enjoy a trip to Havana, that communist oasis in the West, then return. The cover carried a picture of the ship; an inside page even gave the frequencies monitored by the ship's radio.

We worked out a plan. I'd fly the route most communist ships take in making the Havana run—from the Bahamas they go straight toward Palm Beach, then follow the Florida coastline until they've nearly cleared the Keys. Once I'd spotted the ship, I would radio Bob and Eric, who would put out in the *Pequod.* As they closed in on the East German ship, I'd make a low pass in my light plane. That would be the sign for Karl to jump.

The second week of November Eric told us that Karl was aboard the ship. He would be off the Keys sometime on Thanksgiving Day. He would wear a bright jacket for quick spotting by his rescuers and would have a life preserver on under the jacket. But, the younger brother wrote, whether the rescue craft showed up or not, he was going to jump before the *Völkerfreundschaft* veered away from the last bit of America.

To provide day and night surveillance, we had enlisted George Butler, a retired engineer and enthusiastic pilot. For two days he and I had been flying up to Palm Beach and across the 60 miles to the Bahamas, directly over the path the ship should take. We had also worked south along the Keys to American Shoal, an unmanned lighthouse 16 miles off Key West—the usual turnaway point of Russian vessels bound for Cuba. We could report nothing but frayed nerves for our almost nonstop efforts.

At 5:30 on the morning after Thanksgiving, a dejected Eric Bley was leaving his hotel on Duck Key for the airport and still another reconnaissance flight. Suddenly, as he stared out at the blackness across the ocean to the east, he saw lights—*the ship!* He jumped into his car and roared off to the Marathon airport on Key Vaca. I was waiting for him, and the minute we lifted off the runway we could see the ship, its whole stern lighted up like New York. I killed our wingtip lights and the brilliant strobe atop the fuselage so we wouldn't spook our quarry. Flying high over the ship, we took out the brochure with its identifying picture. The sky and water were still dark, but with the deck lighting we had it—picture and ship matched exactly, even to the bright-red line along her hull.

In minutes we were back at Marathon, where a waiting Bob Lowe told us that there wasn't time to go north to Duck Key, get the *Pequod* and still catch the cruise ship, now moving past the city of Marathon at a full 18 knots.

"It'll take a 40-knot boat to catch it," he said. "Come on, Eric! We'll get a boat even if we have to steal it!" A second later their car sped onto the highway, headed for Big Pine Key, 19 miles to the south.

Butler had arrived by this time and was ready to fly the high watch at 2000 feet while I took the low run. Just before we both took off, I asked Butler's wife to call the Coast Guard: "Tell them you got a garbled message that there's a man in the water off American Shoal, and to get help out there right now!" We had to have some kind of backup. I was afraid Bob and

Eric wouldn't get a boat, and that Karl had meant it when he said he'd jump even if there was no signal.

I flew down to Big Pine Key just as a 22-foot fiber-glass outboard skiff came planing out of the Sea Center Marina, charging for the daylight beginning to show in the east. They were taking a brutal pounding as they hit the heavy chop of the open water. I didn't think Lowe could see the ship, and I skimmed over him to set him on an intercept course that would put him ahead of his target.

Just at that point, the skiff went dead in the water! I watched Bob fiddle frantically with the engine until it restarted. Another half mile and it quit again. "Bob's not going to make it!" I barked at Butler over the radio.

As I was debating whether to signal the jump anyway, I saw white froth behind the little boat as Lowe brought the engine alive for the third time. We were still in business!

I headed for my assigned point low and far ahead of the *Völkerfreundschaft* to wait until Butler called that the skiff was closing on its quarry.

"Now!" came the word finally.

"Right. I'm going in!"

Soon I was hell-bent for the bow of the unsuspecting liner, barreling down her port side, white caps only a few feet below me. I caught sight of passengers at the rail as I roared up the starboard side of the ship.

"Nobody jumped!" I bellowed at the mike in my right hand.

Then it happened. A red-shirted figure went over the rail and plummeted to the water. *"He jumped!"* I yelled, frantic with excitement.

There was an abrupt squawk from my radio, and Butler called from overhead: "There's two in the water!"

I gaped in disbelief. From the side window, I now saw not two, but *three*. No . . . *four!* Eric had warned us, "If this boy jumps, look out—you're liable to get more." We had them.

Lord, I thought, what a gamble! None of the three knew of our plot. No one but Karl had a life jacket—only life rings they'd tossed to the turbulant sea just before jumping. I circled the floundering figures below and, as they struggled toward those orange-colored rings in the water, I knew I was looking at raw courage.

Lowe's pilotage of the rescue boat was magnificent. Almost

before the last man hit the water, Bob was past the liner and Eric was pulling Karl into the skiff.

Then came the ship's response. We had known that the Reds were prepared for the possibility of a man overboard, and we'd talked at length about how long it would take the *Völkerfreundschaft* to make a 180-degree turn. We had guessed wrong.

Eric and Bob were still dragging the men from the water when the ship rolled into a tight turn at full speed. It was amazing to see a liner lean like that, and I had the fleeting suspicion the captain wanted everybody overboard.

It was close! By the time the last man was picked from the sea, the ship was bearing down on the tiny rescue craft. Bob raced for shallow water close to shore where the *Völkerfreundschaft* could not follow. Finally she broke off the chase, made an S-turn and took the southerly heading for Havana. It was all over.

Afterward, I sat beside Karl in a room at the Key West Coast Guard station and looked at the earnest face of this slender, dark-haired youth from East Germany. His dream had come true out there in the ocean when he waved his arms in a sign of triumph and screamed at the man in the bow of the rescue boat, "Bruder! Bruder!"

The men who had leaped to freedom with him were Dr. Manfred Kupfer, a 37-year-old neuropathologist from Leipzig; his brother Dr. Reinhold Kupfer, a 33-year-old pathologist from Zwickau; and Dr. Peter Rost, 37, a microbiologist, also from Zwickau. They had come on the cruise with unspoken hopes that just such a chance might be theirs. Karl's bold leap was the inspiration they'd hoped for.

Through Eric's interpreting, I learned that Karl had been on deck since early morning watching the lights along the Keys, studying the shoreline through binoculars for any sign of action. "I saw you when you took off from the airport," he told me. "I saw your bright light go out, and when I heard you in the dark high above the ship I knew Eric was coming."

Looking at this 24-year-old, who I knew now would have made that leap, signal or no, I suddenly realized what freedom means.

An Electric Nightmare

by John Robben

I awoke that Saturday morning knowing something was wrong. Outside our house in Stamford, Conn., the woods were dripping from an all-night rain. But who, or what, had awakened and alerted me? I got out of bed to look around, feeling a curious chill on the back of my neck.

"Dad?" my eldest daughter, Sue, 16, called from her room. "Is something wrong?"

"Did you hear anything?" I asked.

"No. But something woke me up. I'm scared."

On the stair landing, I strained my ears but heard nothing. Perhaps something other than a noise had awakened me. A light? Yes, it had been a light, unusually and oddly white. Or had I only dreamed it?

Then I looked down the stairs, and noticed a tiny light flickering at the base of the double front doors. A firefly? At this time of morning? I went back to the bedroom, slipped on a pair of sneakers and went down to investigate. At the door there were now *two* flickering lights. As I leaned down to take a closer look, the two lights erupted into 10 or 12 and began to *bzzzzz*. Electricity! What had awakened me *was* a flash of light.

I bolted back up the stairs, shouting, to arouse my wife and all five children. My first thought was to get everyone out of the house. I herded them all toward the back door. But as we came into the kitchen, an odd, gurgling sound—like sloshing

57

water—started up from the basement. I yanked open the cellar door, and was greeted with a cloud of blue smoke, shot through with orange and yellow flashes of light. Instinctively I turned on the light switch—and got a terrific shock.

"Don't touch anything!" I yelled. The children began to panic and cry. I slid open the back glass door leading onto the stoop. We stood there a moment, poised in fear. The woods were shrouded in mist, dripping with rain, and in the gray halflight of dawn looked eerie. It didn't seem any safer out there than inside. To run or stay?

Our large and willful dog made up our minds for us. Determined to get out, Trooper made a dash for the door. My wife grabbed him by the collar, but he pulled her out onto the landing.

"Hang onto him, Margie!" I shouted. How strong is habit, even in a crisis. I was worried about his running around, barking, and waking up the neighbors at this hour.

He bounded down the five wooden steps of the stoop, dragging Margie with him. He was pulling her off balance and I yelled at her to let him go. Too late! As the dog's paws touched the wet grass he yelped and leaped away, jerking my wife to the ground. Instantly she began screaming and thrashing convulsively on the grass. I ran down the steps.

"I'm being electrocuted!" she shouted. "Don't touch me!" I froze.

"Oh, God!" she cried. "Save the children."

I saw what looked like a wire beneath her twisting body. If I touched her, I figured, I would be trapped and helpless as she was.

I don't know where I got the strength to leave her and return to the house, but there was no choice. I *had* to save the children first. They were gone from the kitchen. They'd fled back upstairs when their mother screamed. At my order, they came running down again.

"We've got to get out," I said. "Hurry!"

The walls were humming ominously now, the buzzing and sparking from the basement growing louder as I led the children out of the kitchen and down the steps. On the slate walk, single file, we went past Margie. She was still writhing on the grass, screaming for God's help—and for us not to touch her.

"Is Mom dying?" Sue cried.

"I don't know," I said.

The children wailed even louder. I took them down the walk and past the corner of the house, where the grounding rod for our house's wiring system was sputtering and shooting flames like a Roman candle. We ran across a bluestone driveway and through evergreen bushes onto our neighbor's property. Apparently awakened by my wife's screams, Stan and Rhoda Spiegelman were standing on their high porch. I saw terror in their eyes as they must have seen it in ours.

"Margie's been electrocuted. Our house is on fire!" I shouted. "Call the ambulance. Call the police!"

Then, pointing the children toward our neighbors' house, I started back for my wife. But I hadn't taken more than three steps when I heard the children begin to scream. Spinning around, I saw that while three of them had reached the safety of the porch, Sue and her youngest sister, Ellen, were down thrashing on the ground. For the first time I realized the earth itself was electrified.

Suspended between wife and daughters, I stood paralyzed, unable to move in either direction. Any moment now I expected to be grabbed and flung to the ground myself. I could feel a tingling sensation through the soles of my sneakers.

Unlike my wife, whose entire body was pinned to the earth, the two trapped girls, crouched on hands and knees, were able somehow to crawl. Ellen inched toward Stan, my neighbor, who had started out to help her, felt a shock on his feet, and retreated to his wooden steps. His wife ran through her house, flung open a ground-level door and called to Sue from there. When I saw that the girls were going to make it, I started after Margie.

She was still thrashing on the ground. The wire I thought she was lying on was only a piece of rope. But when I bent over and touched her, a terrific shock slammed my arm. I let go. Then I grabbed an ankle and jerked her toward me, letting go as the shock struck again. I continued to grab and jerk, six or seven times, to get her away from the electric field to safer ground. On about the seventh pull I received no shock, and Margie lay still, sobbing. After a moment she was able to raise her head off the ground. I lifted her up and held her in my arms.

"The children?" she asked.

"They're okay."

She wept helplessly.

I helped her walk away from our house, past the now quiescent grounding rod and into our neighbors' back yard. There, waiting at the ground-floor door, were the children. They came running into our arms.

The police arrived a short time later and drove Margie and Sue to the hospital. The firemen came, but the fire was already out. Stan and I inspected the damage. It was remarkable little. The electricity was off, of course, and the clocks stopped at 6:10 a.m. The motor in the freezer in the basement was burnt out. That was the extent of the fire. We opened the cellar windows to let the smoke and smell out. There was no damage upstairs, but the nails in the cedar shingles on the front of the house had charred the wood.

Opening the front door, where I'd spied the first sign of danger, I got a good look at what had happened. The broad trunk of a dead tree, its stability weakened by several days of wind and rain, lay sprawled across our driveway, about 150 feet from the house. In falling it had knocked down a cluster of wires, including—we were told later—a two-cable circuit that normally carried 13,200 volts. Ordinarily these two cables would have touched, short-circuited and blown a power-line fuse, cutting the current off. But for reasons still not entirely clear to us, this failed to happen. Instead, the electricity ran wild.

First it had gone into our well, burning out the pump. "But that didn't satisfy it," said the electrician who came to repair the damage the following day. "So it kept trying to find a ground for its force somewhere else." That's when it slithered into our house like some evil thing, into our food freezer and our wiring. The "fireflies" I had seen were actually droplets of rain which had become energized when they rolled onto the metal stripping at the base of the front door. And, in its relentless hunger, the electricity spread itself over a section of wet ground, creating an "energized field."*

It was probably the diffusion of its energy over this comparatively large area that saved my wife's life. Strong enough to cause her to lose muscular control and keep her pinned to the ground for seven agonizing minutes, the current wasn't concentrated enough to kill her. The doctor who examined her at the hospital that morning said she had suffered no heart damage. However, for months afterward she suffered recurring pains in her arms and legs. Meanwhile, repairs to our electrical system and freezer cost only $437.25.

It was on August 28, 1971, that the accident happened. For the next three nights we slept in the house of friends who were away on vacation. They had a large new house. We each could have had a bedroom to ourselves, but instead we chose to sleep, side by side, on the floor of their playroom. Even together like that, we were uneasy, and we left the lights burning all night.

On the fourth day we returned to our own house, after an electrician had checked it out from top to bottom. The first night there was eerie. My wife turned in with some of the children and I with the others. Finally, toward morning, I fell asleep, but awakened suddenly with a strange feeling. I looked at the clock and saw that it was 6:10—the precise moment when time had stopped for us four days earlier. At breakfast, when my wife proposed selling our house, I agreed immediately.

Two years after that terrifying morning we were still having nightmares about it. However in our new home we chose not to be fearful. As a philosopher once said, "The story of Job is man's lot. But it does no good to audition daily for the part."

Apparently—as electrical engineer Bernard Schwartz explained later— the "hot" cable fell to the earth, while its companion "neutral" cable caught in a tree or came to rest on a non-conducting boulder. Thus for the circuit to be completed, the current had to reach the nearest point where the neutral cable was grounded: at a transformer installation, two poles away. Under the given geology and ground conditions, the route lay through the Robbens' house and yard. As a result, there was a current flow—lasting approximately 20 minutes—which was finally sufficient to blow a line fuse.

An Evening at the Waldorf

by Jean and Bud Ince

Bud: One rainy October evening, 31 years ago, I sat in my room at the Naval Academy in Annapolis, staring at a navigation lesson and thinking of Jean. I had met her the previous August in Chicago and had fallen in love. Three days later I was back in Annapolis, surrounded by rules and regulations, while she was a thousand miles away, surrounded by eligible bachelors. Things looked bleak indeed.

There was one bright spot on the horizon. Jean was coming to Philadelphia for the Army-Navy game in November. We had been invited to spend the weekend with my uncle and aunt in New York. If there was any hope for me, that weekend was going to have to be one she would never forget. I shoved my books aside and wrote the following letter:

The Manager
The Waldorf-Astoria
New York City, New York

Dear Sir:

On Saturday, November 27th, I expect to pick my way across the prostrate bodies of the West Point football team to a seat in Municipal Stadium where a girl will be waiting. We will hie away to the railroad station and entrain for New York. Once there we will take a taxi to your hotel—and that, dear sir, is where you and the Waldorf-Astoria come in.

I am very much in love with this young lady, but she has

not yet admitted to an equivalent love for me. Trapped as I am in this military monastery, the chances I have to press my suit are rare indeed. Therefore, this evening must be the most marvelous of all possible evenings, for I intend to ask her to be my wife.

I would like a perfect table. There should be candlelight, gleaming silver and snowy linen. There should be wine and a dinner that will be the culmination of the chef's career. At precisely midnight, I would like the orchestra to play "Navy Blue and Gold" very softly.

And then I intend to propose.

I would appreciate it very much if you could confirm this plan and also tell me approximately what the bill will be. I am admittedly not getting rich on $13 a month, but I have put a little aside.

> Very truly yours,
> E. S. Ince
> Midshipman, U.S.N.

The minute the letter was gone I regretted having sent it. It was callow, smart-alecky and, above all, presumptuous. The manager of the most famous hotel in the world was certainly not interested in the love life of an obscure midshipman. The letter would be thrown into the wastebasket where it belonged.

One week went by and then another. I forgot about the letter and tried frantically to think of some other way to convince Jean in 36 hours that she should spend the rest of her life with me. Then one morning I found on my desk an envelope upon which was engraved "The Waldorf-Astoria." I tore it open and read:

Dear Midshipman Ince:

Your very nice letter has been receiving some attention from our staff here. Just for fun I am going to attach the suggestions of our Maître d', the famous René Black.

"Black pearls of the Sturgeon from the Caspian Sea, stuffed into the claws of lobsters, and eulogizing the God of the Oceans.

"The Filet of Pompano known as the Demoiselle of the Atlantic, placed in a paper bag with the nomenclature 'Greetings from the Poseidon.'

"The Breast of Chicken served in a little nest to represent the safety of the ketch, with its escort of vegetables and green salad.

"An excellent dessert bearing the nomenclature *'Ritorna vincitor'* from *Aida*, and little galettes. A sweet liqueur to seal the anticipation.

"The price of this *manoeuvre*, including wines, champagne, gratuities, flowers and music, will be in the vicinity of one hundred dollars, with which we hope your little cache is fortified for complete victory."

Frankly, unless you have private resources, I think it is entirely unnecessary to spend so much money. I would be happy to make a reservation for you in the Wedgwood Room and will see to it that you have a very nice table, the best of attention, flowers—and you and your girl order directly from the menu whatever intrigues you. You certainly can have a couple of cocktails and very nice dinners and a bottle of champagne for one-third of what René Black suggests. However, you are the only one who can make the decision so let me know how you would like to have us arrange your little party.

Best wishes.

Cordially yours.
Henry B. Williams
Manager

P.S. I think your delightful letter *inspired* our Mr. Black.

I was thunderstruck with excitement and gratitude. But also dismayed. I didn't have even close to one hundred dollars saved. Regretfully, I wrote Mr. Williams that he had made a closer estimate of my resources than had Mr. Black, and I would appreciate it if he would reserve a table for me.

Days went by with no confirmation of my reservation. I was sure that my letter had never reached Mr. Williams, or that the whole thing had been taken as a joke. Finally, it was the weekend of November 27. The Brigade of Midshipmen watched their inspired team hold highly favored Army to a 21–21 tie in a thrilling football game. Afterward, I rushed to meet Jean, and she was just as pretty and wonderful as I had remembered her.

On the train to New York I showed Jean the letter from Mr. Williams. I told her that I wasn't sure we had a reservation, or whether we should even go to the Waldorf. We decided that we should.

We walked into the lobby. To the right, at the top of some steps, was the Wedgwood Room. There was a velvet rope at the bottom of the steps, and another at the top, with a major-domo posted at both places. A crowd of fashionably dressed couples was waiting for admittance. I looked at Jean, and she at me. Finally, I gulped, "Here goes," and went fearfully up to the first major-domo. "Sir," I said, "I am Midshipman Ince, and I wonder if you happen to have a reservation for me."

Like magic he swept away the rope! "Indeed we do," he said, and we saw the headwaiter at the top of the steps smiling and saying, "Midshipman Ince?" "Yes, sir," I managed. "Right this way," he said, and snapped his fingers. A captain led us across the room toward a beautiful table. Two waiters were leaning over it, lighting tall white candles...

Jean: Walking ahead of Bud, I looked in amazement at the table. Centered between the candles in a low white vase were flowers—white stephanotis and pink sweetheart roses. When the red-coated waiter seated me I saw a box at my place. I opened it and found a corsage of white baby orchids.

The menu was hand-painted in watercolor. A gray Navy ship steamed toward the upper righthand corner, and high-lighted on the left was a sketch of a girl's head with blue lovebirds in her hair.

At the moment our excitement over the flowers, the table and the menu had subsided to a point admitting of intrusion, our waiter said to Bud, "Would you like a cocktail?"

We agreed that we would like a Manhattan, and that was the only question we were asked all evening.

The dinner began. Silver sparkled and crystal glistened in the candlelight. Eddy Duchin and his orchestra played in the background. Service was constant, attentive, unobtrusive, and each course was more lovely than the one that came before it.

About halfway through our dinner a distinguished gentle-man with silvery-gray hair and a large Gallic nose approached our table. "I am René Black. I just came over to make sure that you were not angry with me." Bud leaped to his feet and I beamed, as we poured out our thanks to the man who had planned this evening. He drew up a chair and sat down and talked, delighting us with anecdotes of his continuing love affair with his wife and of the origin of omelets, and a wonderful tale of a dinner party he gave his regiment in France during World War I. When we asked him if he had painted the menu, he smiled, turned it over, and quickly sketched the head of a chef with his pen. Under it he wrote, *"Si l'amour ne demande que des baisers à quoi bon la glorie de cuisinier?"* (If love requires only kisses, of what use is the flame of the cook?)

After Mr. Black left, I looked at Bud. I had made plans to come to see the Army-Navy game and to spend the weekend with him. But I wondered how I would feel about the dashing midshipman I had met so briefly last summer.

Now, here we were in the Waldorf-Astoria in New York. We had just talked with the famous René Black; we had been served a dinner to delight royalty and were sipping wine together. How wonderful!

Bud: A few moments later Eddy Duchin left his bandstand and came to our table. The legendary orchestra leader was warm and friendly as he talked about the great game Navy had played that afternoon; he himself had served in the Navy during World War II. When Jean's attention was distracted for a moment, he leaned over to me and whispered, "'Navy Blue and Gold' at midnight. Good luck!" He rose, grinning, and walked back to his piano.

We were sipping a liqueur when the waiter told me there was a telephone call for me in the lobby. I followed him, wondering who in the world could be calling, only to find the headwaiter waiting just outside the door. He handed me the bill and said, "We thought you might prefer not to have this brought to your table." I turned it over fearfully and looked at the total. It was $33—exactly what I had written Mr. Williams I could afford. It was clear to me that this amount couldn't even begin to cover the cost of the evening to the Waldorf, and equally clear that the reason the bill was presented with such finesse was to save me embarrassment had I not had $33. I looked at the headwaiter in amazement, and he smiled and said, "Everyone on the staff hopes that all goes well for you."

Jean: Bud came back to the table gleaming, and, in answer to my curiosity about the telephone call, said, "It was nothing important. Shall we dance?" I felt his hand on my arm, guiding me gently to the dance floor. Other couples danced about us, chatting and smiling. I saw only Bud. We were living a fairy-tale evening, and it was all real. "I'm in love!" I thought. "How wonderful. I'm in love."

Bud: At five minutes till midnight, we were sitting at our table in a glow of happiness. Suddenly the wine steward appeared at my side with a small bottle of champagne. He opened it with a subdued "pop" and filled two crystal goblets with the sparkling wine. I raised my glass to Jean, and at that moment the orchestra drummer ruffled his drums. Eddy Duchin turned to us and bowed. He raised his hand and brought it down; suddenly we heard the melody of that most beautiful and sentimental of all college alma maters. ". . . For sailormen in battle fair since fighting days of old have proved the sailor's right to wear the Navy Blue and Gold." I looked at Jean, my wonderful Jean, and with a lump in my throat said, "Will you marry me?"

Jean: Bud and I were married the following June. Now, three decades later, with our five children grown and the Midshipman a Rear Admiral, we sometimes turn the pages of the lovely wedding gift we received from Mr. Williams—a handsomely bound limited edition of the history of the Waldorf-Astoria. In it one can read of the princes and potentates, presidents and kings, who have been guests of that glamorous hotel. But there is one evening that is not included there—an evening in which kind, warmhearted, gently romantic men opened a door of happiness for a young couple in love. That evening is ours, and its testimony is Mr. Black's wedding gift. Framed and displayed in a place of honor on our dining-room wall, it is a watercolor sketch of a little chef tending his spit in an ancient kitchen. Printed in Mr. Black's familiar hand across the top, the words are repeated:

Si l'amour
ne demande que des baisers
à quoi bon
la gloire de cuisinier

I Hit and Ran

As Told To Jhan and June
Robbins

Twilight is a bad time to drive. It's difficult to judge distances. Ordinary objects by the side of the road take on strange shapes. Turning on headlights only makes it worse.

That's the way it was on the spring evening three years ago when I was driving home from work. Suddenly, just as I turned into Little Bend Road, I saw this kid—a skinny boy about eight years old—wobbling along on a bicycle. I swerved to avoid him—too late. I felt a slight thump, heard a grinding clatter as my wheels passed over the bicycle.

I braked to a stop so hard my head snapped forward and hit the steering wheel. I started to get out. The little boy was lying about 20 feet away.

"God help me," I thought. "I've killed him!" My stomach started to heave. I put my hand over my eyes until things stopped rocking.

It was utterly quiet on the suburban road. I don't remember what went through my mind. I only know I slammed my door, started the motor and went tearing down the road. I was doing at least 60 and skidding at the curves. I had some crazy idea that if I could just get home everything would be all right.

As I turned into our driveway my car broke the photoelectric beam and the double garage doors flipped open. What a kick Edith and I got out of that gadget! When we were first married, I had only a part-time job. Now we had push buttons, two cars and a fine house. Everything had looked pretty good up to now.

Up to now! I realized what a terrible thing it was to kill a child, but what good could it do him now, I rationalized, for my family to suffer? I looked at my car. There were no dents, no stains. Before I went into the house I reached in the pocket of Edith's car for a flask we had stuck there to take to a football game. I needed something to steady me.

It did the trick. I walked briskly into the house, kissed my wife, then went upstairs with my 15-year-old son, Danny, to check his homework. I went to bed early and soon fell asleep. I refused to think about the accident.

In the morning I didn't feel any different. I couldn't think of myself as a criminal. I knew I was basically a good guy.

I had just sat down at the breakfast table when the announcer on the eight-o'clock newscast said, "Police are searching for a hit-and-run driver who struck a ten-year-old boy on Little Bend Road last night. The boy was nearly run over a second time as he waved his arm and called for help. He suffered a broken leg and severe head injuries and is in serious condition at Community Hospital."

The terrible thing I'd done struck me all at once. I'd hit a child and left him for dead. I had a queer feeling that my body belonged to some heartless coward and that it had somehow betrayed me. I looked across the table at my own bright boy. He was topping off fried eggs with a bowl of cereal. He pushed back his chair and rushed from the room.

" 'By, Dad," he called. "I'm going to ride my bike to school today."

I began to shake all over. "Wait!" I called. "I'll drive you!"

"No, thanks," he yelled back. "I want to ride." I heard the garage doors lift and saw him wheel out his bicycle. Then he put his head in the door.

"By the way, Dad," he said, "did you know your right headlight is broken?"

He pedaled away. I went out to the garage. The glass was missing from the right front headlight. It had shattered so cleanly I hadn't even noticed it. I feared now that they would find me. I didn't dare drive the car. I couldn't have it fixed.

The next few hours were the worst of my life. I borrowed Edith's car, went to my office and tried to work. But my mind pushed me this way and that. I had a bloody vision of Danny being run over by a truck. It would serve me right.

My family was dearer to me than my life, and there was no way I could spare them. I thought of suicide. I could take Edith's speedy little car and slam it against a tree. But I'd put on the brakes at the last minute and only mess myself up. I had already proved what a coward I was. That was strange, too. I was an infantryman. I've got a Bronze Star.

At noon I went to a phone booth and called the hospital. "I want to ask about the little boy who was in the accident last night," I said.

"Is this a member of the family?" parried the floor nurse.

"I'm a clergyman," I lied.

"Pray for him," she said. "He may not make it—he needs your help."

Police headquarters were six blocks from my office. I walked up to the officer at the desk and said, "I'm the hit-and-run driver you're looking for."

They let me call my lawyer. They kept me in jail overnight until I could raise bail. When my lawyer got me out, a bunch of hysterical women were waiting outside. One woman grabbed the lapel of my jacket and screamed, "You should hang for this!"

At home my wife threw her arms around me. She said, "I'll tell them I did it. They'll be easier on a woman."

The boy pulled through, though he will walk with a limp for the rest of his life. The charge I had to face was reduced to assault by auto and leaving the scene. I pleaded guilty. I said I was unable to account for my behavior.

I was sentenced to a year in prison.

The parents of the boy sued me. The court awarded them far more than the liability insurance I carried. To scrape the money together, Edith sold my lumber business and the house. She moved into a small apartment with Danny and went to work as a hostess in a restaurant.

Edith did her best to stand by me while I was in prison. She came regularly to visit me, but she spent the whole time crying. Danny came only once. He had flunked most of his subjects at school and had joined the Navy. Edith had given her okay. She never even consulted me. But why should she?

The prison chaplain told me that if I felt truly repentant I didn't have to worry about my soul. But what worried me most was what I was going to do with the rest of my life.

When I got out of prison Edith made room for me in the apartment where she was living. There isn't much left of our marriage, and nothing at all of my business career. I've thought of moving to some other city, but I guess the story would get around. I still report to a probation officer. They took my driver's license away. No one will give me a responsible job.

I think about my son, Danny. He was going to be an architect or engineer. I don't know what he will make of his life now, and I can't help him. I think about the little boy I ran over, too. I ought to go to see him, but I can't face that right now.

A couple of weeks ago I happened to see the desk sergeant who was on duty the day they arrested me. He shook hands and asked how I was getting along. I asked him a question that had been on my mind for a long time.

"What do you suppose they'd have done to me if I hadn't run?" I said. "Let's say I'd given the boy first aid and called the police—what then?"

"Why, nothing," he answered. "It was an accident. It was as much the kid's fault as yours."

A Girl Named Frankie

by MacKinlay Kantor

It is some years now since the Bravest Woman in America left off living, and I wonder how many people have forgotten her, and how many still remember.

Her name was Mary Frances Housley. She was a stewardess for National Airlines until she relinquished her job (you might say) in 1951.

"Frankie" Housely—friends called her by this nickname—was 24 years old at the time. So, if she were among those present as I write this, in 1966, she'd be 39. I'd picture her residing in a fairly-new ranch-style house in a suburb, arguing with a 13-year-old daughter about whether the little critter should wear stretch-pants to a junior-high-school dance. Or ordering an 11-year-old son to move his model of a lunar vehicle out of the living room. Or some of those things . . .

Stewardess Housley was five-feet-three inches tall. She weighed about 120 pounds, all carried in the right places. She had tender brown eyes and a lovely soft mouth. She did all right with her lovely soft brown hair, too.

The date was Sunday, the 14th of January. The plane was a DC-4, NAL 83, the Norfolk shuttle, proceeding on the first leg of its journey: Newark to Philadelphia. The aircraft had been delayed for minor repairs at Newark while air over much of the northeastern United States thickened with snow and sleet that early afternoon.

Shortly after 2 p.m., the airplane approached the field south of Philadelphia close to the Delaware River. It was a coach trip with only a crew of three: pilot and co-pilot, Capt. Howell Barwick and Edward Zatarain; and Mary Frances Housley, stewardess. Twenty-five passengers in the cabin looked out at the driving storm. The smiling Miss Housley reassured them, as she had hundreds of others in months past, although in truth Mary Frances was no veteran herself. She had been flying only four months. Some of the passengers were soldiers and sailors; there was a Marine; there were mothers and children.

Visibility was close to minimum. Wet snow plastered the ground. At 2:13 p.m. the wheels touched the runway. The DC-4 thrashed from side to side as Barwick fought to bring his braking action to bear. Off the end of the runway, smashing through a fence, the airplane bridged a 30-foot ditch and lurched to a stop with a scream of ripped metal. High-octane gas began to spew, and the first flames boomed.

Start in Knoxville, Tenn., where she was born on the 12th of October. I found there was always a hill in her life, or a height. While she was still a baby her family moved to a handsome brick house on a peak of the North Hills area. And in Knoxville at that time, to live in North Hills was something.

Snapshots show Mary Frances as a chubby child with tousled hair. When she smiled, the smile spread clear across her face. When she grew older, she liked the name Frankie and tried to adopt it, as girls do. She didn't get away with it then.

Later, the family moved to Fountain City, Tenn., to another hill. Seeking the germ of Frankie's greatness, I drove to Central High School of Fountain City—sure enough, another hill. I didn't know quite how to find out what made her tick. Teachers, boy friends, girl friends—I tried them all.

"Yes, I taught Latin to Mary Frances Housley," Mrs. Pace Moore Johnston told me. "But I have never contented myself with teaching Latin as a language. We examine the economics, the political factors of Rome. Often I have taken my classes to city-council meetings, so we might learn something by comparison with the structure of an ancient state."

She smiled calmly. "Sometimes I have been criticized for this. People have said, 'If you are teaching Latin to young folks, you should merely teach Latin.' But on the day when I may not include the wider and more important studies of humanity in my courses, I will walk out of this classroom."

It would seem Mrs. Johnston included those studies of humanity. Frankie appeared to have picked up some ideas along that line.

Perhaps she gained them also from the principal, Miss Hassie K. Gresham. Folks said that Hassie Gresham used to hold her audiences spellbound as she told incidents from the lives of servicemen who once attended Central High. On the wall of the auditorium where she spoke, a marble tablet bore the names of seven Fountain City boys who died in World War I. Above the list was engraved a paraphrase from John XV, 13: "Greater love have no men than this: that they lay down their lives for their friends."

In the quiet of the big, bare room you could very nearly hear Miss Gresham's voice. And in searching amid fancied rows of attentive teen-agers, it was possible to pick out Mary Frances Housley, her face breaking into vivacity as she smiled at something funny Miss Gresham said.

So the record continues. Mary Frances scrambled into momentary disaster in teen-age matrimony, and very shortly scrambled out of it. She worked for a succession of doctors in Jacksonville, Fla., as office assistant. And then—bang—it was 1950, and her current employer was recalled for active duty with the Navy. Several other young doctors for whom she might have gone to work faced the same prospect. That was how it came about that, on September 6, Frankie filled out an application to work as a stewardess. The very next day she was hired.

Home was an apartment in Vernon Terrace, Jacksonville. Her current roommate was a pretty, gray-eyed girl named Peggy Egerton, another fledgling stewardess.

...*Life,* said Peggy. *How she loved it!* People. Life and people, every waking moment.

"Oh, I'm in love," Frankie would cry, coming in at heaven knew what hour. "Peggy, wake up! I've got to tell you all about it. He's the most wonderful man! I'm in love!"

* * *

Eddie George told me about her when we were having dinner. Eddie had been a B-24 pilot during World War II.

"One night I called Frankie and asked her for a date, but she already had one. I was tired and sore. I'd been struggling with the tax return for my tobacco store, and just couldn't lick it. I had to send it in the next day, but I had bogged down.

"I came into this place, sat down, looked around—and there was Frankie. She left her party and came over to me right away. 'Eddie, have you finished the tax?' she asked. I told her it was too much for me; I guessed I'd have to be delinquent. 'But you *can't*,' she said. 'You're supposed to have that done by tomorrow!' I said, 'The hell with it,' and she went back to her party. Next minute here she was by my side again. 'Come on, Eddie. We're going over to your place to work on the tax. I've told my date good-by. Now come along.' It took almost all night for us to work it out."

"Was she in love with you, Eddie?"

"Not me especially. She just loved people."

On Saturday, January 13, Frankie called Peggy Egerton from the place at Jacksonville airport where stewardesses checked in for their flights.

". . . Darnedest luck," Frankie lamented. "I've got to work, so no double date tonight. Some girls were sick, and there was a foul-up."

"Where are you going, Frankie?"

"Oh, up to Newark. Then tomorrow I've got to work the Norfolk shuttle. I'll be back in Jax on Monday." They discussed a future double date, and Frankie's laughter jingled through the telephone.

Thus she flew on her last trip north. She proceeded in Flight 83 to Philadelphia on Sunday, January 14, and she went into the flames.

She forced open the door of the cabin. It was an eight-foot drop to the sleety ground outside. Had she willed, Frankie could have taken that drop then and there, and no one would ever have blamed her. But here were her passengers, and one woman was screaming, and the children were wailing.

People were twisted in their seats. Some of the safety belts seemed jammed from impact. Gasoline flames swathed nearer. Frankie hauled a dazed passenger to the door and shoved him into space. Another. The next was a woman; her coat was on fire. Frankie got her out.

People heard the stewardess's voice. "Just be calm," she said. "Take it easy, and everybody will get out. There's nothing to worry about."

Frankie went back into the cabin 11 times.

Ten passengers she released, and dragged to the miraculous coolness of the hatch opening. The pretty enamel on her nails suffered as her fingers clawed at metal fastenings of the safety belts.

A woman tells it—a woman who found herself mauled through seething space, realized the door was before her, and then wrenched loose from her savior's hands. "No," the woman cried. "You go first!"

Frankie looked at her wide-eyed. "I've still got some passengers back there!"—and the force of her little body shoved the woman out through the door which opened on life itself.

Some of the soldiers and sailors helped, dragging less-able people through the hatch, but they were outside now—bruised and cut, most of them, from the eight-foot fall. It was 90 seconds since the DC-4 came to broken rest across that ditch, and a high-octane-gasoline fire doesn't wait for anybody, even the prettiest stewardess you ever wanted to make a date with.

There were still four women tangled in the forward section of the cabin. Frankie plunged into the reek on her eleventh trip, and there were two babies up there somewhere, and one of them was named Brenda Joyce, and she was four months old. And Brenda Joyce was the one they found in Frankie's arms after the wreckage had cooled.

You go to Fountain City, Tenn., on a warm, sunny day, and the willows rim a quiet section along North Broadway and wave their pliant fingers at anyone who passes by.

You go through an arch marked "Lynnhurst," and birds are thick and flowers, too. You follow a long drive west, and you come at last, past perils of mockingbirds and roses, to an area where you can stand and see hills on many sides.

Frankie lies on a hill now. Toward the north is the hill where Central High School looms, and where her principal used to talk about heroes. Maybe three miles away to the southeast is the house where she spent the first nine years of her life—and that is on a hill also. And away off beyond the environs of Fountain City and Knoxville, bigger ridges stand purple. You might imagine that Frankie was up there somewhere, waltzing; she'd always loved to dance.

She could be, too. Could have been dancing with her darling, and snuggling delightedly with him in bed, running through life with all the verve, perplexity, heartbreak and exultation of any young wife during 5000 nights and days of these past 15 years.

Except that something made her go back into that airplane cabin 11 times, and 11 times was just one time too many.

A crashed airplane is strictly for the stalwart men in asbestos suits and masks. It is not for the petite little Miss Pretty—not unless she is a Mary Frances Housley. Then she has such love in her heart that no high-octane explosion can ever blast it out.

The fir tree makes a long shadow on her hilltop grave when the sun is low in the west, but morning sun can find her sod...as brave a woman as ever breathed. There she lies. Always a hill for Frankie.

Pop's Boy

by Irvin Ashkenazy

In the small hours of a dark September morning I dropped off the truck that had brought me as far as the north Florida town of Lake City. Going into an all-night lunchroom, I let my suitcase drop and ordered a hamburger.

The only other patron was a gaunt, elderly man eating a bowl of soup. An unkempt fringe of graying hair grew down his neck beneath the floppy brim of his ancient Panama. He stared at me a moment and a smile flickered as he noted the University of Florida labels on my suitcase.

"Don't I see ya at the Y in St. Augustine one night last spring?" he asked. "You win the state amachoor heavyweight title."

I nodded, a little surprised.

The old man paused, then added thoughtfully, "Ya don't have them scars over ya eyes then." I'd turned pro, I told him.

"Ya quit school?"

"No, I turned pro in order to stay in school."

After a while the old man swung off his stool. "If you're goin' to the university," he suggested, "I can take ya. I'm goin' through Gainesville."

As his jalopy rattled down Highway 41, Pop strung anecdotes about the pugilistic giants of yesteryear. He'd trained and managed fighters for decades. He was now retired "in a way," but at the moment was helping a promoter by looking for a heavyweight to fight Kayo Billy Terry in a ten-round main bout at Tampa the next evening. Terry's scheduled opponent had broken his hand in training the day before.

After a silence Pop said, "That moniker of yours—what is it, Polack?"

No, I told him, it was Hebrew. Right out of Genesis.

For a long while he stared ahead into the darkness, silent. Always it was the same, I thought. Tell 'em you're a Jew, then wait . . . wait while doors close silently.

"I useta wonder," Pop soliloquized, "what I'da done if I'da been born a Jew."

I'd never encountered this reaction before. My heart suddenly warmed. Why, I told him, he'd have been exactly the same.

He shook his head. "Naaa. I'da had to fight harder to get along. I'da had to have an edjucation. Like you. I'da amounted to sump'n, maybe."

By now the darkness was becoming diluted with dawn. I told Pop, a little uncomfortably, that I wasn't actually stopping at Gainesville. I would hitch a ride from there to Miami. "I thought you was goin' back to school," he said.

I was, but first I had to collect some money from a man named Willie. He was pay-off man for a manager who had taken me with his stable of fighters on a barnstorming tour. At the close of the tour Willie had disappeared. I had about $500 coming to me. (A lot of money in the 1940s.) Miami was Willie's home territory, and if he wasn't there I'd wait for him, picking up fights to keep myself going.

"Forget it," Pop said gruffly. "Charge it off to edjucation."

If I didn't get that money, I said, I wouldn't get any education. I needed $300 to pay off my debts from the previous year so I could get started this year.

Another silence. Then, "Who'd ya fight this summer?"

I mumbled a few names.

"Ya didn't fight *them?* Them's all tough, main-go boys!"

I explained how the barnstorming manager had matched me in ten-round main bouts from the start, endowing me with a mythical record in selling my prowess to promoters.

"The louse!" Pop muttered. "Throwin' in a green amachoor wit' guys like those! You stay the limit wit' any a them monkeys?"

I drew a dog-eared sheaf of newspaper clippings from my wallet. Pop nearly wrecked the car trying to drive and read at the same time. "I'll be damned," he muttered to the windshield.

"Ya win 'em all!" After a few moments he turned to me. "Stay over in Tampa and I'll put ya in against Terry tonight! You'll get your 300 fish!"

Pop's landlady, a little white-haired woman, glanced at Pop with an odd, anxious sadness. "Is *he* the one to fight Billy?" she asked.

"He's my boy," Pop said brusquely. She gave me something to eat, then I went to Pop's room and hit the hay.

When I woke up, the bedroom windows were filled with night. A stocky, baggy-eyed little man was bent over me, his fingers plucking expertly at the muscles in my legs. "This is J.D., my trainer," Pop explained. J.D., it turned out, also drove a cab.

While I was dressing I told Pop that the last I'd heard of Terry was a couple of years before. He'd been pretty good. I wondered what he'd done since.

"He's disgraced the name he's fightin' under," Pop said bitterly. "Tonight he's tryin' to make a comeback. All that means is he's gonna try to win because nobody's payin' him to lay down!" When I asked if he could still fight if he wanted to, Pop nodded slowly. "He might have been heavyweight champ, if he'd listened to me—" I must have shown my surprise. "I useta manage him," Pop said gruffly.

A mounting roar swept through the walls of the dressing room. "The semifinal's over," J.D. commented. Pop threw an arm across my shoulders and said, "This boy you're fightin' is good. He can hit and he can box. But he does his trainin' in dance halls and blind pigs. Hold him for six rounds and he's through! But until then—watch it! He's tricky and he's dirty."

As I moved out at the clang of the bell, Terry charged across the ring in a concentrated assault, designed to crash through a mediocre defense by power and surprise. I stepped back, half-crouching, and caught everything on arms, gloves and shoulder. I let him come, moving in a circle. When he closed in I tangled his arms without clinching, allowing him further to spend his strength in savage attempts to maul me inside.

After that initial flurry Terry knew that I was no amateur. Awareness of that fact must have awakened a sickening desperation in him. He needed a win so badly.

Suddenly a blinding constellation of agony burst in my brain. He'd thrust his thumb into my eye. I hunched against the ropes, unable to see, while Terry's brain-rattling blows jolted against the back of my head and smashed down on my kidneys. I managed to fall into a clinch. Another galaxy of stars exploded as Terry pulled out with a vicious butt of his head to my brow. Then the bell clanged.

Pop vigorously protested the foul to the referee, but the referee only shrugged. Apparently he hadn't seen it.

During the second round, with Terry husbanding his narrow margin of endurance and me waiting for it to trickle away, the fight became static. The crowd began to stamp in metronomic disapproval. Suddenly Terry rushed me, throwing a barrage of leather. I backpedaled, but he closed in, seizing my arms at the elbows. Locked face to face, he snarled, "Fight! Ya yeller Jew!" And he spat full in my face.

For a jagged splinter of time I could only stare. Hatred had never found a place in my emotional pattern of battle. Fear, perhaps. But never personal hatred. I flung him from me; clean across the ring he went, into the ropes—and bounded off them as I came charging in.

Next thing I knew, I lay upon a cloud, floating in space. I heard a distant voice say, "Six!" At the sound of it, the cloud suddenly petrified into hard canvas. "Seven!" At "Eight!" I managed to scramble to one knee, and at "Nine!" I was on my feet. I spat the fragments of a shattered tooth and felt the sharp, quivering pain of a naked nerve.

Terry moved in swiftly, striving for the finishing blow. I smothered his attack, turning so that his back was finally on the ropes. Letting my full 220 pounds sag against him, I dragged him savagely along the strands, knowing they were burning broad, crimson welts across his back. In close, I stamped on his feet, while the referee strove to break us. The punches I was pumping into Terry had little shock power, but I was striking with the heel of the hand instead of the knuckles, and the glove laces left raw places with every blow. When the referee managed to crash between us I struck on the break, deliberately missing, but following through so that my elbow smashed, apparently accidentally, into Terry's face. He staggered and as I charged in again jerked up his knee in such an obvious foul that the crowd broke into a howl. But I half-turned, catching his kneecap on my thigh, my left following through in a hook that cracked against Terry's jaw. He plunged to the floor.

I climbed through the ropes, hardly waiting to hear the end of the count. It gave me a moment's pause, however, to see Pop move suddenly into the ring, lift Terry in his arms and drag him to his corner.

Pop and I went to a little restaurant afterward. He looked very tired as he gave me a roll of bills. I counted $300, then peeled off $75 and handed it to him. "What's that for?" he asked. I told him it was his 25 percent, the regular agent's cut. He pushed the money toward me. "You don't owe me nothin', son."

Presently I said: "I'm sorry I had to fight dirty. You saw what he did." Pop nodded. He wasn't looking at me.

"You figure on graduatin'?"

I told him I guessed so, surprised at the question.

"You graduate. Make sump'n of yourself."

J.D. hurried up and said to Pop, "We'll just about make the Gainesville bus. Ain't ya comin' to the station with us?" Pop just sat there. "Tell ya the truth," he sighed, "I'm kinda beat up." I grasped his hand. "So long, Pop—and thanks a million."

At the bus station J.D. shook my hand. "Pop'll git busy and line up another bundle of easy cabbage for ya pretty soon." I told him that tonight's "cabbage" may not have been easy, but it was certainly the fastest three hundred I'd ever made. J.D.'s baggy eyes for a moment were baffled. Then a sad smile glimmered. "Ya don't have to put on no dog with me, boy. I seen the promoter give Pop the 130 bucks for your 20 percent of the gate."

Before I could go into the subject further, the bus burst into a roar. J.D. shoved me aboard.

Next day I wrote Pop, asking him about the $170 he must have produced for me from his own pocket. I couldn't remember the address of his boardinghouse, so I sent it care of the arena. I wrote him twice more, but all my letters were returned marked, "Not here."

Two months later I received a wire from J.D. offering me a Tampa main-go. He met me at the bus station and hurried me into his cab. "How's Pop?" I asked.

J.D. paused in mid-motion. "Didn't ya know? Pop's dead."

I felt as though someone had kicked me in the stomach.

I asked him when it happened and he said, "The next morning, after ya went back to Gainesville. His landlady found him in bed, dead." He tapped his chest. "Just gave out, I reckon."

It was a moment or two before I could speak again. "Did Pop have any family?"

"Just that one kid," J.D. said.

"What kid?"

J.D. looked at me sharply. And, as he absorbed my bewilderment, a curious expression came over his doleful face.

"Didn't ya know? Billy Terry was Pop's son."

Though the names of individuals and places are disguised, this was an actual experience of the author, Irvin Ashkenazy, once known as "the poet pugilist."

Over the Edge!

by Stephen Johnson

With a grinding screech, the 7300-ton bulk carrier SS *Lake Illawarra* plowed into two piers of the Tasman Bridge—a major structure which connects the Australian city of Hobart with its eastern suburbs. It was 9:28 p.m. on a drizzly Sunday in January 1975. At his cousin's house in Montagu Bay, almost underneath the bridge, police constable William Fair leaped to the front window. He was in time to see 140 yards of roadway and the whirling headlights of a car plummet 150 feet into the dark waters of the Derwent estuary.

Fair ran outside to his patrol car, grabbed the radio microphone and said: "Car 76 here. The bridge has collapsed." Almost at once, a police car on the city side of the river confirmed the dreadful news.

The Tasman, completed in 1964, is Australia's longest overwater bridge, measuring about six tenths of a mile between abutments on either shore. The citizens of Hobart nicknamed their bridge Old Spindly Legs because of its 22 tall, supporting pillars. Swept sideways by the current while trying to pass under the bridge, the *Lake Illawarra* had smashed into first one, then another of these pillars, causing three spans of roadway to buckle and give way. Thousands of tons of steel and concrete crashed down on the ill-fated tanker, sending her, in less than ten minutes, bow first to the bottom.

Just before the *Lake Illawarra* rammed the bridge support, Murray Ling of Bellerive swung his car onto the city-side entrance ramp. With his wife and two young sons, he was hurrying home from a barbecue to help his two daughters, who were giving a supper for their church fellowship.

When the bridge lights suddenly went out, Ling's first thought was for the girls, at home in a power blackout. He put his foot down hard on the accelerator, then noticed that the lights of Hobart and of the eastern-shore suburb of Lindisfarne were still ablaze. Cautiously he slowed again.

As he did so, a car sped past him in the outside lane—and shot on into nothingness, simply disappearing before his eyes. Ling slammed on his brakes and skidded to a stop, one yard from the edge of a black void.

Helen Ling's voice broke the stunned silence. "Back up," she cried. "Back up!"

But in the rear-view mirror Ling could see oncoming car lights. If the approaching car were to hit him from behind, he and his family would be rocketed over the edge into the water.

"Get out of the car!" he yelled. "Quick!"

As Helen and the boys ran for the safety of the pedestrian walk at the side of the four-lane bridge, Murray tried to wave down the approaching car. To his horror, it swerved around him and plummeted into the abyss.

Meanwhile, Helen was hoisting five-year-old Andrew over the rail setting off the pedestrian path. She was about to let go of him when Peter, 12, who had clambered onto the rail, yelled, "Don't, Mum! There's nothing there." An 18-inch water pipe had broken, and the torrents of jetting water had swept this part of the footpath away.

Another car was approaching from behind. In it were Frank and Sylvia Manley, their teen-age daughter Sharon, and Sylvia's brother Dick Fitzgerald. When the bridge lights went out, Sylvia strained to see through the drizzle what was amiss. Now she screamed, "Oh my God, the bridge has gone. Stop, Frank! *Can you stop?*"

Frank rammed his foot on the brake. "I can't," he said. "Too late!" The car skidded, and there was a jolting crunch as the front wheels went over the jagged edge and the undercarriage scraped the roadway. The vehicle hung there, rocking a little backward and forward.

Sylvia looked straight ahead and said, "Do you think we can reverse?"

Frank replied softly, "No, I don't think so."

Dick and his sister and niece flung themselves out through

the passenger door onto safe ground. Frank opened the door on the driver's side, put his foot down gingerly—and found only thin air! Knowing that if he panicked he was gone for sure, Frank reached up and with both hands gripped the molded chrome trim over the doorframe. Rotating his body sideways, but still half in his seat, he worked his hands back along the gutter of the trim. Thus anchored, he stretched his legs until he made contact with the road, then pulled himself from the car.

As the four of them stood on the still-trembling bridge, Peter Ling called out in the neighboring lane, "More cars are coming. We've got to stop them."

Helen Ling and her two sons ran back toward the crest of the bridge. The Manleys started in the same direction, screaming at an oncoming car to stop. The driver showed no sign of slowing.

"Get out of the way!" Frank Manley yelled to his wife. Sylvia flung herself aside as the car rammed into the back of the Ling's car, pushing its front wheels over the edge alongside the Manleys'.

Murray Ling walked on shaky legs to the driver's window and said, "Do you realize if that car hadn't been there you would be in the river?" The woman gazed at him white-faced, unable to speak.

While Manley and Ling stayed at the broken edge of the bridge as a last line of defense, their families remained at the crest. A loaded bus swept past them, ignoring their cries. Murray Ling ran forward waving his arms. The bus still came on. Ling ran alongside the driver's window. "There's a span missing," he yelled. "Get off!"

The bus finally came to a halt. Then it swung into a fast U-turn, bashing its side against the railing. Murray watched in relief as it disappeared over the crest to safety.

By now, police were on the scene. The Lings and Manleys were escorted through the chill drizzle to the western end of the bridge.

Thanks to them and others like them, many people had lucky escapes that night. Heading west toward Hobart, Tim Wark, 18, and his girl friend Rosemary Hickman saw the bridge disintegrate in front of them. Tim did a U-turn and parked in the center of the road. While he charged back on foot, shouting and waving, Rosemary stayed in the car, leaning on the horn and flicking the headlights.

Two other motorists escaped death only by sheer luck.

Traveling toward the city, John McKenzie felt a sudden gust of wind rattle the side of his car. He thought little of it until he arrived at his destination and was told the bridge had collapsed. Only then did he realize the significance of that gust.

Norman Oakes was probably the last person to get across. He recalls: "I heard a loud WHUMP and my car rocked violently. For a moment I thought I'd been hit by the car I'd just passed. But when I looked back, I saw its headlights drop down out of sight. Part of the bridge was missing."

Dr. Thomas Jones was tragically unlucky. He had visited his dying wife in Royal Hobart Hospital that evening, and lingered with her past the nine-o'clock visitors' curfew. Then he headed east across the bridge, home. Neither he nor his car was seen again. Mrs. Jones died four days later without learning of her husband's disappearance.

Below the bridge, brave and resourceful people fought to save lives in the inky black waters. Capt. James Cooper, veteran master of the tug *Cape Bruny*, was on the scene within six minutes. By then, only the stern of the *Lake Illawarra* was still afloat, and Cooper could see men jumping over the side. He picked up 19 survivors. Soon, a whole flotilla of small craft joined the rescue efforts.

In Rosny Esplanade, half a mile from the bridge, Jack Read, 60, was enjoying a family dinner and admiring the view of Old Spindly Legs. Suddenly a crash shook the house, and the reflection of the bridge on the water disappeared.

Read dashed to the phone, but the police emergency number was already engaged. "Come on, Kevin," he shouted to his 36-year-old son.

Experienced yachtsmen, the Reads were soon circling under the gaping hole in the bridge in their 29-foot yacht *Mermerus*. They heard a call for help, and Kevin swung their spotlight on a figure struggling in the water. Together he and his father hauled a seaman aboard.

They were no more than 35 yards from the *Lake Illawarra* when, with a mighty surge, its stern went under. A wave crashed *Mermerus* against a bridge pillar. Looking up, the

Reads could see the headlights of the two cars hanging over them.

From the water came another faint cry—a man without a lifejacket, dog-paddling feebly. They got him, and then six men in an inflatable dinghy who were tangled in a mess of hanging electric cables, some of which were live. The *Mermerus'* own mast became snarled by a heavy cable, but at that point the police launch *Vigilant* chugged up to help.

Hospitalized with exhaustion the following day, Jack Read found himself in a bed next to *Lake Illawarra* seaman John Bush, who had suffered a heart attack. "You yachties have got nerves of steel," Bush said. "Chunks of concrete falling all around, and you didn't turn a hair."

"Tell you what," Jack confessed. "We just didn't notice."

Five crewmen and four motorists are known to have died in the Tasman Bridge tragedy. Two seamen and one motorist, Dr. Jones, were listed as "missing." At an inquiry in April, the *Lake Illawarra* captain, Boleslaw Pelc, 60, was found guilty of careless navigation. Subsequently, suffering delayed shock and a loss of coördination, he was invalided out of the merchant navy.

Three days after her ordeal, Sylvia Manley started weeping uncontrollably for hours at a time. Her husband took her for a rest to a seaside resort—where they found their motel crowded with victims of a disastrous cyclone that, on Christmas Eve, had leveled the city of Darwin. "I saw those poor people who had lost their homes and all they owned," says Sylvia, "and the realization struck me. How fortunate my family and I had been!"

A Bash for the Boys

by James Stewart-Gordon

For weeks, the word had been passed around the sleazy underworld of Astoria, Queens—just over the bridge from Manhattan—that Saturday the 28th was to be the night of the Big Party. It would be a no-holds-barred bash, sponsored by the Mob, to honor Richie the Pawnbroker, their friendly neighborhood fence. There would be booze enough to refloat the *Queen Mary*. And the glamorous centerfold broads whose pictures decorated the walls of Richie's dingy oil-burner-repair shop would be on hand to furnish the stuff of dreams. Every one of the 140 guests would get a crisp $100 bill as a party favor. To top it all, Mr. Big—the Capo of Capos—was going to be there.

During those weeks of early autumn, when the soft haze hangs over New York City's towers and the lights on her bridges sparkle like emerald necklaces, some of the area's most celebrated rip-off artists and strong-arm men trundled into Richie's. As they brought their hot bonds, heisted welfare checks, pickpocketed wallets and credit cards, no one was disposed to argue with Richie over the meager five cents on the dollar he paid them for their merchandise. The lure of the big party had buried even their normal greed.

"Jeez, Richie, will that one be there?" Louis Leftout, a small-time thief, asked, pointing to an over-chested blonde leering down from the wall.

"That's Wanda," Richie told him—while Joey Scarface, Richie's partner, peeled off $25 to pay Louie for a $500 watch stolen an hour before. "She promised me last night she was definitely coming. I'll introduce you."

Daily, as he talked to the prospective guests, building up the pleasures in store, Richie emphasized one point over and over: "No guns, positively no guns. Mr. Big don't like guns. And I don't want no fights over the dames."

Saturday the 28th came September, 1974 and with it torrential rains. Joey and Richie, afraid that the weather might cut down attendance, began phoning their guests, telling them how important it was that there be a big turnout for Mr. Big. They had even arranged for taxis to pick up the partygoers, explaining that too many private cars being parked in one spot might attract the attention of the police.

By 7:30, the thieves—visions of champagne and fun-loving girls dancing in their heads—had begun to assemble at Richie's office, to be met by Joey, wearing a blue tuxedo. Then, by twos and threes, the guests were escorted into waiting cabs and dispatched to the party, which was being held in a remote warehouse near Kennedy Airport—where, as Joey said, "there ain't goin' to be no beefs about the noise."

It was all there, just as had been promised: the block-long warehouse, with music blaring and psychedelic lights swirling. Inside, the party was going full blast—but it was the kind of surprise party that surprise parties are not supposed to be. Suddenly, instead of broads and booze, there were guns and men saying, "We are the police, and you are under arrest."

Within one hour, 42 crook-guests had been arrested, fingerprinted, photographed, and herded into a second room, where they were offered Cokes and cookies instead of the more potent pleasures they had been promised.

As soon as the trap had been sprung, squads of detectives moved out to round up additional criminals who had been Richie the Pawnbroker's suppliers of stolen merchandise. Identification was easy and location swift, because every thief visiting Richie's store had been photographed in the act of selling his swag.

Those arrested included an employee in the computer room of the Human Resources Administration who had access to several million dollars in welfare checks and had lifted $50,000, and a Philadelphia burglar who specialized in stealing bearer bonds. Among the last to be apprehended were two who kept demanding to know when the gag was going to be over and the party would start. "This *is* the party," repeated Richie the Pawnbroker, now properly identified as detective Richard Ledda, and Joey Scarface, now revealed as detective Joseph Fasullo. But the guests still wouldn't believe them.

Two hours after the curtain on the party had been raised, 82 thieves—the largest number ever apprehended by the New York Police Department at one time—had been rounded up and packed off to cell blocks. There, indictments, prepared with machine-like rapidity by the Queens District Attorney's office, assured that trials and justice would be swift. All of them were found guilty. Fifty-nine went to prison with sentences ranging from three months to seven years. Twenty-three got probation and fines up to $4500. "Operation Fence" (as it was known officially to police), or "The Sting" (as it was called unofficially), had ended with a lopsided score: Cops, 82; Crooks, 0.

Operation Fence had its beginning in 1973, when New York City's chief of detectives Louis C. Cottell saw figures estimating that stolen merchandise worth $16 billion was funneled each year through the hands of professional fences. Cottell scrawled a note to Lt. Francis Herron, an aide directing Burglary Analysis, asking, "Can't we do something about this?"

Herron, a 25-year veteran on the force, thought they could. He referred to a study made a year earlier of undercover-fence police operations in New Orleans and reported, "Thieves can't operate unless they have a channel through which to dispose of their loot. If we can set up phony places, manned by our men, we'll not only get those thieves who deal directly with us but make a bust big enough to shake the underworld."

Herron's plan called for special police officers, chosen for their backgrounds, aggressiveness and intelligence, to be detached from regular duty and assigned to work undercover as "fences." From the moment they took the assignment, the men were to talk, act and think like thieves. Sgt. Walter Melnick, 31 years old, six-foot-two and 190 pounds, with an honors degree in chemical engineering, was assigned as Herron's field assistant.

Ordinary storefronts would be rented in areas easily accessible to criminals. The undercover men would run the stores, while backup teams, using sophisticated photographic and electronic-listening equipment, recorded transactions between crooks and the undercover police teams. Each night the photographs would be printed and compared with police files to check for known and wanted criminals, so when the operation was closed down, arrests could be swift, evidence solid, trial and conviction sure.

The first three men—volunteers in spite of the danger—were detectives Bob von Greifenstein, the heavy-set son of an Austrian baron, who had joined the force 18 years before; Artie Matera, a 20-year veteran with a background of diamond-setting in his family's jewelry business; and Ray Gaudenzi, another 20-year veteran, who had been a shoe salesman before becoming a cop. The choice of actors could not have been improved upon by Central Casting. Greifenstein was to be the strong-arm man protecting the store from rip-offs by stickup men. Suave and polished Matera was the leader—the man with Mob connections. And Gaudenzi, his sharp eyes disguised by horn-rimmed glasses and muscular body padded to look flabby, was to be the bookkeeper.

After a dry run in an Upper East Side location, the three "fences" set up shop in what was then New York's hottest crime spot—"Thieves' Row," which ran between 12th and 13th streets on Third Avenue in Lower Manhattan. A rented truck, inscribed with the name "Marino's Precision Trucking" (Artie Matera was Marino), was parked in front of their storefront. Inside the truck teams of police experts, poking cameras through concealed slits, photographed everyone who entered the store.

From the beginning the shop on Thieves' Row was a success, and the techniques learned there were applied in fencing operations in other parts of the city. Within days of Precision's opening, the friendly mailman, Manuel Ortiz, lingered after he delivered the dummy mail arranged to make the set-up look more convincing. "You guys don't do much trucking," Ortiz observed. "You know anyone who wants to buy hot checks?" "Well, we might and we might not," Artie, the method actor, answered. "I got some," Ortiz said, with simple candor. "How much?" "$650," Ortiz answered. "Give you ten cents on the dollar," Artie told him—and so a business enterprise was born, and the trap baited.

Within weeks, crooks were swarming in from all over the city like bees to clover, knowing they could dispose of their merchandise quickly. (Each night the stolen goods were clandestinely loaded into the company truck and taken by circuitous routing to police headquarters, where they were catalogued and checked against reported thefts.)

Meanwhile, in Astoria, Richie the Pawnbroker's operation had taken in $700,000 worth of stolen merchandise, and its roster of criminals tied directly to offenses was sizable enough to make Herron think it was time to blow the whistle there. No one knows who first proposed the idea of a party that would put the crooks off guard, and in one place at the same time; but once it was considered, all other ideas were dropped. When the cops struck, the crooks never knew what hit them.

On Monday, September 30, the fence shop on Thieves' Row was open for business as usual—but there was none. The trio manning the store wondered if the Queens bust had blown their cover. Two days later, Evil Eye Maxie, a gun-toting burglar, came and asked Artie if he had heard about the Astoria bust. Artie shook his head disgustedly. "That Long Island Mob," he told Evil Eye, "they're stupid. They should have smelled cops." Then he jerked his head to a wall map with numerous cities circled. "We operate on a national level." Picking up the phone, he dialed a dummy number, asked for Tony Fats and queried him about what the take had been in Las Vegas the night before. Impressed, Evil Eye spread the word of how important the boys at Precision Trucking Company were—and business became brisker than ever.

Finally, in early February 1975, Herron was ready to pounce. The shop was to be closed. In five months, it had taken in almost half a million dollars in stolen goods and developed cases against 50 thieves.

"We're closing up," Artie told customers. "They're goin' to move us to a new spot. We need more room. We'll let you know when it happens." On February 24, Thieves' Row got the word. Detective squads swept out and rounded up more than 50 crooks.

What had been bad news for thieves was good news for cops. As word of New York's success circulated among other police departments, inquiries poured in from a dozen major U.S. cities, including St. Louis, Philadelphia and Seattle. England's prestigious Scotland Yard sent a chief inspector to visit Herron and study his methods. The inspector remained for a week, took copious notes, and said, "You have a most re-markable body of men here. I only hope we can do as well." Coming from Scotland Yard, that was a compliment—but from the point of view of England's crooks, just more bad news.

Ned's Legacy

by Floyd Miller

Edward and Dedi Taylor lived in Sparta, N.J., with their six children—three boys and three girls. When Dedi became pregnant again, Ned, age nine, was intensely interested and made all sorts of plans for after the arrival of "my baby brother."

In August 1964, Jacqui was born. "Another dang-gone girl!" Ned exploded. "What good are they, anyhow?"

When Edward Taylor reported Ned's disappointment to Dedi in the hospital, she wrote a note: "Dear Ned, I know you're disappointed, but of course it was never up to us to decide the girl-boy bit. It was always in God's hands. So please try to think instead of how very lucky we are to have a healthy, normal baby. And since you are the oldest of the boys, maybe it's time for you to have a special job to do. Would you put yourself in charge of Jacqueline—be her special protector? You know, when she goes to kindergarten no bully will ever dare to bother her because all she'll have to do is threaten to tell *you*, her big brother! We'll talk about it when I see you."

When Jacqui came home, all her brothers and sisters were eager to hold her, feed her, talk to her—all but Ned, who remained a glum spectator.

Ned was in the fifth grade and beginning to lead a very busy life: he had a paper route, camping trips with Scouts, choir, piano lessons. There was baseball to be played, homework to be done; there were model airplanes to be built. There was little room for girls, especially a baby girl who couldn't do *anything*.

Yet, Ned was curious and began to appear in the nursery. "Why does she cry?" he asked. He volunteered to rock her, and one evening his mother overheard him singing a lullaby of his own composition: "Go to sleep, little creep, I'm tired and I'm beat. Go to sleep, little creep, before I drop you."

When Jacqui could toddle, it was toward her big brother Ned that she aimed her uncertain footsteps. It was to him she dragged her stroller when she wanted to go outdoors. It was onto his lap she climbed to bang on the piano. Ned was amused and flattered, and he felt increasingly responsible for her. Then, in 1967, when Jacqui was almost three, Ned fell ill.

The year had started triumphantly for Ned. He had had his heart set on professional voice training—something the family could not afford. But in March he won a competitive scholarship to the summer camp run by the Columbus Boychoir School in Princeton, N.J. There he was named "best choir boy" and awarded a $1500 scholarship for the Columbus seventh grade in the fall. He would become a member of the famed choir, "America's Singing Boys," and be taken on their world tour.

Shortly before he was to leave for school, the family had a picnic in the backyard. It was a time of happiness touched by regret, pride mixed with consciousness of impending loss.

Ned was tending the charcoal fire when Dedi noticed that the whites of his eyes were streaked with yellow. The rest of the family gathered around, and a mirror was produced so Ned could see himself. He pulled his eyelids into a slant and announced, "Hey, I'm going Oriental." His brothers and sisters laughed.

A routine blood test indicated hepatitis, and the doctor ordered Ned to bed, isolated from the rest of the family. At the same time, he assured the worried parents that their son's natural good health and vitality would have him back on his feet in time for school.

One Taylor was delighted with these developments—Jacqui. Now she and her big brother would be home together all the time. True, she was prevented by a folding gate from entering his room, but from opposite sides of the barrier they would talk and laugh. As Ned's skin took on a yellowish cast, he assumed the name Mr. Foo Yong, and from time to time he would shake the barrier and call out to a laughing Jacqui, "Open the gates of the temple!" When time came for her third birthday party, she insisted it be held in the hall outside his room.

Ned began to look pregnant, which gave rise to new hilarity among his brothers and sisters. His "pregnancy," however, was not hilarious to the doctor, who said it was ascites, an accumulation of fluid in the abdomen, and Ned should be hospitalized.

Jacqui was desolate. The "gates of the temple" had opened, and Mr. Foo Yong was gone. Even with the presence of all her other brothers and sisters, her father and mother, the house was empty.

In New York's skyscraper Columbia-Presbyterian Medical Center, Ned was no longer an Oriental potentate attended by loving subjects; he was suddenly a very small boy engulfed in impersonal bustle and coldly gleaming equipment. After days of tests, all the doctors could say for sure was that he was gravely ill with a form of hepatitis, his liver barely functioning.

"How long do I have to stay in the hospital, Mom?" he asked.

"Only until you get well," his mother replied.

He thought for a moment, then asked, "When does Jacqui go to kindergarten?"

"Oh, not for a couple of years."

He seemed relieved. "I think it would be a good idea for me to go with her the first day."

"A *very* good idea," his mother agreed.

Ned was placed in the intensive-care unit, where he always seemed to be plugged into something—tubes to feed him, to add blood, to remove fluid. The days stretched into weeks, then into months as he went from crisis to crisis. Through it all he maintained a cheerful, clinical interest in everything that happened, asking the doctors and nurses endless questions. When his parents visited him each day, he gave them an objective medical report on the previous 24 hours, much as if he were the doctor rather than the patient.

Only once did his cheerful façade crack. At the beginning of the third month he said, "I'm tired of being sick. I wish I could hurry up and get this over." Immediately contrite, he said, "Don't worry, Mom. Things always turn out all right."

By now the parents realized things were not going to turn out all right. The doctors simply did not know what was destroying Ned's liver. Ned died at 3:30 on Thanksgiving morning, 1967. The baffled doctors asked permission to perform an autopsy. Permission was granted.

A year and a half after Ned's death, when the family had once again begun to trust life, a letter arrived threatening another shattering blow. It was from a man they had never heard of but who seemed to know their family very well—Dr. I. Herbert Scheinberg, of the Albert Einstein College of Medicine in New York. He wrote that he knew why Ned had died, and there was a possibility the disorder—known as Wilson's disease—would develop in another Taylor child. Stunned, the parents read the long letter several times before they were able to comprehend it fully.

Dr. Scheinberg and a research team at Einstein were studying this rare inherited disease. Tissue from Ned's autopsy had been sent to Dr. Scheinberg, and he had now confirmed that Ned died from Wilson's disease.

Research had shown that this illness, which is due to copper poisoning, occurs only in children who have inherited a pair of faulty genes. Both father and mother must have the rare gene and, though they do not become ill, the children may. The chances of two such adults marrying were one in 40,000, but it had happened in the Taylors' case. While such parents do not necessarily produce children with the flaw, the odds were better than even that one of the surviving Taylor children had inherited a faulty gene from each parent. Dr. Scheinberg urged they have a blood analysis, called a "ceruloplasmin test," which spots the presence of an important sign of Wilson's disease.

They did this at once, and the next day Dr. Scheinberg reported five of the children were free of the disease—but there was strong evidence that one of them had it: Jacqui. He asked the despairing Taylors—faced with the possibility of losing another child—to bring Jacqui in for an exhaustive series of tests. These confirmed that Jacqui did indeed have Wilson's disease, and copper was accumulating in her liver; but the doctors were also able to determine that her liver had not suffered irreparable damage. A treatment had recently been developed. If Jacqui took four capsules of medication daily and stayed on a special diet, the excess copper in her body could be drained off and a proper balance could be maintained. She would be able to have a normal life!

During the drive home, Jacqui slept while her parents talked softly of her deliverance from death. "It was Ned who saved her, you know," Edward said. "Without the tissue from his body, they never would have diagnosed her case in time."

Dedi was silent. Then she asked, "Remember the letter I wrote Ned, asking him to take care of his baby sister?"

"I remember," her husband said.

And that was the end of the story as Dedi Taylor told it to me. Some months later, though, I received a letter in which she told of a visit that she and Jacqui had made to Ned's grave.

"Sadness and a sense of loss will forever be a part of my being," she wrote. "But that day with Jacqui—sunbeams dancing off her long, shining hair, sturdy legs bent as she concentrated on digging a proper hole for a chrysanthemum plant— I felt the sweet, sad joy of acceptance, of having come to terms with life. The sacrifice had been completed. Ned was indeed doing his job well."

Which Was the Real Linda?

by J. Anthony Lukas

The windows of Dr. Irving Sklar's reception room at 2 Fifth Avenue, New York City, looked out across Washington Square—from it a patient could watch pigeons circling Stanford White's dignified Washington Arch, children playing hopscotch on the square's wide walkways. Dr. Sklar had long been the family dentist of the Irving Fitzpatricks, who lived in a 30-room home a mile from the Greenwich, Conn., Country Club, and for them "the Village" had always been the Henry James scene they saw out his windows. But for their 18-year-old daughter, Linda—at least in the last ten weeks of her life—the Village was a different scene whose ingredients included crash pads, acid trips, freaking out, witches and warlocks.

If the Fitzpatricks' knowledge of the Village stopped at Washington Square, their knowledge of their daughter stopped at the unsettling but familiar image of a young, talented girl overly impatient to taste the joys of life. Reality in both cases went far beyond. In mid-October of 1967, a week after Linda's murder, the Fitzpatricks were still unable to believe what their daughter had gone through in her last days.

Which was "the real Linda"—the Linda of Greenwich, Conn., or the Linda of Greenwich Village? As the New York *Times* investigated, it found her a mixture so tangled that Linda herself probably did not know.

The forces at work on young people like Linda in recent decades have been the source of puzzlement for many other parents, and of studies by social workers and psychologists. Until a few months earlier, Linda—or "Fitzpoo," as she was known to family and friends—seemed a happy product of wealthy American suburbia. "Linda is a well-rounded, fine, healthy girl," her mother, a well-groomed woman in a high-collared chocolate-brown dress, said during the three-hour *Times* interview in which she often used the present tense in talking of her daughter.

Born in Greenwich, Linda attended Greenwich Country Day School, where she excelled in field hockey, swimming and riding. She went on to Oldfields, a four-year college-preparatory school in Glencoe, Md. A blonde tending to pudginess, she never quite matched the striking good looks of her mother or of her elder sister, Cindy. At country-club dances she often sat in the corner and talked with one of her half brothers; but, apparently more interested in sports and painting than dancing, she never seemed to mind very much.

In June 1967 Linda returned from Oldfields and, after several weeks in Greenwich, she left with the family for a month in Bermuda. "We always do things as a family," said Irving Fitzpatrick, tall, athletic-looking, a wealthy spice importer.

The family included seven children—Linda and nine-year-old Melissa (Missy) from this marriage; Perry, 32; Robert, 30; Carol, 27; and David, 25, from Fitzpatrick's previous marriage, which ended in divorce; and Cindy from Mrs. Fitzpatrick's first marriage, which also ended in divorce. But this time only Linda and Missy accompanied their parents to Bermuda, while Cindy and her husband joined them later for ten days.

As the Fitzpatricks remember it, Linda spent "a typical Bermuda vacation"—swimming in the ocean; beach parties; hours of painting; occasional shopping expeditions to town.

On July 31 the family returned to Greenwich, where Linda spent most of August. Again, the family insists she was "the girl we knew and loved." They say she spent most of her time painting in the studio in the back of the house. But she found plenty of time for swimming with friends in the large robin's-egg-blue pool. If Linda went to New York during August, it was "just a quick trip in and out—just for the day."

Linda's friends in the Village had a different story of her summer.

"Linda told me she took LSD and smoked grass many times during her stay in Bermuda," recalled Susan Robinson, a

small, shy girl who had run away in May from her home on Cape Cod, Mass. "She talked a lot about a fellow who gave her a capsule of acid down there and how she was going to send him one."

The two-room apartment of Susan and her husband, David, served that summer as a "crash pad"—a place where homeless young people could spend the night. "Linda first showed up one evening early in August with a guy named Pigeon," Susan said. "She'd just bought Pigeon some acid. She stayed maybe a couple of hours and then took off.

"A few nights later she came back with a kid from Boston. She turned him on, too. She was always doing that. She'd come into the city on weekends with $30 or $40 and would buy acid for people who needed some."

David Robinson, a gentle, black-bearded young man who worked in a brassiere factory, recalled how Linda turned him on, on August 22. "We went to this guy who sold us three capsules for $10 apiece," he said. "She put one away to send to the guy in Bermuda, gave me one and took one herself. We were out in Tompkins Park and we dropped it right there. Around midnight we walked over to Cooper Union Square where we had a very good discussion with a drunk. By then we were really flying. She was very, very groovy. At 8 a.m. Linda took the subway up to Grand Central and got on the train to Greenwich. She must still have been flying when she got home."

That weekend Mrs. Fitzpatrick was getting Linda ready for school. "We bought her almost an entire new wardrobe," she recalled, "and Linda even agreed to get her hair cut."

For months Fitzpatrick had complained about Linda's hair, which flowed down over her shoulders, but Linda didn't want to change it. Then at the end of August she agreed. "We went to Saks Fifth Avenue and the hairdresser gave her a blunt cut, short and full. She looked so cute and smart. Hardly a hippie thing to do."

The first day of school was only 11 days off when Linda went to New York on September 1. Next day she told her mother she didn't want to go back to Oldfields—she wanted to live and paint in the Village. "We couldn't have been more surprised," Mrs. Fitzpatrick said.

"We talked about it all through the weekend," Fitzpatrick

added. "Finally, on Sunday night, we gave her our reluctant permission, though not our approval."

"After all," her mother said, "Linda's whole life was art. She had a burning desire to be something in the art world. I knew how she felt. I wanted to be a dancer or an artist when I was young, too.

"Linda told us that she was going to live at the Village Plaza, a very nice hotel on Washington Place, near the university. 'I'll be perfectly safe, Mother,' she kept saying. 'It's a perfectly nice place, with a doorman.' She said she'd be rooming with a girl named Paula Bush, a 22-year-old receptionist from a good family. That made us feel a lot better."

Linda left for New York the next morning. The family never saw her alive again.

The Village Plaza had no doorman. The stooped desk clerk said, "Sure, I remember Linda." And riffling through a pile of thumb-marked cards, he came up with one that had Linda's name inked at the top in neat schoolgirl penmanship. Below it in pencil was written: "Paul Bush. Bob Brumberger."

"Yeh," the clerk said. "She moved in here on September 4, Labor Day, with these two young guys. They had Room 504. She paid the full month's rent—$120—in advance. Of course she had lots of other men up there all the time. Anybody off the street—the dirtiest, bearded hippies she could find.

"I kept telling her she hadn't ought to act like that. She didn't pay me any attention, but she never answered back real snappy like some of the other girls. She had something, I don't know—class. The day she checked out—oh, about September 20—she said, 'I guess I caused you a lot of trouble,' and I said, 'Oh, it wasn't any trouble, really.' You want to see the room?"

The elevator was out of order. The stairs were dark and narrow, heavy with the sweet reek of marijuana. A knock, and the door to 504 swung open. A bearded young man took his place again on the swaybacked double bed that filled half the room. He and three girls were plucking chocolates out of a box. On the mirror above the dresser with one drawer missing was scrawled, "Tea Heads Forever," and in lighter pencil, "War Is Hell." Red plastic flowers hung from an overhead light fixture.

* * *

"Would you like to see Linda's room?" her mother asked. On the third floor Mrs. Fitzpatrick opened the red curtains in the large room. "Red and white are Linda's favorite colors," Mrs. Fitzpatrick said, taking in the red-and-white-striped wallpaper, the twin beds and red bedspread, the red pillow with white lettering, "Decisions, Decisions, Decisions."

On the shelves, between a ceramic collie and a glass Babmi, were Edith Hamilton's *The Greek Way* and Agatha Christie's *Murder at Hazelmoor*. Nearby was a stack of records. In the bright bathroom hung ribbons from the Oldfields Horse Show and the Greenwich Riding Association Show. "As you can see, she was such a nice, outgoing, happy girl," her mother said. "If anything changed, it changed awfully fast."

The Fitzpatricks said they had been reassured about Linda's life in the Village because she said she had a job making posters for a company called Poster Bazaar at $80 a week.

The records show Linda worked for $2 an hour selling dresses at a shop called Fred Leighton's Mexican Imports, Ltd. On the third day she was discharged. "She was always coming in late," a salesgirl said.

David Robinson said Linda supported herself from then on by panhandling on Washington Square. "She was pretty good at it," he said. "She always got enough to eat." Yet "she had a thing about money. Once she told me she wanted to get a job with Hallmark cards drawing those little cartoons. She said she'd make $40,000 a year, rent a big apartment on the Upper East Side and then invite all her Village friends up there."

"Linda was very shy," her mother said. "When a boy got interested in her, she'd almost always lose interest in him. She got a proposal in August from a very nice boy from Arizona. She told me, 'I like him, but he's just too anxious.' The boy sent flowers for the funeral. That was thoughtful."

The Robinsons and her other friends in the Village said there were always men in Linda's life there: first Pigeon, then the boy from Boston, then Paul Bush, who carried a live lizard named Lyndon on a string around his neck. Bush, in San Francisco, was interviewed by telephone.

"I met Linda at the Robinsons' about August 18—a few days after I got to town," he recalls. "We wandered around together. She said her parents bugged her, always hollering *at her. So I said I'd get a pad with her and Brumberger, this kid from New Jersey.*

"She said she'd tell her parents she was living with a girl named Paula Bush. That was okay with me. I only stayed a week anyway, and Brumberger even less. Then she brought in some other guy—tall, with long hair and a beard."

This may have been Ed, a tall young man the Robinsons saw with Linda several times in mid-September. Later came James L. (Groovy) Hutchinson, the man with whom—in less than a month—she would be killed.

Toward the end of September, Susan Robinson says, Linda told her she feared she was pregnant. "She was very worried about the effect of LSD on the baby, and since I was pregnant too we talked about it for quite a while."

"I don't believe Linda really had anything to do with people like that," her father said. "I remember during August we were in this room watching a CBS special about the San Francisco hippies. I expressed my abhorrence for the whole thing—and her comments were much like mine. I don't believe she was attracted to them."

Her friends say Linda was fascinated by the San Francisco scene. Susan recalls that suddenly on October 1 Linda turned up at her pad and said she had been to Haight-Ashbury. "She said she stayed out there only two days and that it was a really bad scene; that everybody was on speed [methedrine]. She said she got out and drove back, with two warlocks she met out there. They could snap their fingers and make light bulbs pop.

"This didn't surprise me," Susan said. "Linda told me several times she was a witch. She discovered this one day sitting on a beach when she wished she had some money, and three dollar bills floated down from heaven."

One of Linda's self-styled warlock friends, who called himself Pepsi, was in his late 20s, with long, sandy hair, a scruffy beard, heavily tattooed forearms, wire-rim glasses and high suede boots. "My buddy and I ran into Linda in a club in Indianapolis called the Glory Hole," Pepsi said. "You could see right away she was a real meth monster. We were two days driving back. We got in on October 1, and she put up with me and my buddy in this pad on Avenue B. She was supposed to keep it clean, but all she ever did all day was sit around. She had this real weird imagination, but she was like talking in smaller and smaller circles. She was supposed to be this great artist, but it was just teeny-bopper stuff.

"It sounds like I'm knocking her. I'm not. She was a good kid, if she hadn't been so freaked out on meth. She had a lot of, what do you call it—potential. Sometimes she was a lot of fun to be with. We went out on the Staten Island Ferry one day at dawn, and surfing once on Long Island."

Pepsi saw Linda at 10 p.m. on October 8 standing in front of the Cave on Avenue A with Groovy Hutchinson. She said she'd taken a grain and a half of speed and was "high." Three hours later she and Groovy were dead—their nude bodies stretched out on a boiler-room floor, their heads shattered by bricks. The police charged two men with the murders and were continuing their investigation.

"It's too late for the whole thing to do *us* much good," her brother, Perry, said after he had been told of her life in the Village. "But maybe somebody else can learn something from it."

The Glories I've Seen!

by Maud Jackson

I was sitting on the kitchen floor washing the linoleum when the telephone rang. Carefully, I slid the pail of water beneath the table before going to answer the phone. A friend's voice said, "We had company yesterday, and too much food was prepared. May I bring some of it to you? We can visit for a while and have lunch together."

Hurrying now to finish the cleaning, I looked with first one foot and then the other for the pail. Blind people look for things on the floor with their feet as well as their hands, and I had been blind for 20 years, ever since I was 50.

From my earliest years my eyes had troubled me. By the age of ten I suffered from severe myopia (nearsightedness), and then I developed a disease of the retina in both eyes that caused progressive loss of vision. As if that were not enough, cataracts began to form, but surgery to remove them was impossible because of the condition of the retina. In time I retained only a minute amount of light preception, and was declared legally blind. I learned Braille and all the tricks blind people develop to help themselves.

Where *is* that pail? I was now saying to myself. Losing patience, I reached down quickly to look with my hands—and struck my cheekbone a sharp, glancing blow on the back of a chair. Stunned for a moment, I sat down until the pain had passed. Then I found the pail of water and finished washing the floor. I thought no more of the bump.

Four days later, while I was sitting in my living room—I

lived alone in the apartment my daughter added to her home in Dallas, after my husband died four years earlier—I opened my Braille watch to determine the time. It was 9 p.m. I closed the watch and placed my hand on the arm of the chair. As my hand passed my face, I saw movement! I raised my hand again and found I could actually see it. I held both hands up. At first they had a strange, transparent appearance, but as I stared they began gradually to look like normal hands.

I turned my head toward the table next to me and realized a lamp was on. The light shining on the table top made a golden glow. I *saw* the design on the metal base of the lamp, which always before my fingers had traced.

My eyes rested on a tiny orange pitcher. A gift from a friend, it had been displayed on the table so she would know it was cherished, but this was the first time I had *seen* it. Near it, a crystal candy jar sparkled brilliantly.

I looked at my watch again, but it was not necessary to open the Braille window. I could see the hands. The time was just 9:30. There was no doubt now of my vision. But sight had come so suddenly I wondered if it might not leave as quickly. Frightened, I really expected to go blind again at any moment.

I had to see my daughter. When I phoned her, I found myself speaking in a hoarse whisper. My voice held such urgency, however, that she came at once—still holding in her hand the carton of milk she had picked up just as the phone rang. As she walked toward me, I said calmly, "Darling, I see you." She was so amazed she was speechless.

"You have a milk carton in your hand." I said. "Will you turn it around so I can see it better?" I read the words on the carton. I was reading words for the first time in 20 years!

At that moment, my grandson walked in. "How handsome you are!" I said. He just stood there and smiled, a disbelieving smile. "That's a beautiful shirt you have on," I went on. I began to spell: U-N-I-V-E-R-S-I-T-Y. White letters on a light-blue background.

My daughter ran to get things to show me. There were pictures of my son's children in Colorado, grandsons I'd never seen. She also brought me knickknacks and long-treasured possessions to look at. I was astounded when she handed me a flyswatter. The ones I had seen so long ago were made of wire mesh. This one was bright-colored plastic with a flower on it!

We discussed phoning my son in Colorado. But sight had come so suddenly we were afraid it might be gone again by morning, and decided to postpone the call.

At midnight, when my daughter left, I looked about the room. Now for the first time I could see what my apartment was like. I opened the door of the big clothes closet, climbed on a stool and put a floodlight in the socket. What wonderful colors in those clothes!

I examined everything in my bureau and desk—everything I could think of, until 3:30 in the morning. When I stopped to rest, I glanced out the window and saw the moon. It was such a breathtaking sight I sat down just to look at it.

I had never walked in the backyard alone. Now I stepped out into the moonlight and examined every shrub, every flower, every tree—everything in the yard over and over again. I watched the sun rise that morning, and as I write this, 15 months later, I still watch it every day.

The next day, which was Friday, was grocery-delivery day. The grocery boy had been trained to arrange packages and cans carefully in a certain order on the table so I could place Braille labels on them. When he arrived that day, I was astonished at the colors and ingenious labels on the cans and boxes, and examined them all eagerly. My favorite was the Quaker Oats label. That Quaker in the huge hat smiling at me reminds me of my childhood. When I was small, my mother, if she caught me frowning, would make me look at myself in a mirror. I never liked what I saw and always tried to smile, but now I don't have to try. I can't stop smiling.

The next afternoon, my son flew in from Colorado. "Is everything still all right, Mother?" he asked. I was able to tell him how wonderful he looked. He had brought a motion-picture projector and screen, and films from the time of his marriage to the present. That evening I saw my grandchildren grow from infancy.

Sunday, my daughter prepared the most colorful dinner I have ever seen. She used all her best silver, china and crystal. It was one of the happiest days of my life.

On Monday we went to see my eye specialist, who tested my vision. When he asked me to read a poem in fine print,

I could see every word. It was such a joy to be reading, he literally had to take the paper away from me. He was the happiest-looking man I had ever seen.

Now the doctor explained what had caused my miracle. The blow on my cheekbone the morning I was cleaning the floor had caused the cataracts to shift so they no longer covered the retina. Although retinal disease had destroyed the sight in my left eye, this had not occurred in the right—where I now had about 75-percent vision.

When my friends learned of my good fortune, they began taking me to visit every place I had wanted to see for so long: my church, the new buildings in Dallas, the airports, the parks. The night trips were like a journey to fairyland.

In October, my son took me by car to Colorado, and along the way we stopped to see all the things I remembered. My husband and I had taken this trip on our honeymoon many years before.

My son and his family live in the Grand Valley, their home surrounded by mountains. Every night we sat and watched the stars hanging over those gorgeous mountaintops. I was there when the Christmas season arrived, and was able to see the children's Christmas pageant, and to help trim the tree. It was as if I were doing these things for the first time; all of life had taken on a new meaning.

Every day I think of what the doctor told me after I regained my sight: "This may last the rest of your life, or it may not. Enjoy your sight every minute, every hour, every day." I do. I will never be able to satisfy my eyes' hunger.

Many of my friends, after hearing of my miraculous experience, have told me they have begun to observe more fully the beauty of God's world and to give thanks every day for their power of sight.

In contemplating the Great Resurrection, we think of glorious light and the wonderful visions we shall see. I can tell you there is nothing on this earth more like the Resurrection than the sudden restoration of the precious gift of sight.

When the Grain Elevator Exploded

by Norman Spray

It was a cloudless, 100-degree July afternoon in Brownfield, Texas. There was nothing to foreshadow the catastrophe that, before nightfall, would bring horror and sorrow to the townspeople and test the courage of Brownfield's lean, sun-hardened men. From a stranger the town would learn something about love, and from one of its citizens something about heroism.

The stranger was 17-year-old Philip Reeves, who had followed his fiancée, Sandra Wilson, also 17, to Brownfield from their home town of Cotton Valley, La. He had found a job at the grain elevator of Goodpasture Grain & Milling Co., and she was living with her sister and brother-in-law. In two weeks they would marry.

Now, five minutes before quitting time on that hot afternoon in the summer of 1960, Philip was on the topmost floor of the elevator's "headhouse." This superstructure rose 70 feet above the concrete storage bins, which themselves towered 102 feet. From his dizzying height he could see mile after mile of the flat, sandy, sun-baked farmland of Terry County.

At that moment, 28-year-old Donald Ethington, line foreman for the city's electric utility, was sitting with his crew in the Best Yet Café, two blocks down the street. Just as the waitress set their coffee on the table, the building shook violently. Ethington heard two muffled whooshes.

"The elevator's blown up!" someone yelled.

"Let's get there, boys," Ethington said. "There'll be hot

wires to cut down." For Ethington, there was to be more. Much more.

Seconds before, observers in the street had seen what looked like a flash of lightning as a spark set off highly explosive wheat dust that had accumulated during the two-day unloading of the bins. Feeding on the dust, the blast shot through the tunnel beneath the huge storage bins. Two explosions followed, like freight cars crashing—shattering windows three blocks away and hurling concrete and timber 500 feet in the air.

Four men working at an unloading ramp next to the bins were dashed to earth as the blast knocked out the wall. Bombarded by concrete and steel, two of them were killed instantly; another died several days later. Beneath the storage bins, the tunnel operator was buried alive in a sea of grain.

Fire and smoke roared up through the headhouse so furiously that the townspeople who gathered at the scene were sure no one caught there could be alive. They were astonished when a man's face appeared through the smoke and flame at a first-floor headhouse window.

There was no ladder outside, no rope—no way down. It was impossible for a man to jump beyond the jutting storage-tank roof into a safety net. Yet he had no choice but to try. He was trapped by fire on all sides but one. Horrified, the crowd watched him leap. He hit the tin roofing of a catwalk and rolled off onto the roof of a grain tank.

It was only then that they saw Philip Reeves in the topmost window of the headhouse, 163 feet above ground. "Help me!" he cried frantically. "For God's sake, help me!" He was in agony, and people just stood there, watching! He screamed to a man he recognized: "Shorty! Shorty! Are you going to let me burn to death?"

"Who is he, Shorty?" demanded a man who feared it might be his own son.

"His name is Reeves," Shorty said. "A new kid in town."

The man's taut face relaxed—and those around seemed relieved that he was not a son, husband or brother of someone they knew. At the same time, they were ashamed. Somewhere this fellow Reeves had parents or kin.

The suspense was almost unbearable now. How long could the boy hold out in the fearful heat before jumping to his death? Desperate, people began to think of things that could be done.

By two-way radio, firemen who had arrived on the scene

called crop-dusting pilot Chick Clark, who in an old biplane was spraying cotton just outside town. Could he drop a rope to the trapped man? Clark got four 100-foot lengths of one-inch rope. A pilot-employe, Bill Dempsey, rode in the front cockpit. As Clark approached the burning elevator from the southeast, diving in at 120 m.p.h., Dempsey let one of the lengths of rope trail—hoping to drape it over the headhouse where Reeves could reach it, tie it to something and lower himself to the top of the bin. On two successive tries, the rope floated like a kite in the hot, rising air.

Meanwhile, Weldon Callaway of the Brownfield *News* was telephoning Reese Air Force Base at Lubbock, 40 miles away, to ask for a helicopter. The call was received at 5:10 p.m. At 5:15, a tandem-rotor H-21 helicopter was airborne.

In an effort to keep Reeves from jumping, the Rev. James Tidwell of Brownfield's First Methodist Church was now talking to him through an electronic bull horn. "Hold on, boy," he shouted. "We are pulling for you. We're going to get you down."

Reeves was rapidly losing strength. He moved the upper half of his body out to the point where it seemed he must fall, then went limp. His head struck the wall beneath the window.

"He's dying!" a woman shrieked, and fainted. The crowd hushed.

Tidwell thought fast. "Get your head up, Reeves," he ordered. "A helicopter is on the way. Look to the north, boy. Do you see it?" With what seemed enormous effort, Philip lifted his head.

But as the helicopter approached, the pilot immediately saw a problem the townspeople hadn't foreseen—a radio antenna reared 50 feet above the top of the headhouse, preventing any attempt to work in close to the structure. He was further hampered by the turbulent air above the burning elevator. The rotors beat air down into the fire, and flames roared back 50 to 100 feet high. Even so, the pilot moved in to a point where his lowered cable sling was a scant three or four feet from Reeves. To those on the ground, it looked as if Reeves could leap into space and catch it.

The helicopter inched closer, still closer. Then *whap!*—one of the rotor blades struck the antenna and, as the pilot veered off to land his crippled machine, Reeves cried, "They've left me."

"No, they haven't, boy!" the minister shouted back. "The pilot is radioing for another helicopter. It'll be right down."

Reeves seemed not to hear. He lifted one leg over the sill, as if intending to jump. For two minutes he remained poised, while Tidwell talked frantically. Reeves made no acknowledgment of the minister's pleas, but it was obvious to the crowd, now 3000 strong, that he was changing his mind. It was as if he had found new courage from some unseen source. He dropped his leg back inside the headhouse.

At Reese Air Force Base a second helicopter crew was assembling. And at a landing strip outside Brownfield the two crop-duster pilots, Clark and Dempsey, were preparing to go after the menacing antenna. They tied a grappling hook to a rope, and Clark aimed his ancient biplane straight at the headhouse. The plane bobbled as it roared into the turbulent air over the inferno; then there was a crash as the grappling hook hit the antenna, another, as 20 feet of it fell to earth.

Now Reeves was again hanging limply at the window. He could never hold to a sling, even if the second helicopter should reach him with one. In this moment of crisis, the line foreman, Don Ethington, father of four children, pushed through the crowd. Ethington did not know Reeves, and he had never been in a helicopter in his life; but he asked the fire chief to instruct the helicopter to land before attempting a rescue. "I'm going after the boy," he said simply. Ethington, carrying a lineman's safety belt and a 100-foot length of rope, jumped into a pickup truck.

Capt. Keaver Holley landed his helicopter in a nearby field just as the pickup arrived, and the wiry, 145-pound Ethington leaped up into the gaping midsection door. "Tell the pilot to hover well above the antenna," he said to the flight surgeon. To S/Sgt. James Holloway, the hoist operator, he said, "Let me down beside the north wall of the headhouse. Put me as close to the window as you can."

Captain Holley was already in flight when Ethington tied his safety rope to a metal support inside the helicopter. Sergeant Holloway handed him the sling. Ethington slipped into it and snapped his own safety belt to it. Then, as the aircraft fought for position in the turbulent air above the headhouse, Ethington kicked his safety rope out the door. "Lord, go with me," he said.

The crowd watched as Ethington was lowered from the helicopter. When he stopped, the pilot moved the machine over slightly. The effect on Ethington, 80 feet below, was to send him arcing through the air as if he were riding a giant swing. At the apex of this swing he grabbed the headhouse window. It was impossible for the pilot to observe the action below. He took instructions from Sergeant Holloway, who even at this altitude was severely hampered by heat and smoke. "Right!" Holloway shouted. "Right." Then, "Hold it, hold it!"

As Ethington held to the window sill with his left hand, he slipped a loop of the safety rope over Reeves with his right. Then he put his arm around Reeves and pulled him out of the window. He saw Reeves' fire-blistered flesh tear off as his burned body scraped over the sill. Both men dropped sickeningly for about eight feet—the sling line had slackened when the pilot adjusted the position of his helicopter—but Ethington kept his grip on Reeves.

"He's got him!" Holloway shouted to the pilot, and began hoisting the two men up. When they reached the helicopter door, Ethington lay in on the floor and pulled Reeves on top of him, forming a human cushion.

Down on the ground the people of Brownfield put all the suspense of the last hour and 40 minutes into one great cheer for Ethington and for the young man who was still a stranger.

At the hospital the next morning Reeves told Sandra Wilson, a sparkling-eyed brunette, how she had kept him from leaping to certain death. "I started to jump," he said. "Then I thought of you. I promised myself I wouldn't go until I could see you just once more—at least to say good-by." He asked to see Ethington and thanked him for what he had done.

Brownfield virtually adopted Philip Reeves as he fought for life in the days that followed. Visitor after visitor came with flowers and gifts, and comforting words for Sandra, who stayed at his bedside constantly. Then, on the night of August 3, he cried out and Sandra moved to his side. "There isn't any use in getting a doctor or anyone else," he said. "I just want you."

Two days later Philip Reeves was dead. Even after an autopsy, doctors couldn't say exactly why. It looked as if he had succumbed to sheer exhaustion.

In her grief Sandra accepted this explanation. She knew that but for his love of her, and Don Ethington's heroism, Philip Reeves would have departed this life without telling her again as he did so often in the hospital: "I love you, Sandra."

Donald Ethington was nominated for the Carnegie Hero Medal. And the town itself finally came to see a meaning behind the tragedy. The Rev. James Tidwell, the man at the bull horn, expressed that meaning. "Life is not great in terms of length," he said. "It is great in terms of quality. Every day this boy lived—of those few short days we gave him—was a sign of victory, of a power beyond ourselves and yet within ourselves. He showed us the quality of love, and the power of love's determination; most of all, he showed us the power of ourselves.

"In our own town we found there were men who could do more than they thought they could. To help a young man they didn't even know, men did what had to be done—even the impossible. We cannot learn how to be heroes. But we can learn to accept nothing less than the best of ourselves. Philip Reeves taught us this."

A Bullet From Nowhere

**by Albert A. Seedman
and Peter Hellman**

It is 8:40 on Friday morning, July 8, 1967: a dazzler of a day in Brooklyn—not a cloud in the sky, just a hint of breeze blowing in from Sheepshead Bay, traffic moving well on the Belt Parkway toward Manhattan. For several minutes now, Detective Lieutenant Vito DeSiero, on his way to work on Staten Island, has been following a bright-yellow Camaro sports car driven by a teen-age girl. He likes watching the way the soft air off the bay swirls her blond hair.

As they pass a spot called Plum Beach, the girl begins to drift from the passing lane toward the center lane. She keeps drifting to the right, and DeSiero assumes she'll get off at the next exit. Except that she keeps drifting . . . drifting . . . and suddenly with a crackle and splinter she is sideswiping the bushes at the edge of the parkway. The bumper bashes in, the hood crumples. In a tangle of foliage and a hiss of steam, the Camaro stops.

DeSiero is on the scene in seconds. The girl's head is bowed; she is moaning. He raises her head. Though her eyes are open, the eyeballs are rolled back. DeSiero knows, from too much experience, that it is useless to talk to her. Her license reveals she is Nancy McEwen, 17. Nothing in her wallet to warn of epileptic seizures, or diabetic collapse. Her body is unmarked. What has happened to her?

DeSiero calls for an ambulance, and the girl is taken to Coney Island Hospital. There the doctors try everything—electrical stimulation, adrenalin injections, manual heart massage.

Nothing works. At 11:15, Nancy McEwen is declared dead. And only then do the doctors discover, hidden by the long hair on the left side of her head, a small, bloodless bullet hole.

At the same hour, with the sun hot now on the Belt Parkway, an unmarked black Ford sedan pulls up to the scene of the accident. Albert Seedman, puffing his second cigar of the morning, gets out of the back seat and strolls over to the Camaro. He is a broad-shouldered man of 48, hair silvery-gray and lightly oiled, lips well-sculpted and slightly down-turned, eyes cold-green. The cops respectfully make way for the unsmiling commander of all Brooklyn South detectives.

Lt. Bernie Jacobs, commander of the local 61st Detective Squad, quickly explained to Seedman the little they knew about Nancy McEwen. She had been on her way to her summer job at her father's construction firm in Brooklyn. Except for what DeSiero saw as she passed Plum Beach that morning, what happened to her was a mystery.

"Jeez," said Jacobs, shaking his head, "who would want to shoot a sweet young kid like that?"

"Nobody," snapped Seedman. "At 45 m.p.h., nobody—not even the best marksman in the world—could make such a perfect head shot. He would have to fire from a car pulling alongside at the same speed—but Vito would have seen that. This thing had to be a crazy, one-in-a-trillion, pure fluke." He stared at the Camaro. "Did anyone roll the windows up or down?"

"No, Chief," answered Jacobs. "That's the way it was—just the left rear window open."

Since the glass in all other windows was intact, the left rear window was the only possible source of the bullet. So it must have been shot from somewhere behind the Camaro on the side of the parkway facing Sheepshead Bay. It could have come from the reeds and low dunes that sloped down to Plum Beach, or from the public bathhouse 200 yards back from the highway, or from the parking lot alongside the eastbound lanes. The shot might also have been fired from a boat on the bay. Or even from any of the three 28-story steel apartment-tower skeletons two miles across the bay.

Seedman ordered Emergency Service and Ballistics units to comb the beach and dunes for the shell casing. He knew it was an awful place to look for anything so small, but if they could find the casing, it would tell them where the shot had come from. "Tell those guys to bring their swim trunks," said Seedman. "Losing their weekend won't seem so bad if they can take a few dips."

All during the long daylight hours of the weekend, search teams scoured the sand at Plum Beach. They found no shell casing. On Monday morning Seedman called in a special Army Ordnance team from Fort Monmouth, N.J., to work with metal detectors. Still nothing. As the sun went down on Monday evening, a tired, disgusted Seedman stood on the beach scanning the marshy spur of dunes to the east, Fort Tilden and the towers of Breezy Point across the bay. "That bullet could have come from so many places besides this beach you can't even count them all," he said to Lieutenant Jacobs.

On Tuesday morning, Seedman sent detectives to Nancy McEwen's Requiem Mass in the hope that the man who fired the shot would turn up. One nervous young man nobody knew did take off fast after the service, but detectives found he was just a school chum of Nancy's in a hurry to get back to his office. A dozen citizens called the police that same day to say they also had been shot at as they drove to work on the Belt Parkway. But the "sniper" turned out to be a mowing machine that had been pelting stones from its whirring blades.

On Tuesday, too, the FBI returned a report on the death bullet. It had been fired from an Enfield .303, a model manufactured in England about 1940 on an around-the-clock production schedule. *Millions* of the rifles were still in circulation.

Five days of work by dozens of detectives, and Seedman was still nowhere. His men had turned up no gun dealer who had recently sold an Enfield .303. They had covered all the marinas, climbed the skeletons at Breezy Point, crawled around the dunes and marshes at Plum Beach, called in the Army, checked out every wild tip that came in on the "hot line"—and still had no idea who had shot Nancy McEwen, or why, or even where the bullet had come from.

Seedman was well aware how much taxpayers' money had gone into the case so far with no results. But he was not ready to quit trying to find the person who killed Nancy McEwen. Not quite yet.

"We're going to make a canvass," he announced to his men. "Starting tomorrow morning, we're going to knock on every door in Brooklyn until we find the guy who has that Enfield. He isn't talking now, but when a detective comes calling he's going to figure we've traced the gun to him somehow. And then he'll come clean."

The detectives looked at one another. Covering just a single block of the city can be time-consuming, but Seedman was talking about a borough of three million people! It would take longer than their lifetimes. "You've got to be kidding, Chief," Jacobs said. "Where would we start?"

A large map of Brooklyn was pinned to the office wall. Seedman ran his finger slowly up and down the lower half of the borough. Suddenly, the finger stopped. "Start . . . right . . . *here.*"

Jacobs marked the block: Knapp Street north of the Belt Parkway, about a mile in front of where the Camaro had run off the road. It was not a direction from which the bullet could have come. Why had Seedman's finger jabbed that particular spot? The Chief himself could not explain, then or later.

The next morning two detectives began working the block on Knapp Street. The third place they came to was a Mobil station. In the office they found the proprietor, a chunky man of 46 named Theodore DeLisi, working over his bills.

"Do you own a rifle?" the detectives asked.

"Oh, I have one down in my boat, locked away."

"What kind?"

"It's . . . an Enfield," DeLisi said, his eyes glued to his bills. "One of those British jobs."

DeLisi felt the silence, and looked up in dread.

"That girl, she was killed by a .22 rifle, right? That's what I read in the paper. Please tell me she got it from a .22 . . ."

This is the story Theodore DeLisi told during seven hours of questioning on Wednesday. Two weeks earlier, at the end of June, he had gone out in his boat *Luau* to fish for bluefish off Rockaway Beach. The blues were there, but so were sharks, and they scared the blues away. Frustrated, DeLisi remembered that when he and two other men had bought the *Luau* a few years back, a rifle had been thrown into the deal—just the thing to deal with those sharks. On his return, DeLisi picked up the gun from the partner who had been keeping it.

July 8 was a great day for fishing. No clouds, just a hint of wind on Rockaway Inlet. As he chugged by buoy No. 7 in the channel to the ocean, DeLisi reached for the Enfield. "Might as well see if the damn thing works," he said. He saw a beer can bobbing near the buoy. He took aim, and hit the can with his first shot. Pleased, he raised the rifle and fired one more shot before putting out to the open sea.

The second bullet missed the can, smacking the water beyond it at a shallow angle. To a bullet at that speed, the surface of the water is as hard as a sheet of steel. It ricocheted with a pop and headed north across Rockaway Inlet. It whistled along at almost four feet over the blue, flat water, and remained at that height as it crossed the sand, the dunes and the reeds of Plum Beach. Far ahead of the sound of its own report, it sped across the parking lot and the eastbound lanes of the parkway, and just cleared the fence divider on the median strip. As it approached the yellow Camaro—nearly a mile from the *Luau*—the bullet had begun to lose momentum. Had the rear left window of the car been closed, it would probably have glanced off. As it was, the bullet had just enough force to penetrate behind the left ear of Nancy McEwen.

On July 18, 1967, in Brooklyn Criminal Court, Theodore DeLisi was charged with the homicide of Nancy McEwen and with discharging a rifle within city limits. The homicide charge was later dropped, and DeLisi was fined $100 on the lesser charge. Incredibly, it turned out that he and the dead girl were acquainted, and had once been neighbors in northern Queens.

Detectives still talk about the Belt Parkway Case because of its three amazing coincidences. The first, obviously, was that after traversing a mile-long sweep of water and sand, the bullet had found the one place where it could do fatal damage. The second was that out of the city's millions, the families of shooter and victim knew each other. But what appeared to be the greatest coincidence of all was not dismissed as such by the detectives.

Over the years their Chief had demonstrated an uncanny ability—call it instinct, luck, intuition, whatever—suddenly to come up with the one element needed to solve the seemingly unsolvable. Now, in the 240 square miles of the borough, he had put his finger precisely on the one block where the Belt Parkway Case could be closed. His men had seen it happen too many times to call it anything but a particularly mysterious example of Albert Seedman's special instinct.

"IF WE STAY HERE, WE'LL DIE...."

by Franklin R. Jones

The gray New Hampshire landscape writhed in a slow, snake-like dance as I stared through the rain-streaked kitchen window. All that November morning, a fine drizzle had been falling.

"It's a rotten day," I grumbled. My nine-year-old daughter, Carolyn, resting her chin against my shoulder, had just reminded me of my promise to take her to see the porcupine caves. "Look, Carolyn, I'd like to. It's just that you'd get soaked."

"Oh," she said softly.

There was a long silence and I should have dropped the whole thing. Instead, I said, "Well, I suppose we could—if you take a hot bath when we come back."

We left the house just before noon. Carolyn wore dungarees and two light sweaters under a wool shirt. I had on wool pants, the top to my insulated underwear and a cotton shirt. Carolyn had made some peanut-butter sandwiches, and I had a few chocolate bars in my pocket.

We drove to the Flintlock farm, left the car by the main road and followed the old tote road into the woods. Walking in the warm rain, we made our way south through the woods, crossed the thick alder swamp, and climbed the ridge to a big outcropping of rocks. On the far side we found the porky caves—low, horizontal crevices cutting deep into the ledge. We explored them, but no animals were home.

The caves were not large enough to serve as a shelter, so

I suggested we build a little lean-to. Long-dead branches served as a framework, and we gathered hemlock boughs to thatch the roof. We scrunched our wet bodies into this regal mansion and dined on soggy sandwiches and sticky chocolate bars, conversing on the splendors of nature and the benefits of being a wild animal.

As we talked, it occurred to me that the temperature had changed, and I was suddenly very chilly. "Let's go," I said. "It's two o'clock, anyway."

We had moved only a hundred feet when I felt the cold bite at my cheeks and seep through my wet pants. Then we saw the first flakes of snow mingled with the rain. By the time we reached the swamp, the sky was a whirling mass of blinding white snow.

Even in good weather, it's difficult to cross the swamp unless you take a bearing on the opposite shore. I had always sighted on a tall pine that stuck up above the rest of the woods. But now, engulfed by snow, I could hardly make out bushes 20 feet ahead.

We crossed the swamp and headed through the woods, fighting the wind, trying to watch the way and keep the snow out of our faces at the same time. Then Carolyn stopped. "There's our house," she said, nodding her head toward the right.

"What house?"

"Our little house—right there."

"You mean our lean-to? No, that's just some old branches...."

She crossed the clearing, stopped and spun around. Her voice was calm, quite matter-of-fact. "It *is* our lean-to."

"Now, that was pretty bright," I said, trying to smile. "You know what happened? I was too busy fighting the snow to pay attention. We've walked in a circle."

Carolyn showed little interest in my theories. She was shivering. "I'm cold," she said.

"Okay—we'll just have to try again." We went back to the swamp, and again I led her to the far side. Carolyn stomped one foot and then the other. "My sweater's freezing," she said.

"Look, honey, you stand here a minute. I'll go along the edge here and find the big pine." I walked slowly, keeping her in sight. I kept talking so she would not be scared. Gosh, she was good. Not a complaint about my blundering.

There was no tree. I went back and tried the other direction. Everything looked strange. I didn't recognize a single landmark.

It was almost four. Hard to see my watch. Better move out, only this time I'd bear to the left more, toward the main road. We walked, and the snow whipped about us so thick that Carolyn couldn't look up. She took hold of my shirttail, and I pushed my way through windfalls and dragged her up snow-covered slopes.

Darkness was quick in coming, but the white of the snow made it possible to see the black branches that reached out for us. Carolyn fell and I pulled her up. A sob burst from her lips. "My feet hurt, Dad."

I ran my hand over her face and felt the crust of ice that encased her hair. "It's all right...you cry if you want to...I know you're cold."

"I...I'm all right."

We walked faster now. I literally dragged her along as she clung to my shirt. "I can't walk. I don't feel anything," she said.

It must have been the newspaper item I had read that first distorted my thinking. Just a little item I'd glanced at with only passing interest—about a man and his young son lost in the woods. It had been raining and the father tried to keep his son warm by holding him against his body. But the boy died of exposure before morning.

As we stumbled aimlessly through the woods, this news item flashed again and again across my dull mind. I wasn't kidding myself—I was in the same spot, maybe worse. The temperature had dropped fantastically since two o'clock. Both of us were encrusted in a thin layer of ice. My hands were numb with cold, and Carolyn was certainly colder.

I could see a dark mass against the sky. "Let's get to that ledge. I'll build a fire."

Suddenly, I stopped and stared through the trees. A gray piece of land, darker than the snow, had caught my eye. Even in the oncoming night I knew it was the swamp. I left Carolyn and stumbled toward it. I had to find out which side we were on. I walked a few yards, first in one direction and then the other. And then I knew—it wasn't the same swamp. This was the big swamp, deeper in the woods. But which side was I on?

I helped Carolyn to the rocks. I gathered leaves and twigs from under the crevices. Green pine needles were tenderly set on top of this tinder. I took out my lighter.

Until this moment, I was sure that my daughter had no doubts of my ability to handle the situation. Now she looked at my hands as I fumbled with the lighter. I struck violently at the wheel, again and again. There were sparks—feeble sparks that quickly died. A sob welled up from Carolyn's throat. She shook convulsively, then cried. I looked down at the little girl and realized that I was responsible for her life, and wasn't doing well at all.

Perhaps my insulated underwear would keep her warmer than her sweaters. I unbuttoned my shirt and told her to take off all her upper clothing. We threw the wet sweaters aside and she stood naked to the waist with the snow falling on her quivering body.

To my amazement, the inside of my underwear was perfectly dry, even though we had been exposed to hours of rain and snow. Almost instantly Carolyn felt the warmth of the garment as I put it on her and fumbled to fasten the snaps. My own cotton shirt was less inviting as its icy wetness hugged against my flesh.

I needed a moment to think—to stand alone and try to unravel this terribleness I'd created. I climbed to the top of the ledge and stared into the gray, snow-filled sky. Never in my life had I faced a danger so real. Not for myself. I could keep walking all night to keep warm. But for my child. The newspaper article kept flashing like a neon sign. I had to do something.

Then I heard a sound. I turned my head quickly to pick out the direction. There it was again—the bark of a dog off to my right. It sounded a million miles away.

The silence that followed made me ill. Then I heard it again. For the first time during the storm my mind seemed to function clearly. It was only a chance—that dog might never let out another yap—but anything was worth trying now.

Carolyn lay huddled against the rocks and I knelt beside her. "Carolyn, you've got to listen. If we stay here, we'll die. We're going to walk out. There's a dog barking . . . we can follow the sound." She didn't answer.

I would have to make her walk. I'd never be able to carry

her up and down the snow-covered ridges. "You've got to walk. Understand?"

She moved her head slowly from side to side, sobbing softly. "I didn't . . . hear a . . . dog."

"No mind, you can't hear him except on a ridge." I helped her to her feet. She held on to my shirttail, and we stumbled over the rough ground and half crawled up the slope of the next ridge. We couldn't hear anything but our own breathing. Then the dog barked again.

The regularity of that blessed dog's voice each time we struggled to the crest of a ridge became eerie. Always we stood for a few moments, then a couple of deep barks and silence.

But on the fifth hill there was no sound—only the gurgle of an underground brook somewhere. The soundless curtain of snow continued to fall. "We've got to try for another ridge," I said. "We just can't stand still too long."

I slid down the slope with Carolyn hanging on, and then we carefully moved ahead through the trees. We came into a clearing and I was about to cross over, when I realized we were standing in a road. A tote road! "We did it, honey, we did it!"

But I wasn't sure. Was it the right road—and which way should we go? I decided to turn left and we moved slowly, guided by the light strip of snow. We'd gone about 20 yards when I felt logs under my feet. I stomped my foot and knew by the sound that I was standing on a bridge.

We had walked over a bridge on the way in. I got down on all fours and ran my stiff fingers over the end of each log. Then I repeated the same thing on the other end.

"What are you doing, Dad?"

"Here it is, Carolyn—the nail! I remember a nail on the far end of this bridge. I caught my boot on it once. We're going the wrong way—*that's* the way out. We made it, Carolyn!"

We made it, all right, and found our car at the end of the old road. A dog up at the farm barked as I slammed the door. It was the same deep bark, bless his soul.

I was sure we'd been lost most of the night, but it was only six o'clock and supper was being set when we got home. We couldn't tell them—not just then. We went in and I helped Carolyn take off her wet things and she got into a hot tub. Then I carried her to the living room bundled in a blanket and had her drink some warm wine.

As I was lighting my pipe, she reached for my sleeve and pulled me close, and kissed my cheek. "Thanks, Daddy, for bringing me out."

The Four-Minute Mile

by Roger Bannister

John Landy of Australia startled the world in December 1952 by running a mile in 4 minutes, 2.1 seconds. He made no secret of the fact that his goal was the four-minute mile, the mark athletes and sportsmen had dreamed of for 30 years.

I had been running seriously since 1946, my freshman year at Oxford, and my best time for the mile was 4 minutes, 7.8 seconds. I decided to set out after the same "Dream Mile" that was Landy's goal.

The lowest I could get during the summer of '53 was 4 min. 2 sec. Then in December I began training every day between 12:30 and 1:30, picking up a quick lunch before returning to my work as a medical student at St. Mary's Hospital. With Chris Brasher, a fine British distance runner, I started out by running a series of ten consecutive quarter-miles, each in 66 seconds. We speeded them up gradually, keeping to an interval of two minutes' rest between each. By April we could manage these quarters in 61 seconds, but no matter how hard we tried we couldn't reach our target of 60 seconds per lap.

Meanwhile, John Landy had won six races in less than 4 min. 3 sec.—a record no other athlete in history had ever achieved.

Discouraged, Brasher and I drove up to Scotland for a few days' mountain climbing. There the air was calm and fragrant, and we had a complete mental change. The climbing probably did us more harm than good physically, for we used the wrong muscles in slow and jerking movements. But when we tried to run those quarter-miles again in London the time came down to 59 seconds!

It was now less than three weeks to the Oxford University *vs.* Amateur Athletic Assn. race, the first opportunity of the year for us to tackle our objective. My good friend Chris Chataway had decided to join Brasher and me on the A.A.A. team. He doubted his ability to run a three-quarter-mile in three minutes, but he generously offered to attempt it.

I abandoned the severe training of the previous months now, and began to concentrate entirely on gaining speed and freshness. Each trial I ran became a joy. I no longer thought of length of stride, or style, or even my judgment of pace. All this had become ingrained. On April 24, 12 days before the race, I ran a three-quarter-mile trial in three minutes.

Now that the crisis was approaching I spent most of the time imagining I was developing a cold and wondering if the high winds would ever drop. Each night in the week before the race there came a moment when I saw myself at the starting line. My whole body would grow nervous and tremble. I ran the race over in my mind. Then I would calm myself and sometimes get off to sleep.

Thursday, May 6, was the day of the race, on the Oxford track. A wind of gale force was blowing, which might slow me up by as much as a second a lap. Should I try it?

At 5:15, just before race time, I glanced at the flag. It was fluttering less and less. The wind was dropping. I made my decision. The attempt was on.

The gun fired—then fired again, indicating a false start! I felt angry that precious moments during the lull in the wind might be slipping away. We lined up again; the gun fired, and we were off.

Brasher went into the lead and I slipped in effortlessly behind him, feeling tremendously full of running. My legs seemed to be propelled by some mysterious force. But we were going so slowly! Impatiently I shouted, "Faster!" Brasher kept his head and did not change the pace. I went on worrying until I heard the first-lap time—57.5 seconds.

In the excitement, my knowledge of pace had deserted me. Brasher could have run the first quarter in 55 seconds without my realizing it, but I should have had to pay for it later. Instead, he was making success possible.

At one and a half laps I was still worrying about the pace. A voice insisting, "Relax!" penetrated to me above the noise of the crowd. Unconsciously I obeyed. If the speed was wrong, it was too late to do anything about it, so why worry?

I barely noticed the half-mile, passed in 1 min. 58 sec., nor when, round the next bend, Chataway went into the lead. At three-quarters of a mile the time was 3 min. 0.7 sec., and by now the crowd was roaring. Somehow I had to run that last lap in 59 seconds. Chataway was still leading. Then, at the beginning of the back straight, 300 yards from the finish, I pounced past him.

I had a moment of mixed joy and anguish, when my mind took over. It raced well ahead of my body and drew my body forward. I felt that the moment of a lifetime had come. Here was my chance to do one thing supremely well. I drove on, impelled by a combination of fear and pride. I had now turned the last bend. Only 50 yards remained.

My body had long since exhausted all its energy, but it went on running just the same. The physical overdraft came from will power. With five yards to go, the tape seemed almost to recede. Would I ever reach it? The arms of the world were waiting to receive me if only I could finish without slackening my speed. I leapt at the tape.

My effort was over, and I collapsed, almost unconscious, with an arm on either side of me. It was only then that pain overtook me. I felt like an exploded flashbulb. Blood surged from my muscles and seemed to fell me. It was as if my limbs were caught in an ever-tightening vise. I knew I had made it, though, before I even heard the time.

The announcement came: "Result of one mile . . . Time: 3 minutes . . ." The rest was lost in the roar of excitement. [The time was 3 min. 59.4 sec.] I grabbed Brasher and Chataway, and together we scampered round the track in a burst of joy. We had done it—the three of us! We shared a place where no man had yet ventured.

It would not be long, however, before John Landy from Australia or Wes Santee from America broke the barrier too, perhaps lowering my record as well. We had proved the four-minute mile was possible, and now the progress would continue.

Landy, in search of ideal record-breaking conditions, arrived in Finland soon after my Oxford run. He ran four races close to the four-minute mile, but he seemed unable to cut down those last two seconds.

Then one day Chris Chataway surprised me by saying he had decided to go to Turku, Finland, to race against Landy. They raced on June 22, and weather conditions were ideal. Landy led from the end of the first lap onward. At the beginning of the final lap he glanced behind him. Seeing Chris right on his heels, he took fright as he had never done during his solo runs. Under the stimulus of real competition he unleashed a tremendous finish, which at last brought him below four minutes. He set up a magnificent new world record of 3 min. 58 sec. So, after having pulled me from in front at Oxford, Chris Chataway pushed Landy from behind at Turku.

I was waiting for the news at home. For a few minutes I was stunned. The margin of 1.4 seconds by which he had broken my record was greater than anything I had feared. I had held the world record for only 46 days.

Now the struggle between Landy and myself would begin. The four-minute mile, however perfect it had seemed at Oxford, now meant nothing unless I could defeat John Landy.

In six weeks Landy and I were scheduled to race against each other in the Empire Games at Vancouver, B. C. We were the only two runners to have broken the four-minute barrier, and we were both at the peak of our training. There had never been a race like this.

Landy did all his training on the main track and often had two sessions a day. Details appeared in the newspapers, and very disturbing reading it was for me. His "hard work" school of training made my own preparation seem most inadequate. When I felt depressed, however, I reminded myself that my training had been good enough to run a four-minute mile when conditions were far from ideal, and was content to leave it at that.

I was mainly resting for the final struggle. I did most of my running on a golf course. I took longish walks. I screwed up my determination to win. The result was, almost for the first time in my life, I could say the day before the race I was really looking forward to it.

My plans were extremely simple. I must force Landy to set the pace of a four-minute mile for me. I must reserve my effort of will power for the moment when I would fling myself past him near the finish. Until then I would be entirely passive.

I believed that Landy would try to run me off my feet. I had to consider how great a lead I could allow him to establish. There were times when he had misjudged the pace and run a first lap in 56 seconds. If he were to do this he would play into my hands. By running evenly I might have a greater reserve left at the finish.

On the day of the race, Saturday, August 7, the stadium was filled with an enthusiastic crowd. The setting was perfect. We lined up for the start, Landy on the inside. The gun fired.

William Baillie of New Zealand went into the lead. I stayed some yards back, at Landy's shoulder, until Landy took over the lead at the 220-yard mark. Gradually he drew away now; at the end of the first lap I had allowed a gap of seven yards to open up.

In the second lap this lead increased at one time to 15 yards, and at the end of the half-mile I was ten yards behind. Yet my time was 1 min. 59 sec., and I felt complete detachment, prepared for relaxed running until my final burst.

But Landy was not slowing down as I had expected! This was the moment when my confidence wavered. Was he going to break the world record again?

To have any "finish" left, I must be able to follow at his shoulder throughout the early part of the last lap. How could I close the gap before then? I would have to abandon my own time schedule and run to his. This decision was the turning point of the race.

I quickened my stride, trying at the same time to keep relaxed. I won back the first yard, then each succeeding yard, until his lead was halved by the time we reached the back straight on the third lap. How I wished I had never allowed him to establish such a lead!

I had now "connected" myself to Landy again, though he was still five yards ahead. I was almost hypnotized by his easy, shuffling stride—the most clipped and economical I have ever seen. I tried to imagine myself attached to him by some invisible cord, and with each stride I drew the cord tighter, reducing his lead.

At the three-quarter-mile mark I was at Landy's shoulder. With the rest of the field 20 yards back now, I was so absorbed by the man-to-man struggle that I heard no lap time called out. The real battle was beginning. The two of us were running alone.

The third lap had tired me; ordinarily, this is the lap when a runner expects to slow down a little to gather energy for the finish, but I had been toiling hard to win back those painful yards. Now I fixed myself to Landy like a shadow.

He must have known I was at his heels, because he began to quicken his stride as we turned into the last back straight. It was incredible that in a race run at this speed he should start a finishing burst 300 yards from the tape! If he didn't slacken soon, I would be finished.

As we entered the last bend I tried to convince myself he was tiring. With each stride now I attempted to husband a little strength for the moment at the end of the bend when I had decided to pounce. I knew this would be the point where Landy would least expect me, and if I failed to overtake him there the race would be his.

When the moment came, my mind would galvanize my body to the greatest effort it had ever known. I knew I was tired. There might be no response. But it was my only chance.

Just before the end of the last bend I flung myself past him. As I did so I saw him glance inward over his left shoulder. This tiny act of his gave me confidence. I interpreted it as meaning he had already made his great effort along the back straight. All round the bend he had been unable to hear me behind him because of the noise of the crowd. He must have hoped desperately that I had fallen back. His last chance to check on it came at the end of the bend.

Here, because of the curve of the track, he could see behind him with only half a turn of the head. He knew that to challenge now I must run extra distance, and therefore he did not expect it. The moment he looked around he lost a valuable fraction of a second in his response to my challenge. It was my tremendous luck that these two happenings—his turning around and my final spurt—came absolutely simultaneously.

In two strides I was past him, with 70 yards to go. But I

could not accelerate further. Though I was slowing all the time, I managed to reach the tape, winning by five yards, in 3 min. 58.8 sec. Once again the four-minute mile had been broken— this time by both of us in the same race.

This last lap was one of the most intense and exciting of my life. John Landy had shown me what a race could really be at its greatest. He is the sort of runner I could never become, and for this I admire him. Before Vancouver he achieved a record of solo mile races that I could never have equaled. At Vancouver he had the courage to lead at the same speed in a closely competitive race.

After this experience I knew that, just as the barrier of the four-minute mile had proved mythical, so our own times would be lowered. Men will go on breaking records as long as they run. To the great thrust of the human spirit there is no limit.

One Year to Live

by Jhan and June Robbins

Lucile McFarland Fray, of Ottumwa, Iowa, was 33 years old when her tenth child, Stephen, was born. While in the hospital she noticed a small lump in her left breast, but did not report it to her doctor. "It's just a skin irritation," she told her husband, Ivan. "It'll clear up when I get home."

Home was a rented three-room cottage on the edge of town. Five days later she was back there, caring for the baby, her nine other children and her husband, who was all but crippled by arthritis.

Ten months after Stephen's birth the breast lump had enlarged, and Mrs. Fray consulted a doctor. The diagnosis: cancer. It still seemed localized, however, and after the breast was removed Mrs. Fray returned home confident she had nothing more to worry about.

During the next year, at the Frays', the struggle to live became acute. Ivan Fray's arthritis forced him to spend weeks in bed. The family savings vanished. And in the spring Lucile had to have another operation. It revealed that the cancer had spread. She had only a few months to live, the surgeons told her—at best a year.

There is no evidence that Lucile Fray ever wept or accepted her own fate with anything but stoic regret. But what would become of the children?

"One night I was giving Stephen a bath," Lucile later told her minister. "I was turning the problem over in my mind. I couldn't bear to think of my children living in an orphanage. Suddenly I got a feeling that there was some kind of wonderful presence right beside me. And I knew then what I must do. There were enough good people in the world to provide loving homes for all my children. I had to find them myself, before it was too late."

Although she often read the Bible to her children, Lucile Fray was not a deeply religious woman. But to the end of her days she was convinced that on that night, in her extremity, she received divine guidance.

Ivan Fray, now almost a total invalid, reluctantly agreed to his wife's plan. In the next few weeks Lucile Fray explained to each child what was to happen. "We are all going to have new homes," was the way she put it to Linda, then not quite five. "I can't take care of you any more because I am going to heaven to be with Jesus. But I'm going to find you another mommy who will love you just as much as I do!"

Word spread quickly that there were ten bright, fair-haired children available for adoption; after a story appeared in the local newspaper, many couples came to the Frays' door. But Lucile and Ivan weren't giving their children away to just anybody. Lucile had drawn up a list of formidable check-points for judging each couple: 1) Will you help the child to keep in touch with his brothers and sisters? 2) Does the adoptive father earn a steady living? 3) Are you happily married? 4) Do you believe in education? 5) Do you go to church?

Couples who seemed qualified were permitted to take the child they wanted for a few days' visit. When the child returned, Lucile asked him how he liked them.

"I know it wasn't very reliable, but I just had to take my child's word for it," she explained. "Besides, I think children have an instinct about these things. Once Warren, my three-year-old, said he didn't want to live with one woman because she wouldn't let him holler. 'Not even a teeny bit!' he said. Well, I think he was right. Kids need to holler some!"

Baby Stephen was the first to go. "We didn't really believe it was true, until we said good-by to Stevie," Joann, the eldest, told us. "Then we all got a little scared. Nobody cried, though. Instead we formed a family council to see what we could do to make Mother feel happier."

The council—Joann was elected president—decided to take over most of the household chores. "We knew Mom wanted to be able to spend her time with us." Pauline, 11, explained. "Mom spent hours drawing and painting with the little ones. And she went hiking and berrypicking with the rest of us. I guess she was in pain, but she never let us know it."

Baby Stephen was adopted by Betty and Kenneth Handy, a young farm couple who lived outside Fremont, Iowa. When Betty Handy took him from his mother's arms she felt a pang. "There were tears in her eyes," Betty recalls. "After all, he was her youngest!"

Little Linda was next to go. Lucile Fray, who had taught school for a year before her marriage, was especially happy about Linda's adoptive father, Clifford Keizer. A chemistry professor at Central College in Pella, Iowa, he and his wife, Ruth, had one adopted child, Richard, six years old; Linda, then five, seemed an ideal sister for him. Linda left her parents' home shortly before Thanksgiving, taking with her one memento of her family—a Santa Claus made out of an old light bulb and a salt box.

Alfred and Clara Johnson, who own a farm near Kinross, Iowa, had helped rear six foster children, but wanted one of their own. When they arrived at the Frays' they had a hard time making up their minds which of the children to take. All of them looked so attractive—especially Pauline, whose happy disposition delighted the visitors. The Johnsons finally decided they wanted Pauline.

As always, though, Pauline herself was given time to think about the adoption. The little girl made three weekend visits to the Johnson farm. She was pleased when they gave her a spotted calf of her own. She told her mother it was fun to sit in the Johnsons' large, sunny kitchen and do fancywork. When at last her mother asked her gently, "Do you want to go back there to stay?" Pauline nodded vigorously.

The Johnsons legally adopted Pauline the following March. When we saw her, more than a year later, she had recently finished an embroidered dresser scarf that her mother had started. "Mommy gave it to me the morning the Johnsons came to get me," Pauline told us. "And she said, 'Be a good girl, just as you always have been.'"

The pleasant couple who adopted Joyce Fray had three grown children and were grandparents. Joyce's new father had a good job and owned and operated a farm near Ottumwa. "We lost a little girl of our own when she was about Joyce's age," he explained. "We wanted another child to love."

As winter came, Joann, Virginia, Carl, Ivan, Jr., Warren and Frank were still waiting for homes. But Mrs. Fray, now in constant pain, refused to lower her standards. A wealthy farm couple who wanted a son were turned down because they said education wasn't important. Another well-to-do couple, who drove up in a fancy new car, were also sent away. "They wanted to take Warren," Mrs. Fray told the family council, "but they wanted to cut his ties with the past. They were even going to change his first name! But don't you worry," she added, "you'll all get good homes!"

Then Richard Thomas, a prosperous contractor in a town 200 miles from Ottumwa, arrived with his wife. They wanted Joann. "She was a lovable girl, and just the right age," Mrs. Thomas said.

The oldest of the Fray children, and presumably "set" in her ways, Joann Fray Thomas made the greatest transition. Living for years on the edge of hardship, she moved into a secure, prosperous environment and the life of a typical teenager. Although she lost a year of schooling during her mother's illness, two years later she stood at the top of her high-school class.

The Thomases were so pleased with their good fortune that they set about finding homes for the remaining Fray children. Within a week Virginia, Carl and Ivan, Jr., had found good homes among the Thomases' friends and neighbors.

A few days later a young school superintendent and his schoolteacher wife adopted Warren. Lucile Fray stood dry-eyed in the doorway as she watched the next-to-last of her children leave her forever.

The last was six-year-old Frank. For him Lucile Fray was resigned to the idea of institutional care. "It's too much to hope," she admitted. "They tell me Frank is epileptic. It's no use explaining what a darling he is—no one is going to take on such a burden." The following week she placed Frank in a hospital for physically incapacitated children.

By late spring Lucile Fray realized the end was near. Suddenly she was overwhelmed by the desire to see her children once more. Her doctor and husband protested, but she packed a suitcase and boarded a bus.

At the nine homes, Mrs. Fray seemed to find everything satisfactory. "I thought her visit would be difficult," Mrs.

Thomas said, "but she made it extremely pleasant. She acted like a visiting aunt."

A few hours before her death, on June 15, 1954, Lucile Fray asked for and received baptism. "My house is in order," she told her minister.

That summer the couple who had adopted Warren went to California to live. Before leaving they took Warren on a round of farewell visits, and at the children's hospital, when he said good-by, Frank asked, "Why don't *I* have a new mommy?"

No one answered him. "But when we got home," Warren's new father said, "neither my wife nor I could eat dinner. We just sat at the table, not saying anything, but each thinking the same thing.

"Then I said, 'It's an awful shame. He's such a handsome little boy!'

"And she said slowly, 'Epilepsy is caused by some kind of brain injury, isn't it? It could happen to anybody. If we had a child of our own—who could say he'd be perfect?'"

When the couple and Warren moved to California, they took Frank with them. He, too, became their legally adopted child. His seizures were increasingly rare and milder. His doctors held out hope of full recovery.

The good news traveled back to Iowa. Everybody said it's too bad Lucile Fray couldn't have known about it. We believe she does.

I Catch a Burglar

by John Berendt

Early one morning in February 1976, I found myself dreaming of a window-washer raising a window. The squeaking and scraping of the window became louder and clearer until I woke up to discover that the sounds were real—and that they were coming from the next room.

The two living-room windows were a tricky but not impossible climb from the garden one floor below. Burglars had come in through them twice before. After each break-in, I had put a new lock on the window they'd used and considered myself lucky I had not been home. Then for several years I had no burglaries, and I became complacent. Only the other day, for instance, I had noticed that one of the locks had rusted open, and I hadn't bothered to do anything about it.

Now I lay in bed stark-naked, straining to hear every sound. There was the hollow clomp of someone stepping onto the window seat, and then a pause.

I couldn't think of anything to do. A call for help would probably go unheard, except by the burglar. Making a run for it was out of the question, because the burglar stood between me and the front door. And there were no weapons at hand—only a heavy ashtray that would have been difficult to grasp and clumsier to wield.

I could only wait and listen, first to the sound of feet dropping to the floor, then to the thud of a potted plant falling over, followed by an interminable freeze-frame pause. At length, the footsteps resumed, stealthily creaking across the parquet toward my door.

A hand grasped the knob. The door brushed against the nap of the carpet as it opened. I could make out the shadowy outline of a man, a lumpy shape in a bulky jacket and baggy pants. He made a move toward me. I coughed, to let him know someone was there. He stopped and waited. Then he took one step backward. Then another, back into the living room.

He might be leaving. He might think I was asleep and try to rob the place quietly. Or possibly he was going to the kitchen to get a knife. That's what I'd heard up-to-date burglars in New York were doing: breaking into apartments unarmed to minimize chances of being caught with deadly weapons, and then availing themselves of the kitchen's culinary arsenal if need be, leaving it all behind on the way out.

I was not going to wait to find out what he was up to. First I reached for a pair of undershorts on a chair by the bed and slipped them on. Then I picked up the phone, a Touch-Tone dial with buttons instead of a dial wheel. Not only can one dial on it with the speed of a touch-typist, there is something even better for moments like this: the dial is perfectly silent—no ratchets, no clicks. Somebody standing two feet away wouldn't have known I was making a call.

Suddenly it occurred to me I should not call the police. They would be stymied at the apartment-house door downstairs, since I would be unable to get past the prowler to the buzzer to let them in. Instead I called an upstairs neighbor, who answered on the fifth ring.

In a whisper so soft that even I could hardly hear it, I managed to say, "It's Berendt. Second floor." He understood. I went on: "Somebody just broke into my apartment. He's here now. Call the police. Tell them to ring your apartment so you can buzz them in, but have them come straight to mine." He said he would, and I hung up.

The burglar was moving around quietly now, taking things off shelves, opening and closing cupboards. Abruptly, everything fell silent. The ensuing eternity lasted maybe five minutes—until at last the doorbell rang. It rang again.

Suddenly, I heard tiptoeing coming toward my bedroom at a quick pace. I jumped out of bed, snatched up the ashtray, and sprinted for the bedroom door. I swung at him as I headed toward the doorway, flinging butts and ashes over both of us. He darted into the bathroom, and I rushed past. He must have discovered instantly that the bathroom was windowless, but I now had a clear field to the front door and reached it in a matter of seconds.

I opened the door and saw a platoon of policemen in the hall. "There's a burglar in the bathroom," I said.

Three of the policemen moved to the far wall and drew their guns. The one in the lead stepped sideways through an archway that lay at right angles to the bathroom door, quickly reached in and switched on the light. "Come out or we'll blow your head off!" he said.

The burglar, a black man in his late 20s, came out silently. The policemen handcuffed him and relieved him of burglar tools, a pair of scissors, and a small tape recorder that belonged to me. He stood by the fireplace, sullen and a little dazed by the squad-room-like din of squawking two-way radios and the banter of at least seven policemen.

"This guy's been around," the policeman in charge told me. "Are you going to press charges?"

"Of course," I replied.

"Thanks," he said. "Every now and then we get someone who wants to forget the whole thing."

I did not look forward to sending a man to jail, or to spending months in court to seal his fate. But letting him skip off into the midst of unsuspecting victims, to be ferreted out all over again by the police, would have been the height of callous ingratitude. So I would press charges and just hope the man was not a vengeful sort.

What I did not know was that, within hours, a computer in the basement of the New York Criminal Courts Building would be easing my role by flagging the burglar, one James Harrison, for something called the Career Criminal Program. It was, I later learned, a hard-nose unit in the district attorney's office, set up with federal funds in October 1975 to deal exclusively with unregenerate repeaters who have become savvy in the ways of beating the rap. The idea was to select a few hundred of these professional offenders from the thousands of felony defendants in Manhattan and lead them at a gallop through the judicial system without giving them a chance to escape into the legal underbrush they know so well.

Primarily, the Career Criminal Program is notable for what

it does *not* do. It does not plea bargain just to expedite a case. It goes for felony convictions every time, and its record after its first year was 161 convictions (including guilty pleas) and only one acquitted.

Samuel Linderman was one of seven assistant district attorneys assigned to the program. "You may not be aware of it," he told me in his office a week later, "but the man who tried to rob you constitutes a one-man crime wave. Not only is James Harrison an accomplished and prolific burglar, but in the past seven years he has been arrested a total of 14 times, 11 times for burglary. On two occasions, he managed to have the case dismissed. Nine times he got off with a misdemeanor. Only once has he been convicted of a felony, for which he served one year and 11 months. He's not some kid on a lark; burglary is the way he makes his living. We've got him in jail now, and I want to see that he stays there a reasonable length of time."

Linderman next consulted a date book. "Ordinarily it would take a month or two to get him before a grand jury. But since we are considered something of an elite outfit, we can speed things up a little."

That was an understatement: the next day, at 2 p.m., the grand jury convened to consider the Harrison case. At 3:10, Linderman called to tell me I would not even be needed to testify and that an indictment could be expected in a few days.

Events took an odd turn the following day. A man purporting to be a friend of James Harrison telephoned and asked me not to press charges. His tone was not threatening, but it was unnerving to know that someone was at large with a grievance against me.

I called Linderman. He was certain the caller had been Harrison himself, talking from a cellblock pay phone. "You can be pretty sure he'll call again," I was told. "And let me warn you: he will try to establish a rapport with you, find out insignificant details about your life, and you would be shocked at what could happen next."

Linderman went on to describe what might happen: "Harrison would refuse to plead guilty. He would go to trial and claim that you and he were intimate friends. He's desperate, but very shrewd. He knows that at this stage the whole system is weighted in his favor, and he is looking for some kind of leverage. So if he calls again, tell him you've informed me about it, then hang up. And don't worry; he isn't a violent person. It's unlikely he'll ever retaliate. But let me know if he contacts you again."

A second call came a few days later. This time the man owned up to being Harrison. He professed to being sorry for what he had done, but I held my ground firmly when he asked to be let off. The call was followed by a long letter from Harrison. It was contrite and imploring, yet skillfully avoided the use of a single self-incriminating sentence. That was the last I heard from him.

Linderman later told me that Harrison had sent up a small blizzard of legal paperwork in the form of motions before bowing to the intransigence of the Career Criminal Program and being convicted of a felony—by pleading guilty to third-degree burglary. He was sentenced to two to four years.

Sending Harrison to jail was not a pleasant thing to have to do; doubtless, jail will do nothing to improve his lot, and the odds are he will go right back to burgling when he gets out. But if he was breaking into just one apartment a week (a conservative estimate, according to Linderman), then his sentence can be looked upon as 100 or 200 burglaries he would never get a chance to commit. And that, at least, is reassuring. So is the fact that the judicial system *can* move swiftly at times.

The Undelivered Letter

by Fulton Oursler

Some years ago there lived in an English city a man whom I shall call Fred Armstrong. He worked in the local post office, where he was called the "dead-letter man" because he handled missives whose addresses were faulty or hard to read. He lived in an old house with his little wife, and even smaller daughter and a tiny son. After supper he liked to light his pipe and tell his children of his latest exploits in delivering lost letters. He considered himself quite a detective. There was no cloud on his modest horizon.

No cloud until one sunny morning when his little boy suddenly fell ill. Within 48 hours the child was dead.

In his sorrow, Fred Armstrong's soul seemed to die. The mother and their little daughter, Marian, struggled to control their grief, determined to make the best of it. Not so the father. His life was now a dead letter with no direction. In the morning Fred Armstrong rose from his bed and went to work like a sleepwalker; he never spoke unless spoken to, ate his lunch alone, sat like a statue at the supper table and went to bed early. Yet his wife knew that he lay most of the night with eyes open, staring at the ceiling. As the months passed, his apathy seemed to deepen.

His wife told him that such despair was unfair to their lost son and unfair to the living. But nothing she said seemed to reach him.

It was coming close upon Christmas. One bleak afternoon at work Fred Armstrong sat on his high stool and shoved a new pile of letters under the swinging electric lamp. On the top of the stack was an envelope that was clearly undeliverable. In crude block letters were penciled the words: "SANTA CLAUS, NORTH POLE.". Armstrong started to throw it away when some impulse made him pause. He opened the letter and read:

> Dear Santa Claus: We are very sad at our house this year, and I don't want you to bring me anything. My little brother went to heaven last spring. All I want you to do when you come to our house is to take Brother's toys to him. I'll leave them in the corner by the kitchen stove; his hobby-horse and train and everything. I know he'll be lost up in heaven without them, most of all his horse; he always liked riding it so much, so you must take them to him, please, and you needn't mind leaving me anything, but if you could give Daddy something that would make him like he used to be, make him smoke his pipe again and tell me stories, I do wish you would. I heard him say to Mummie once that only Eternity could cure him. Could you bring him some of that, and I will be your good little girl.
>
> Marian

That night Fred Armstrong walked home at a faster gait. In the winter darkness he stood in the dooryard garden and struck a match. Then as he opened the kitchen door he blew a great puff from his pipe, and the smoke settled like a nimbus around the heads of his startled wife and daughter. And he was smiling at them just as he used to do.

"We're Too Close to the Falls!"

by James H. Winchester

Thousands of tourists crowded both the American and Canadian shores of Niagara Falls. At the eastern tip of Goat Island, on the U.S. side of the Niagara River, Bill Faust was resting in the ticket booth at the Prior Aviation sightseeing heliport. Only a few hundred yards away, 100,000 cubic feet of rushing water makes a showy 161-foot drop over the Horseshoe and American falls every second. It had been a busy day, that first Sunday of October 1973, and the three-passenger helicopter was now away refueling at Niagara Falls Airport.

Glancing idly toward the Canadian shore, Faust was electrified. Mid-river, already wrapped in spray, a small boat was sweeping toward the lip of Horseshoe Falls. His first thought: *My God! Nothing can keep them from going over the falls.*

Four people were in the boat. In the bow were Lee Sweitzer, 21, of Buffalo, N.Y., Jo Ann Horn, 21, of Tonawanda, N.Y., and her 18-month-old son, Michael. Jerry Land, 20, also from Buffalo, was at the tiller of the outboard motor in the stern.

Totally unfamiliar with the Niagara River, the group had blithely started out from Buffalo two hours earlier. Moving downstream in a 15-foot boat borrowed from Jerry's mother, they somehow hadn't seen the huge warning signs three miles back from the falls banning all boating beyond that point.

Between Goat Island and Canada, the Niagara River is only three to four feet deep in most places, but filled with great boulders and boiling rapids. The boat was less than a half-mile from Horseshoe Falls when the outboard motor's propeller blade struck a rock, tearing itself loose from the drive shaft. "No control! No control!" Jerry cried. Suddenly aware of the roar of cascading water, he yelled another warning: "I think we're too close to the falls!" He tried to steer toward Goat Island, 100 yards to the right, but the boat was already caught in the river's accelerating 20 m.p.h. downhill race.

Leaving little Michael, the only one wearing a life jacket, alone in the craft, the two young men and Jo Ann jumped into the river and struggled desperately to hold back the boat in the waist-high water. It was impossible. The solid-stone river bottom was slick as glass, and the current's inexorable force tore Jo Ann and Lee off their feet, ripping their hands from the boat. Jo Ann's scream was piercing: "The baby!"

Jerry still held on to the boat, but it was plunging uncontrolled toward the falls. Letting go, he grabbed Michael by his life jacket, lifting him clear. He held him high above his head and fought to keep his balance. Jo Ann and Lee didn't regain their feet until they were 150 feet closer to the falls; now they braced against each other for shaky support.

Alerted by phone, at 3:33 p.m. the Niagara Frontier State Park Police radioed a report that a boat had been sighted off the east end of Goat Island. With siren wailing, patrolman James MacNeil drove to Goat Island's eastern tip in less than two minutes—three other Park policemen just behind him. As they watched, the boat shot over the brink of Horseshoe Falls, dropping to destruction in the rock-filled whirlpools below. "In front of me," MacNeil recalls, "were the people from the boat. The girl kept stumbling, and the fellow with her kept grabbing her before she could be swept away. The guy holding the baby was closest, maybe 300 feet out."

Looping a coil of quarter-inch nylon rope around his waist, with the three officers holding the other end, MacNeil waded toward the stranded boaters. But even this powerful 210-pound man couldn't keep his balance in the rushing river. Time after time he was knocked off his feet—and finally had to be pulled back to land.

At this point, the police saw the sightseeing helicopter approach its landing pad 100 yards away. Pushing through the gathering crowd, MacNeil and Sgt. Joseph Boyd raced to the heliport and shouted an explanation of the situation to pilot Dale Hartman. He kept the blades turning as the patrolmen removed two pins from their hinges, tore off the right door and tumbled into the small cabin, then he lifted off. Seated in the open door, MacNeil planted his feet on the landing skid, while Boyd held him from behind by his belt.

As the chopper hovered over Jerry Land and baby Michael, MacNeil leaned out and grabbed the baby's life jacket. He flipped the child back over his shoulder. "I've got him!" Boyd shouted. "Take off!"

Seeing the helicopter begin to move away—and not realizing that it could carry no more passengers—Jerry Land lunged in panic at the skid rising above his head. He gripped it hard, and for an instant it seemed he would be lifted clear of the clinging current. Feeling the sudden dragging weight, the pilot frantically tried to compensate on the controls. He was too late. The tip of one of the rotor blades, yanked down by Land's 150 pounds, slashed into the water and shattered.

Dropping like a rock, the helicopter smashed into the water with such force that the just-filled fuel tanks ripped apart. The volatile gasoline, spraying in all directions, struck the exposed, red-hot exhaust pipes and exploded in a gigantic, deafening burst of red flame.

Never had young mother Jo Ann experienced such a "gone" feeling. *The baby is dead for sure,* she thought and went limp, rolling another 50 feet closer to the falls before Lee could help her back to her feet.

As the plane exploded, Land's grasp on the skid was torn loose, and he was thrown back into the water. Semiconscious, the pilot dangled forward, held by his seat belt and shoulder harness. Patrolman MacNeil found himself "face down on the bottom of the river, being scraped along by the current." When he managed to surface, he was in the middle of a 50-foot-wide pool of blazing gasoline. Trapped, with his left arm almost useless from hitting something and with his hair and eyebrows singed from the heat, he ducked back under the water.

Sergeant Boyd, with the baby in his grasp, was also propelled into the flames. "I was turning over and over," says the six-foot-four, 200-pound Boyd. "When I realized I no longer had the baby in my grip, it was the worst moment of my life!"

Downstream, MacNeil surfaced again—this time out of the flames. He caught a flashing glimpse of Michael's bright-red jacket as the child, buoyed face-up by his life jacket, swept past. Lunging from his feet in pure reflex, the patrolman grabbed for him. "I just caught him by his foot," he says. "Thank God my grip held. It was a miracle!"

The fiery gasoline, moving swiftly on the current, headed for Jo Ann and Lee. "I thought the flames would cover us," she says, shuddering. Instead, they swept past just inches away. Seconds later, the sheet of fire passed MacNeil, fighting to get back on his feet with the baby.

Where the wrecked helicopter rested precariously in the riverbed with part of its bubble cabin exposed, pilot Hartman loosened his seat belt and climbed out, dazed and bleeding from a deep scalp wound. Boyd stood 60 feet away, and Land a little beyond. Farther out, Jo Ann and Lee couldn't move against the strong stream. Below them, the baby was held tight by MacNeil. "I didn't dare shift my feet," he says. "I had them wedged in a crack in the stone bottom."

The time was now 3:45 p.m. Police, fire engines and other rescue vehicles filled the afternoon air with the sound of sirens as they raced to the scene. From the Canadian side of the river, in the joint control room of the New York State Power Authority and the Ontario Hydro Corp., the supervisor on duty watched through binoculars. International agreements strictly limit the amount of water the two companies can take out of the river to make electricity: any extra withdrawals require the approval of both countries. Despite this legal barrier, knowing the waist-high current was strong enough to sweep those in the river to their deaths, the supervisor flipped switches opening a dozen extra gates, slowly decreasing the water level by one third.

Thus aided, Sergeant Boyd and Land wallowed back to the helicopter, from which the policeman salvaged a length of quarter-inch rope. He tied one end to the wreck and floated the line downstream toward his partner. Finally grabbing the rope, MacNeil inched his way back along its taut length to the wreck, dragging little Michael with him. Climbing into the partly submerged bubble, he slumped down exhausted, the baby in his arms. "I thought he was dead," he says. "I started breathing into his mouth and shaking him. In a minute or so, he began to cry. I just hugged him close, and pretty soon he went off to sleep."

Real rescue, though, was still far away. On Goat Island, police readied a line-throwing gun that shoots a projectile pulling 600 feet of thin nylon cord behind it. This in turn is used to pull a half-inch line, followed by a heavier one-inch manila rope.

Sgt. Lyle Newberry made a perfect shot across the top of the helicopter 300 feet away, but when Boyd and Land started pulling the cord toward them it broke. Another try. Another perfect shot. This time the line remained intact. But it would take over an hour to work the one-inch line out to the helicopter. Meanwhile, the current threatened to dislodge the wreck and send it over the falls. And the line used to pull MacNeil and the baby back to the wreck was lost in efforts to get it to Jo Ann and Lee.

The police decided to try their boat, an 18-foot craft with 110-h.p. main motor and 10-h.p. auxiliary berthed a mile back up the river. It had never been taken this far downstream.

At 4:32 p.m., with both motors running for better steering, the white police boat moved cautiously downstream. Newberry was at the wheel in the bow while Lt. Joseph DeMarco, commanding officer of the Park police, and patrolman Anthony Larratta handled the motors in the stern. A hundred yards from the wreck, the big motor broke its shaft on the rocky bottom and the auxiliary motor stuttered to a stop. When the anchor wouldn't catch, the two men in the stern leaped into the rushing water, shouting, "Get out!" at Newberry, who was still trying to restart the auxiliary motor.

Jumping over the side, the 48-year-old sergeant was swept off his feet. Vainly he fought for a grip on the slippery rocks. The tips of his fingers were scraped to bloody stumps, and his wedding ring was torn from his finger as he was swept on in the frothing rapids. The empty police boat had already gone over Horseshoe Falls. The commanding officer's heart almost stopped as Newberry disappeared, too. His only thought: *He's gone!*

Somewhere in Newberry's brutal tumble, the straps of his life jacket snapped. Pushed down around his legs, it bound them together like a rope. Unable to kick, he got some help from the current as it curved toward Brother Island, the last solid surface before the drop over the falls. "I was just a couple of feet away from the bank, and moving fast," he says. "I grabbed at some overhanging shrubs and caught one about the size of a broom handle with my right hand. How I held on!"

Getting both hands on the branch, he inched his way out of the water. "I just lay there, numb and battered," he says, "thanking God over and over." (He was rescued later by firemen with an extension ladder.)

Nine people were still in the water off Goat Island, five of them at the wrecked helicopter. At 4:56 a Canadian sightseeing helicopter moved into position near patrolman DeMarco and Lieutenant Larratta, and dropped a 3/4-inch manila line. The other end of this line was then dropped to the people at the wreck. Using this lifeline, the two policemen worked their way upstream to the others. Then they floated the rope down to Jo Ann and Lee. Ten minutes later they, too, had been pulled back, and baby Michael was handed to his sobbing mother.

By 5:31, Sergeant Boyd and Lieutenant DeMarco completed the backbreaking task of pulling the dragging one-inch manila line, out through the water from shore. Now the stranded group was ready to try to get to land.

DeMarco, holding baby Michael in one arm and clinging to the line with the other, went first. Behind him came Jo Ann, assisted by patrolman Larratta. Helicopter pilot Hartman, his head bloody, was next, with Lee and Jerry behind him. In the rear, patrolman MacNeil, who couldn't use his injured left arm at all, was assisted by Sergeant Boyd. It took 20 minutes to get to shore, but they made it.

The thousands of tourists who had watched the spectacle cheered wildly. From hundreds of cars on both sides of the river, horns blared. What a Niagara Falls *Gazette* reporter called "the most involved and dangerous rescue ever made at the falls" had ended in success.

All of the Niagara Park police who so risked their lives were soon back on the job, their everyday work more concerned with traffic than thrillers. When Jo Ann expressed her thanks to them, their reaction was "That's all right, it's part of our job. But *please*, don't do it again!"

Rescue From a Fanatic Cult

by Charles H. Edwards, M.D.

Unless it happens to you, you can't possibly imagine the anguish of losing a son or daughter to one of the extremist religious cults. I know because it happened to Betty and me. It was a nightmare neither we nor our boy, Chris, will ever forget.

Our son join a cult? "Impossible!" I would have said before it happened. Here was a young man who had been an excellent student from prep school through college. He was a religious youth, though not a zealot. He held strong moral views, had lots of friends, a good home, and an older brother he was close to.

During the few days he was home after graduation from Yale in 1975, Chris appeared mentally drained and exhausted. And though anxious to be off to California to investigate graduate schools, he was still uncertain what he wanted to do with his future. It was an unsettling time for him—one, we would later learn, in which a young person is particularly vulnerable to cult indoctrination.

Prior to leaving for the Coast, Chris promised to write or call every few weeks. It was a pledge he lived up to. But we began to notice something in his voice and in his answers to our questions about where he was living and his new friends that gave us an uneasy feeling.

After four months, Chris wrote and enclosed a clipping that he said would explain what he was doing. It was a description of "Creative Community Projects," an organization we'd never heard of. A few days later a local paper ran a story reporting that Rabbi Maurice Davis of White Plains, N.Y., was holding a meeting for parents whose children had run off and joined religious cults. Among the groups mentioned was Creative Community Projects—one of a number of groups sponsored by the Unification Church.

When Betty and I attended the meeting, we found ourselves among almost 500 distraught parents. After talking with some of them and listening to Rabbi Davis, we could no longer have any doubts. Chris had become a disciple of the Korean self-ordained Rev. Sun Myung Moon and his Unification Church—commonly referred to as "Moonies."

Immediately after the meeting, Betty and I told our story to Rabbi Davis, a calm, soft-spoken man who had helped numerous parents with similar problems. He explained that the Moon organization is highly selective about the boys and girls it recruits. Blacks and Hispanics are usually ignored: they're considered too "street-wise." Instead, the cult seeks out well-educated, religiously oriented, white middle-class youngsters who appear to have relatively well-heeled parents.

The Moonies, we were told, convert recruits into cultists by programming every minute of their waking hours. Hard-core Moonies are assigned to all novices, talking to them incessantly, never giving them a chance to talk or ask questions. Underfed, and with only four or five hours' sleep at night, these youngsters are psychologically worn down until they're brought under complete mind control and fall into a trance somewhat like an autohypnotic state where their wills aren't their own—they belong to Moon.

The first step in getting our son back, Rabbi Davis advised, was to keep a good relationship with Chris and not antagonize him about his Unification Church affiliation. He also suggested that Ted Patrick, one of the most successful "deprogrammers" of young cultists, might be able to help us.

Patrick, who first started fighting these groups when his own son joined a cult, was sympathetic when we phoned him at his headquarters in National City, Calif. But he told us he was so busy we'd have to wait at least two and a half months before he could handle our case.

Meanwhile, we tried to continue with Chris as though nothing had happened. But it became increasingly difficult. Cued by some of the Moonies (we could hear them in the background when Chris called) he began pressing us for money, stocks or an automobile—assets we knew would be turned over to the organization. Chris was growing more and more alienated from us: he turned down an invitation to come home for Thanksgiving, then ignored the funeral of a favorite great-aunt.

Just before Christmas, he suddenly began calling daily instead of every other week. Sometimes as he was talking we'd hear a Moonie come into his room and Chris would hang up. Betty and I got the feeling he was subconsciously signaling us that something was wrong.

When we told Patrick, he agreed it was urgent and said he would attempt to free Chris as soon as possible. I was now committed to an act that put my name, reputation and profession on the line. I was going to abduct my son from a religious cult—quite possibly against his brainwashed will. Law or no law, I felt it was my moral right and duty. The Unification Church had taken away my son's will and ability to think for himself. Chris deserved to have those things returned, whatever the cost.

During the first week of January 1976 I flew to California. It took five tries before I finally got to see Chris. Each time I'd go to the Moonie house where he was staying, I was told a different story. Finally, I was told Chris would be waiting for me at a Moonie-owned coffee shop a few blocks from the house.

He was with a dozen or so others who worked in the place. At first glance they seemed like nice, normal kids. But then I noticed the glazed, faraway look in their eyes. It was as though I'd walked into a room filled with zombies. And there was Chris, just like them. He looked up and said, "Hello, Dad." No emotion, not even a smile. I broke down and wept like a child.

Chris came over, and I hugged him. He patted me on the back. "That's all right, Dad," he said, still without emotion. "Go ahead and cry if you have to." When I finally got hold of myself, he invited me to have dinner with him and the Moonies that evening at their communal dining hall.

There were other outsiders there, mostly kids the Moon missionaries had picked up off the street that day. As the evening wore on, I felt myself being caught up in the experience. All that talk of "love" and "fellowship," that rhythmic sermonizing and singing were hypnotic. I even got up and sang. I could see how, after an initial encounter, Moonies were able to spot a prospective convert and induce him to spend a weekend at one of their isolated retreats where the organization's thought-programming takes place.

Chris agreed to lunch with me the following day. When I picked him up, he was with another hard-core Moonie, a girl. I drove the rented car to a rendezvous where two of Ted Patrick's associates were waiting. As I stopped, one of the men opened the front door and asked the girl to step out. She first refused, but was finally persuaded. In a flash, he jumped in front next to Chris, and the other man got into the back.

As I sped away, I could hear the girl screaming. Chris, however, just sat there like a mummy for about half a minute, then turned to me and said softly, "Thank you, Dad." I'm still not sure whether he was sincere or had been programmed to say that in order to put us off guard and later escape. But he was now safely in our custody, and the initial phase of the deprogramming could get under way in the motel rooms I'd reserved.

As Ted Patrick started talking quietly, I realized what a traumatic experience was in store for my son. Ted's aides and I sat rapt as Ted mentally worked Chris over, trying to get him to respond to his questions. The first session lasted five horrible hours. As Ted talked, Chris chanted prayers to block out anything that would challenge the Moon philosophy.

"What do you think Moon does with all this money?" Ted asked. "Do you know any good he's done? Do you know anybody he's helped?" The idea was to get Chris to use his mind. Trained not to think for themselves, some deprogrammed Moonies even have to ask whether they can go to the bathroom.

Under normal conditions deprogramming is difficult, but in Chris's case it was especially so. He knew enough about pyschology and psychiatry so the techniques initially had little effect. But Ted kept at it for three days, and in one final 14-hour session he got Chris to respond and challenge him at last—a sign he had begun to think for himself again.

After that breakthrough, the deprogramming was taken over by two former Moonies. This phase continued for three weeks. Even though Chris seemed to be responding well, he was never left alone for fear he might try to escape.

Meanwhile, at home, Betty spent her days trying to locate a psychiatrist or psychologist who could help with Chris's rehabilitation. Eventually, she found Dr. Hardat Sukhdeo, a Newark, N.J., psychiatrist who is also an expert on cults—one of a handful in the United States. She arranged to have Chris see him five days a week.

We brought Chris home in February. Almost immediately, the Moonies began harassing us with calls 24 hours a day, even after we switched to an unlisted number. The organization was trying to get through to Chris. At this stage, we were told, he was still subject to posthypnotic suggestion and could be induced to rejoin the group.

When Chris didn't answer or return the calls, the Moonies began threatening Betty and me—threats we took seriously enough to hire round-the-clock armed bodyguards. Even so, the organization kept us under constant surveillance.

Thank God, the phone calls and the harassment gradually tapered off, though we continued to maintain our vigilance. We'd shown that we wouldn't give up our son regardless of intimidations. More than a year later we still didn't feel entirely safe. But what was important was that Chris regained his self-identity and confidence. He was seeing old friends again, working at a temporary job, and actively thinking about a career. Moreover, he had begun helping deprogram and rehabilitate other cultists.

Betty and I? We were emotionally exhausted and, because of the extraordinary expenses, financially all but wiped out. But we'd got Chris back to the point where he could stand on his own and lead a normal life. Nothing else really mattered.

Strange Encounter With a Blue Jay

by Thomza Zimmerman

I don't expect anyone to put credence in the story I am about to tell. Then why do I write it? I'm not quite sure. Maybe because a remembered experience is more easily put aside for all time after it is written down. Maybe because I walked through the yard this morning and picked up a blue jay's feather.

The story has to do with a jaybird that lived with us for more than two years. We called him Pesty.

But not at first. At first he was just the unfortunate ball of gray fluff that fell from the nest in the maple tree. I didn't relish the thought of the hapless creature being devoured by a passing cat, so I took him in.

As I put him into a box lined with toweling, I hoped he would not be too uncomfortable during his few remaining hours of life. My husband, Lyman, came in from his work in the fields, peered into the box and grinned. Without knowing it, we had been taken over by a jaybird.

The name Pesty came as he grew older, when he began to catch bugs and happily store them away in my freshly done hair, lift the blossoms from a bouquet and take a bath in the bowl, and object in no uncertain terms when a guest unwittingly sat in Lyman's chair.

But this is not what makes the story so different or so strange. The unbelievable part came later. More than a year after Pesty was gone.

From the day Lyman brought a fat earthworm from the garden to supplement Pesty's diet of boiled egg yolks and baked pie crust, Pesty became Lyman's bird. He perched on the arm of his chair and waited, with no sign of impatience or boredom, while Lyman read the paper. If Lyman napped, Pesty sat quietly on his shoulder. Though Pesty didn't like being fondled ("I'll make the advances," his manner quickly told you), at bedtime Lyman would pick him up from wherever he happened to be—the mantel, the top of a curtain, the back of a chair—and hold him a moment against his cheek, where Pesty actually snuggled. Then Lyman carried him to his night-time perch, a bathroom towel bar.

When daylight edged its way through the east windows, I would feel a soft touch on my pillow and then a bobby pin being slipped gently from my hair. Pesty knew I got up first to start breakfast. It was time.

Although his food and water were always in the kitchen window, Pesty preferred eating at the table. "He thinks he's people," our neighbor would say. And Pesty's favorite meal, like most country people's, was breakfast. He drank coffee from a butter-pat-size saucer, and ate scrambled eggs—with butter, thank you. When he was finished, he hopped to Lyman's shoulder and waited politely until we were through too.

Like a boy following in the footsteps of his father, Pesty took up smoking. In one quick movement he could have a cigarette from the pocket in Lyman's shirt. At first, we thought it was clever and enjoyed telling people about it. But when he made attempts to light his cigarette, a scorched rug resulted. After that, the matches were kept in a drawer.

Pesty's level of intelligence never ceased to amaze us. He learned the sound of Lyman's tractor and the car. When he heard either of them coming he went quickly to the door to welcome Lyman home.

Pesty chose his own friends, and he preferred men. When Lyman had company over to play cards, Pesty sat in on the game from the safety of Lyman's shoulder. The cards fascinated him, and with his dexterity he had to be watched. He could take a card quickly and make off with it. This brought about a chase and sometimes a scolding from Lyman, but it heightened the evening's fun.

We never confined our bird to the house. We wanted him to know the outdoors and expected that someday he would join his kind. But the yard birds resented him intensely, and he usually preferred to stay in the house.

There was a day, however, when he chose to stay outdoors. It was a balmy, summer-scented morning, and Lyman and I were going to join friends for an all-day picnic. When we were ready to go, Pesty was outside. We tried to bring him in, but he wasn't ready.

Pesty seemed not to have an adequate supply of oil in his feathers. After a bath he could never fly, and walked around like a decrepit little old man until he was dry again. For this reason Lyman scanned the sky. "There's no sign of rain," he concluded, and we left. Before we returned there was a severe downpour.

Lyman called and looked and hunted for days, but we never found Pesty.

The summer ended, the harvest was in, we made ready for winter. In due time the snows melted, the crocus came up, spring passed and again it was summer. The wild rose was blooming in old fence rows; the smell of honeysuckle was heavy on the morning air.

I was busy in the kitchen when I heard the birds making a great commotion. The raucous cries of the blue jays had brought them all: the robins and cardinals, the mockingbird and wrens, the brown thrasher and the orioles. Even the indigo bunting came from the raspberry border, and I went too. They were gathered over and around the garage where a lone blue jay was sitting on a crosspiece above the door. The hostility of the other birds told me he was a stranger.

With my arrival the yard birds settled down and went back to their various concerns, but the new bird remained. His shorter tail marked him as a young bird, hatched just that spring. His eyes were bright, his beak strong and straight. A bird analyst would have called him a fine, healthy specimen.

The young blue jay looked at me with a show of interest that held no fear. *He may be hungry,* I thought, and brought a cookie. When I offered it, he bent down and nibbled.

Rabbits live and frolic at random in our garden. Squirrels feed in our corncrib and then play on the roof. In winter, birds eat from feeders with only a windowpane between them and us. There is a joy in being accepted and trusted by a creature of the wild. I knew that joy now, but overriding it was the knowledge that the young jay's behavior was anything but normal. There was something here I didn't understand.

I went around the house and sat on the patio. The bird came and sat on the arm of a chair close by. Later, when I went inside, the bird came with me. He went immediately to the window over the kitchen sink where Pesty used to sit and was there when Lyman came in for lunch.

Lyman stopped halfway across the kitchen and looked at the bird in the window, then turned and looked at me, with his eyes wide and full of questions. I told him what little I could.

When we sat down to eat, the strange bird came and perched on the back of a chair at the table. After a few seconds he hopped up onto Lyman's shoulder. At this, Lyman stiffened visibly, and I thought his face paled. After another minute or two, the bird went back to the window.

The meal ended sooner than it should have. Dessert was refused. Lyman got up and without a glance toward the window started back to work. The bird followed him to the back porch, sat in the window and watched him go.

I cleared the table, left the dishes in the sink and went outside. *I'll go for a walk,* I thought. *I'll go to the pasture fence and see if berries are ripening.*

I walked through the pasture but forgot to look for berries. When I came back to the house, the blue jay was still in the back-porch window. He was dead.

I held the small, limp form in my hand, and tears flowed down my cheeks. A flood of questions crowded my mind. Questions . . . without answers.

"I Died at 10:52 A.M."

by Victor D. Solow

When I left home with my wife that morning to go for a ten-minute jog, I did not know I would be gone for two weeks. My trip was the one all of us must make eventually, from which only a rare few return. In my case a series of events occurred so extraordinarily timed to allow my eventual survival that words like "luck" or "coincidence" no longer seem applicable.

It was a beautiful Saturday morning—March 23, 1974. We had jogged and were driving back home to Mamaroneck, N.Y., along the Boston Post Road. It was 10:52 a.m. I had just stopped at a red light, opposite a gas station. My long, strange trip was about to start, and I must now use my wife's words to describe what happened for the next few minutes:

"Victor turned to me and said, 'Oh, Lucy, I . . .' Then, as swiftly as the expiration of a breath, he seemed simply to settle down in his seat with all his weight. His head remained erect, his eyes opened wide, like someone utterly astonished. I knew instantly he could no longer hear or see me.

"I pulled on the emergency brake, pleading with him to hang on, shouting for help. The light changed and traffic moved around the car. No one noticed me. My husband's color had now turned gray-green; his mouth hung open, but his eyes continued seemingly to view an astounding scene. I frantically tried to pull him to the other seat so I could drive him to the hospital. Then my cries for help attracted Frank Colangelo, proprietor of the gas station, who telephoned the police."

It was now 10:55—three minutes had elapsed since my heart arrest. Time was running out. In another 60 seconds my brain cells could start to die.

Now came the first of the coincidences: Before police headquarters could radio the emergency call, officer James Donnellan, cruising along the Boston Post Road, arrived at the intersection where our car seemed stalled. Checking me for pulse and respiration, and finding neither, he pulled me from the car with the help of Mr. Colangelo, and immediately started cardio-pulmonary resuscitation.

In the meantime, the police alert reached officer Michael Sena, who chanced to be cruising just half a mile from the scene. He reached me in less than half a minute. From his car Sena yanked an oxygen tank and an apparatus with a mask which is used to force air into the lungs. Within seconds he had the mask over my face. Donnellan continued with heart massage. Sena later told me, "I was sure we were just going through the motions. I would have bet my job you were gone."

Police headquarters also alerted the emergency rescue squad via a high-pitched radio signal on the small alert boxes all squad members carry on their belts. When his warning signal went off, Tom McCann, volunteer fireman and trained emergency medical technician, was conducting a fire inspection. He looked up and saw officers Donnellan and Sena working on a "body" less than 50 yards away. He raced over, arriving just ten seconds after his alarm sounded.

"I tried the carotid pulse—you had no pulse," McCann later said. "There was no breathing. Your eyes were open, and your pupils were dilated—a bad sign!" Dilated pupils indicate blood is not reaching the brain. It can mean that death has occurred.

It was 10:56. McCann, who weighs 270 pounds, began to give me a no-nonsense heart massage.

The strange coincidences continued. The emergency-squad warning beeper went off at the exact moment when Peter Brehmer, Ronald Capasso, Chip Rigano, and Richard and Paul Torpey were meeting at the firehouse to change shifts. A moment later and they would have left. The ambulance was right there. Everybody piled in. Manned by five trained first-aid technicians, the ambulance arrived three minutes later. It was 10:59.

When I was being moved into the ambulance, United Hospital in Port Chester, six miles distant, was radioed. The hospital called a "Code 99" over its loudspeaker system, signaling all available personnel into the Emergency Room. When I arrived, two internists, two surgeons, two technicians from the cardiology department, two respiratory therapists and four nurses were waiting. Dr. Harold Roth later said: "The patient at that point was dead by available standards. There was no measurable pulse; he was not breathing; he appeared to have no vital signs whatever."

11:10 a.m. A cardiac monitor was attached; a tube supplying pure oxygen was placed in my windpipe; intravenous injections were started. An electric-shock apparatus was then attached to my chest.

11:14. The first electric shock was powerful enough to lift my body inches off the operating table. But no result: my heart still showed no activity.

11:15. A second electric shock was applied—a final try. Twenty-three minutes had elapsed since my heart had stopped. Now, excitement exploded around the operating table as an irregular heart rhythm suddenly showed on the monitor. To everyone's amazement, I sat bolt upright and started to get off the table. I had to be restrained.

Sometime later I was aware that my eyes were open. But I was still part of another world. It seemed that by chance I had been given this human body and it was difficult to wear. Dr. Roth later related: "I came to see you in the Coronary Care Unit. You were perfectly conscious. I asked how you felt, and your response was: 'I feel like I've been there and I've come back.' It was true: you were there and now you were back."

A hard time followed. I could not connect with the world around me. Was I really here now, or was it an illusion? Was that other condition of being I had just experienced the reality, or was *that* the illusion? I would lie there and observe my body with suspicion and amazement. It seemed to be doing things of its own volition and I was a visitor within. How strange to see my hand reach out for something. Eating, drinking, watching people had a dream-like, slow-motion quality as if seen through a veil.

During those first few days I was two people. My absent-mindedness and strange detachment gave the doctors pause. Perhaps the brain had been damaged after all. Their concern is reflected in hospital records: "Retrograde amnesia and difficulty with subsequent current events were recognized. . . . The neurologist felt prognosis was rather guarded regarding future good judgment."

On the sixth day there was a sudden change. When I woke up, the world around me no longer seemed so peculiar. Something in me had decided to complete the return trip. From that day on, recovery was rapid. Eight days later I was discharged from the hospital.

Now family, friends and strangers began to ask what "death was like." Could I remember what had happened during those 23 minutes when heart and breathing stopped? I found the experience could not easily be communicated.

Later, feeling and thinking my way back into the experience, I discovered why I could not make it a simple recital of events: when I left my body I also left all sensory human tools behind with which we perceive the world we take for real. But I found I now *knew* certain things about my place in this our world and my relationship to that other reality. My knowing was not through my brain but with another part of me which I cannot explain.

For me, the moment of transition from life to death—what else can one call it—was easy. There was no time for fear, pain or thought. There was no chance "to see my whole life before me," as others have related. The last impression I can recall lasted a brief instant. I was moving at high speed toward a net of great luminosity. The strands and knots where the luminous lines intersected were vibrating with a tremendous cold energy. The grid appeared as a barrier that would prevent further travel. I did not want to move through the grid. For a brief moment my speed appeared to slow down. Then I was in the grid. The instant I made contact with it, the vibrant luminosity increased to a blinding intensity which drained, absorbed and transformed me at the same time. There was no pain. The sensation was neither pleasant nor unpleasant but completely consuming. The nature of everything had changed. Words only vaguely approximate the experience from this instant on.

The grid was like a transformer, an energy converter transporting me through form and into formlessness, beyond time and space. Now I was not in a place, nor even in a dimension, but rather in a condition of being. This new "I" was not the I which I knew, but rather a distilled essence of it, yet something vaguely familiar, something I had always known, buried under a superstructure of personal fears, hopes, wants and needs. This "I" had no connection to ego. It was final, unchangeable, indivisible, indestructible pure spirit. While completely unique and individual as a fingerprint, "I" was, at the same time, part of some infinite, harmonious and ordered whole. I had been there before.

The condition "I" was in was pervaded by a sense of great stillness and deep quiet. Yet there was also a sense of something momentous about to be revealed, a further change. But there is nothing further to tell except of my sudden return to the operating table.

I would like to repeat that these experiences outside the dimensions of our known reality did not "happen" as if I were on some sort of a voyage I could recollect. Rather, I discovered them afterward, rooted in my consciousness as a kind of unquestionable knowing. Being of a somewhat skeptical turn of mind, I am willing to grant the possibility that this is a leftover of some subtle form of brain damage. I know, however, that since my return from that other condition of being, many of my attitudes toward our world have changed and continue to change, almost by themselves. A recurrent nostalgia remains for that other reality, that condition of indescribable stillness and quiet where the "I" is part of a harmonious whole. The memory softens the old drives for possession, approval and success.

*Postscript:*I have just returned from a pleasant, slow, mile-and-a-half jog. I am sitting in our garden writing. Overhead a huge dogwood moves gently in a mild southerly breeze. Two small children, holding hands, walk down the street absorbed in their own world. I am glad I am here and now. But I know that this marvelous place of sun and wind, flowers, children and lovers, this murderous place of evil, ugliness and pain, is only one of many realities through which I must travel to distant and unknown destinations. For the time being I belong to the world and it belongs to me.

Ordeal in the Desert

by Evan Wylie

"We'll be back for lunch," Laura Scott called as the Ford sedan, over-flowing with children, pulled out of the William Prescotts' driveway in Moab, Utah, one summer morning. The Scott family—Virl Scott, a husky man in his middle 30's, his slight, blonde wife Laura (Barbara Prescott's sister), and their six children ranging in age from four to 12—were down from the Salt Lake City area for a weekend visit. Now, right after breakfast, they were setting out for Dead Horse Point, a lofty bluff which provides a breath-taking panorama of the gorges and canyons of the Colorado River.

By 11 a.m. that morning in July 1959, they had reached the Point, spent an hour admiring the view and taking snap-shots, and started back toward Moab. All about were scores of little roads made by uranium and oil prospectors during the boom which centered around Moab in the early 1950's. Spot-ting one marked "To the Neck," the Scotts, eager for still more spectacular scenery, followed it down into the canyon. Un-knowingly, they were on a road to nowhere, a trail which led into as wild, desolate and treacherous a region as exists in all of the United States. Here, for thousands of square miles, there is nothing but a chaos of deep canyons, lonely rock towers, dry basins and naked, burning desert. It is an area where the sun, blazing with a ferocity that sends temperatures to nearly 125 degrees, dehydrates and shrivels human tissue in a matter of hours.

Following the rough, rocky trail, the Scotts had dropped more than 2000 feet to the bottom of the canyon, far west of Dead Horse Point, when they heard a sharp, metallic clash coming from beneath the car. Leaping out, Virl Scott saw the car's radiator, bent backward by a rock and gashed by the blades of its fan, spurting antifreeze from a dozen small holes. Before he could rip off a hub cap to catch the liquid, it had vanished into the hot sand.

Suddenly aware of the frightful heat and malevolent silence of the canyon, Scott said to his wife, "I think there's still some water inside the engine. It's too far for us to turn around and go back. We'll keep on and get out of here as fast as we can."

He had made perhaps ten miles more when, with a tooth-rattling jolt, the car struck another rock and stalled. Underneath, heavy black oil poured onto the sand. The crankcase was punctured.

So swiftly had events turned against them that the Scotts' plight seemed almost unreal. Without oil and water the car could not be driven more than a few hundred yards. Between them and Moab lay some 50 miles of burning desert. No one would know where to look for them.

Virl Scott spoke calmly to his hot, dusty, thirsty children: "Now Bryan, Virlene, Laurene—everybody listen carefully. Our car is broken down, and we're going to have to stay right here until Aunt Barbara and Uncle Bill send someone to get us. You must be quiet and brave, and do exactly as your mother and I say."

For the rest of the afternoon the Scotts crouched in the meager shade of an overhanging rock, eying their green Ford sedan baking in the sun, realizing that whatever it contained might count toward their survival. As soon as a lengthening twilight shadow enveloped it, they ransacked it. There was not a particle of food, not a drop of water.

Nevertheless, the Scotts got busy. As a full moon rose over the desert, Laura used wire cutters from the tool box to cut two blankets into narrow strips and fashioned the letters SOS in the sand. Virl removed the spare tire, rolled it out onto the desert and left the inner tube and a pair of old galoshes with it, to have a signal fire ready to go. He took out the back seat to use as a sunshield, unscrewed the rear-view mirror for signaling, spread the hub caps about to catch any night moisture.

The Scott children, with the discipline often found in large families, helped or sat quietly watching. Only Leland, just four and too young to understand, had begun to whimper through parched lips, "Want a drink. . . . Want to go home now."

In Moab, Barbara Prescott waited with growing anxiety. "I'm scared," she said to her husband when he came home from work at 5 p.m. "Something has happened to them."

"Oh, I'm sure they're all right," Prescott replied. "I'll go out to Dead Horse Point and round them up."

For two hours he searched. Then he drove back to Moab and called Sheriff John Stock. After an unsuccessful preliminary investigation, Stock flashed an alarm to highway patrols and led them on a search. Finding nothing, Stock used the short-wave radio in his car to call the Utah Air Police. "We may have some people down in the canyon," he said. "I'd like to fly with you in the morning."

Says Stock: "Even we natives are afraid of that White Rim canyon country. In summer the sun and heat are so terrific in there that you don't find a living thing—not a snake, not a rat, not a toad."

In the moonlight, the steel cool to their burning bodies, the Scott children slept, draped over hood, fenders and roof of the Ford. Virl and Laura made every moment of darkness count. Sighting on the North Star, they marked in their minds every ledge and rock that might provide a few minutes of shade next day.

In the desert the day comes with a rush. By 5 a.m. it was daylight. By 7 the Scotts' battle for survival had begun.

Laura and the children crept under an overhanging ledge and lay still. Down in the canyon Virl braved the merciless heat as he knelt and flashed the car's mirror futilely at high-flying jet bombers. When a small plane appeared in the northwest, he soaked his road map in gasoline from their camp stove, tucked it around the galoshes and spare tire, and ignited it. The pyre gave off a plume of black smoke, but an errant breeze directed it into a shadow beside a canyon wall. The plane vanished.

To counter despair, the Scotts turned to another resource. They were a steadfast Mormon family, and Virl was a member of the Mormon priesthood. "Come, everyone," he now said. "Let us pray together." Kneeling in the dirt, the children and

Laura joined in as he prayed to God for the strength and will to survive the day. From then on, whenever he sensed that hysteria was seizing his family, Scott would say, "Come now, let us pray together."

Since Dawn, search operations had been pressed with desperate urgency. But, as the day wore on, the desert air became so turbulent that further flying was out of the question and search parties were restricted to the ground. Over the entire effort hung one inescapable fact: if the Scotts were stranded in the desert without water, they would be dead or dying before sunset the next day.

The Scotts crouched motionless under their ledge, peering into the sky, straining their ears for the sound of automobile or aircraft engine. Laura took her lipstick and coated the blistered, swollen lips of her husband and children. On their faces she patted rouge from her compact. She gave them spoonfuls of the rusty fluid—half antifreeze, half water—that had been left in the radiator.

Absently thrusting his fingers into the dirt, Virl was startled—it was cool. "Laura! Children!" he cried. "Get down into the dirt. Cover yourselves with it." The family scooped up handfuls of dirt, rubbed it on their arms and faces.

As the sun's rays reached deeper under the ledge, the children cowered closer together. Virl said, "I'm taking up too much room." He went out into the scorching sun, came back with branches ripped from a bush cedar. "Peel the bark and suck the wood," he told the children. "There may be a bit of moisture."

By midday the canyon was an inferno, and the children were dehydrating rapidly. Throats parched, tongues swollen, they lay listless, still.

Virl Scott and his wife now undertook a measure they had put off as long as possible. Earlier they had announced that everyone would urinate only into an empty milk pail they found in the car. Dipping her children's shirts and blouses into the pail, Laura now bathed their bodies and faces with the fluid, wrung out the garments and put them back on the children. The desert breeze blowing through the damp clothing cooled their chests and arms. Covered with dirt, foul-smelling, weirdly theatrical in lipstick and rouge, they lay under the ledge like animals, numbly enduring.

In mid-afternoon a solitary cloud put the car in shadow. Virl Scott was roused by his children running toward the car. They squirmed into the sand beneath it and waved to him to join them.

Scott was too weak to move. "Keep those kids in the shade," he shouted to his wife. "I'll throw stones at anybody who moves around down there!" His cracked voice had a frenzied quality to it.

As she sprawled in the dirt, Laura remembered that the children had four packages of coloring crayons in the car. She got them, read the label: "Harmless vegetable dyes—non-poisonous." She peeled the paper from a red crayon, chewed and swallowed it. The waxy flavor was not too unpleasant.

"Children," she said, "look what I've found to eat."

Dutifully the Scott children peeled the crayons and ate them. Then they ate the contents of a tube of white glue which Laura had discovered was made from a milk-products base. The sight of them gravely licking the glue from their fingers drove Laura to dry sobs. She crawled to the other side of the car so they wouldn't see her.

After sunset Virl, and his wife conferred. "Virl," Laura said, "we may not all get through tomorrow. I want to walk down the road tonight. Maybe I'll find something for the children—some water—something."

"All right," Scott said. "But take Virlene with you. And let me give you my blessing."

Kneeling with his wife and children in the desert twilight, Virl Scott blessed them with the ceremony of the laying on of hands. Then Laura and her eldest daughter started out.

Moonlight soon flooded into the canyon, transforming rocks, ledges and bush cedars into monstrously misshapen images. The vast emptiness of the desert lay wrapped in eerie silence. Mother and daughter trudged, stumbled, lay still in the dirt, dragged themselves to their feet and walked on. Whenever the trail forked, they piled stones to mark their way back.

It was after midnight when, footsore and much weaker, they came upon a wind sock, a length of silk on a short stake. Nearby there must be an airfield! In the moonlit shadows Laura thought she saw the silhouette of an aircraft. They struggled toward it—but wings, tail, propeller turned out to be a mocking deception of rocks and moonlight.

Mother and daughter stopped and turned around. They knew they must get back to the car before the sun rose. But Laura Scott, like her husband, had pushed herself to the brink. "My mind was filled with confusion, and I couldn't concentrate," she recalls. "Far off I could hear the children crying. Right before my eyes I could see foaming glasses of cold root beer, and I could smell hamburgers cooking. When Virlene said firmly, 'No, Mama, not that way—this is the way to the car,' I just followed."

For three hours they reeled forward, fell, rested and wobbled on. The moment came when Virlene did not get up. In racking sobs she cried, "Why don't we die here, Mama? I can't face Leland and the others without bringing them something. I want to die here with you."

Laura drew her daughter's head into her lap and stroked it. "Come on, baby," she said. "We'll go back to our family."

As the eastern sky lightened, they finally made it to the car. The children greeted them weakly. "Did you find anything, Mama?" they asked.

"No, we didn't," said Laura Scott. Then, without a pause, she added cheerfully, "But I thought of something for us to do. We're going to make a fire and cook up some of that old cactus, just like a barbecue."

It was 4:15 a.m. In a grim parody of a picnic, Virl and his wife set up the camp stove, sliced the thorny cactus in strips and laid it on the grill. The children, puffy-faced and glassy-eyed, watched as the mass of gummy fibers cooked.

"How is it?" Laura asked Bryan.

The boy put a strip between his swollen lips, gagged, and spat it out. "Not very good, Mama."

As daylight entered the canyon, Virl and Laura herded the family up to the ledge and prepared for a last-ditch stand beneath it. With tire irons they hacked a hole in the dirt, buried four-year-old Leland up to his neck in it. Husband and wife kept scraping with all their might to deepen the space for the rest of them. Finally, Virl Scott, half blind, mumbling deliriously, thrust his face into the cool dirt and lay still. Laura continued to dig, punching feebly at the red dirt and rock, dimly aware that she was probably digging a common grave for her family.

"Does it hurt to die, Mama?" asked Laurene, ten.

"No, darling, you'll just go to sleep."

"Will we get a drink of water from the angels in heaven?"

"Yes," said Laura. "Now you just rest. Try to sleep."

Laura Scott was still jabbing at the dirt with the tire iron when the silver fuselage of an aircraft flashed by, a few feet overhead. With a roar that shook the canyon, it shot over the car and disappeared. Soon another plane appeared and dropped a penciled note: "Help will come."

But the closest place for aircraft to land was several miles away, and it was two more hours before Laura saw two men running toward them, felt water being splashed on her. Another hour, then a rescue truck appeared, laden with milk, oranges, tomato juice. There was a bumpy ride to the rescue planes, and then the family was flown to Moab.

There a doctor awaited them. He examined them carefully, shook his head in astonishment. When asked if they should be flown to a hospital he answered slowly, "No, I'd suggest home, a bathtub, then bed." To Virl Scott he added, "You're all in much better shape than you should be. You must have worked pretty hard to stay alive."

"We worked at it and we prayed for it," said Scott wearily. And then he fell sound asleep.

Ride for the Money!

by Merna McMillan Hailey

There we were, in a strange cold city 3000 miles from home, dead broke, our chances of raising getaway money mighty slim, and all I could think about was getting Jim a $20 coat.

Life is like that. When you're down and out, the first small step back up the ladder is often the hardest, the most important. For my husband and me, that $20 coat was the one thing that counted.

It was the fall of 1953 and Jim, a 24-year-old professional cowboy, was riding in the rodeo at the old Madison Square Garden in New York. That's where the big money was, and Jim was good; we knew he was. We had driven day and night across the country for this big chance.

This was to be our last rodeo. Jim loved the excitement, and so did I, but we knew this dangerous, nomadic life wasn't really for us. So we were out to make our big score. With the prize money we'd settle down on a farm in California and raise a family.

But in the bulldogging, that dangerous business of wrestling a steer to the ground, Jim had drawn "cheaters," erratic and unpredictable. In the bronc riding he drew only "runaways," horses that wouldn't buck enough to give a cowboy a chance to show what he could do. In the wild-horse races there was always a stumble or a brush that bumped him out of the running. His luck had been bad.

We had been to New York once before, and as we drove across country we had chatted gaily about the treats we would enjoy after each victory—tickets to a show, meals in a nice little restaurant we remembered. But "shows" turned out to be walks along grubby West Side streets. "Restaurants" were a can of beans in the shabby hotel room across the street from the Garden. On top of it all, I was pregnant. I yearned to tell Jim because it would make him so happy. Yet I didn't dare. It would have been too much.

On the last night of the Garden rodeo, we took our usual walk up Eighth Avenue. It was chilly, and I saw Jim shiver under his denim shirt. "You need a coat," I said, and he mumbled, "Yes."

We turned into a little store, and Jim tried on a few without much enthusiasm. Then he smiled. He'd found one he liked. The store-owner said $40. Jim handed the coat back quickly. $35? $30? Okay, special for a cowboy, $20. Jim nodded. "We'll come back after the performance to get it."

Back to the Garden we went. Broke? Stranded? Hungry? Pregnant? Discouraged? None of these things mattered. Only the coat.

As we turned into the Garden entrance, Jim's shoulders were squared and he was very quiet, concentrating. He barely smiled as I kissed him and whispered, "Good luck."

He was in the bareback bronc-riding. This was our last chance, and he'd have to put on a whale of a performance to make the kind of money we needed. He was out of the "average"—that is, he had no chance to pick up a prize for high average score. He could only shoot for the "day money"—the top prizes of this go-round of the event.

Day-money riders are the desperate ones. Each tries to be flashier than the next to grab the judges' eyes, and this means each tries something more dangerous than the one before. Jim, I knew, would go all out now. I was frightened for him. But I kept thinking of his winning that nice warm $20 coat.

I ran up the stairs to where the other wives sat. There's a false calm in that sorority. Every wife is fearful for her husband, terrified at each erratic move that could send him crashing under the stomping hoofs. Every wife is also pathetically eager for the prize money, which is the only difference between steak and beans. But under the unspoken code of the rodeo, each frantic wife puts on a façade of utter serenity. Fear shows only in the high-pitched voice, the nervous laugh.

I played the game. I sat down and exchanged the nonchalant

pleasantries of a tea party, while the corner of my eye found Jim getting ready in the chute. For this ride he had drawn the dreaded Madame Pompadour. She had been ridden successfully only once that season, and the only good thing you could say about her was that her meanness was consistent. Just the day before, Jim had spent a solid hour talking to the cowboy who had ridden this devil, analyzing every jump, every spin the horse took.

The announcer explained the rules to the audience. The bronc rider had to stay on the horse for eight seconds. He could hold on to the rigging (a broad strap around the horse's body) with only one hand. He would get a goose egg, a zero, if his other hand so much as brushed the horse. His spurs had to be exactly in place, just above the point of the horse's shoulders, as they left the chute or else another goose egg. Then if he did all of that perfectly, he'd be judged on the over-all style and quality of the ride.

I saw Jim pulling on his big glove and dusting it with the resin bag. A uniformed SPCA man reached down to check that the rowels of his spurs were properly dulled.

Jim would be the last one to go. The first cowboy got as far as the second jump, then went tumbling. He limped back toward the chutes, dusting his pant leg with his hat. The next brushed his horse with his free hand and was goose-egged. After that there were a couple of good rides, not spectacular but good.

Finally it was Jim's turn. While the announcer was calling out his name, he slipped down on the horse's back, gave his hat an extra, nervous tug, nodded and yelled, "Outside!"

I stopped breathing. The chute gate swung open, and then— nothing. Madame Pompadour didn't move. There was a split second of absolute stillness. Wouldn't she go? Just when it seemed the horse had frozen in the chute, she leaped out like a big cat, with all four feet off the ground. It was all so sudden I couldn't tell if Jim had been able to keep his feet in the proper position.

On the next jump she kicked high and twisted back to the right, toward the corner of the arena. Then she began that bucking spin which had made her the terror of the rodeo. Around and around she went, digging her front legs into the ground and kicking up behind.

I guess I prayed; I don't know: it was too fast and furious and frightening. Jim was not riding safely. He was spurring her high and loose. His neck snapped back and forth each time she lunged forward, and my throat tightened in fear.

At first there was a harrowing rhythm to the mare's bucking and the man's spurring, but then they seemed to meld into one frenzied living machine. Once I saw Jim lunge upward and off on an angle. *Oh, God,* I thought, *he won't make it.* He crunched back down, but at a crazy angle—I knew he was going to topple—but no, he caught his balance. I tried to tick off eight seconds with my fingers against my palm, but in the middle of the count I just dug my nails into my hand and froze. The horse jumped higher and harder.

The crowd was beginning to react. They screamed as Jim was flung upward, and gasped when he landed back on the horse with a teeth-jarring thump. When the whistle finally blew to mark the end of the eight seconds, I could hardly hear it.

The pickup men swooped in on both sides of the bucking mare. Jim slid over onto a pickup horse and jumped off on the other side. The crowd let out a deafening cheer.

But it was up to the judges, not the crowd. I waited, and now I *know* I prayed: "That coat. Please let us get that coat. I don't know how we're going to get back home, but we've just got to have that coat."

The announcer started to speak. "Well, folks," he started slowly, and my heart stopped. He was going to explain a goose egg again, and what it meant despite that spectacular ride. But no. "Folks," he said, "you have just seen the high-mark ride of this go-round. This young cowboy just made $840 in eight seconds."

$840! I brushed away the tears that were burning into my eyes and headed for the aisle. Jim came up the stairs two at a time with a big boyish grin, picked me up and swung me around, then kissed me.

"Let's go get the coat," I said.

"Yes, the coat—and a steak."

We ran for the door, hand in hand. We got the coat, and the steak. And over the steak I told him the other good news— our child. So that was it for the world of rodeo. We paid our hotel bill, made the long trek back to California and put a small down payment on the farm.

We still have the farm, and love it. We have the child, too, plus three more. And we still have the coat. Once, years later, Jim was going through his closet and held it up. "I suppose we can get rid of this old thing now?" he said.

I glanced at him and the faraway look in his eyes reminded me of that night in 1953.

I shook my head. "Never."

A Woman Attacked

Anonymous

The first intimation I had that someone was in my house was the clicking of the latch on the door of my first-floor bedroom. A professional woman, I was in my 50's. My house was in a rural section and, my children all married, I lived alone. There were no neighbors within sound of my voice, none in a position to see or take alarm at any unusual happenings in my house. In our quiet little community, several women lived alone. We had not considered that we were in danger.

This night, sometime after I had turned out my light, I thought I heard movement outside, as if something had brushed against the house. Sitting up in bed, I looked out the window. I saw nothing except my car beside the house in the bright moonlight. A little later I heard the dull boom my heavy cellar door makes when it is opened. Still I was not alarmed. Deer come to my door. Trees and old houses produce strange sounds of their own. I attributed this sound, too, to some innocent cause.

Perhaps 20 minutes after that—it must have been around midnight—the latch rattled on my bedroom door. I got out of bed and started toward the door, calling out, "Who is it? Who is there?"

I was halfway across the room when the door was thrown open boldly, and a man entered, half crouching. He was in his shirt sleeves, and he was young. This was nightmare—but real, and it was happening to me!

As I stood there, momentarily paralyzed, the man straightened to full height and catapulted himself upon me, forcing me back across the room to my bed. Into my mind came the certainty that I was going to die. I concentrated all my force on fighting as long and as hard as I could.

I saw his face above me, white in the moonlight, completely expressionless. His hands came down to my throat. I thought, "Now he will kill me." I didn't propose to die tamely. Finding a strength I had not dreamed I possessed, I seized his hands, pulled them from my throat. That was the only intentionally hurtful gesture he made. I realized it was not his intention to kill me, at least not now.

I managed several times to wriggle off the bed. He would seize me and throw me back, but as he stooped over me I lashed out at him with both feet. Once I slammed him against the dresser, then against the wall, so hard the iron foot of the floor lamp was bent out of shape when he crashed against it. I can see him now on the floor, staring up at me with that expressionless face. It was the first time in my life I had ever kicked anybody.

Finally, he threw me down so hard that when my head hit the window sill I was partially dazed. I was half lying, half sitting against the wall, trying desperately to get my wits back, when my assailant suddenly collapsed on the floor. He stayed there, leaning against the bed, making no further move toward me.

The battle must have lasted half an hour. Somehow I knew it was over. I must have said something about not reporting the affair if he would leave at once. He snarled. "Yeah, you would just get me for breaking and entering," and reeled off a string of charges to which he evidently knew he had laid himself open. I stood up, and he made no move to stop me.

Now, however, he got to his feet, too, and before my eyes I saw a new personality appear. The man who stood there seemed mature and poised. In his new mood he did not wish to harm me. The problem now was his fear that if he left me alive I would call the state troopers. I earnestly assured him I would not—hoping to placate him and get him out of the house.

We walked into the kitchen, and he went to the sink for a drink of water. Bending over the counter until his head almost touched it, he exclaimed in what seemed an agony of self-loathing, "Would you believe I was married once to a good woman?" I said I could believe it.

There was an awkward pause; then he said, "I wish I could talk to you."

Perhaps this was where I made a mistake. Hesitating only briefly, I replied that I would be glad to talk with him.

I was shivering violently, partly from nervous reaction, partly from cold. I had on only a nightgown and was barefoot. In a matter-of-fact voice I said, "I'm going to get a robe and slippers."

I don't know how I got the courage to go back into the bedroom. I didn't linger. I pulled a warm robe out of the closet. Not seeing my bedroom slippers. I snatched up a pair of sneakers and put them on. Then I went back to the kitchen.

We sat down at the kitchen table across from each other.

My work was in vocational guidance, but I had never dealt with a young person as deeply troubled as this. So, even though I knew he might have killed me, and might still, I was not untouched by his plight—and in his present state he seemed capable of being helped.

He told me he had been on the road for four days. In answer to my questions he said he had no place to go; he would now go over to the railroad and hop a freight. He said he was sorry for what he had done and wished we could be friends. He betrayed curiosity about me, asking who I was, what I did.

His trouble, he said, was he had never been able to adjust to society's requirements. I asked if he'd ever had anyone to help him with his problems. He said no. I learned later that a number of attempts had been made to help him. But perhaps in a deeper sense what he said was true, for it requires more than good intentions to get at the problems of a seriously disturbed person.

Thus far his conversation had been completely rational. So I was quite unprepared for what happened next. Suddenly he said, "What I would like to know is, why have you been haunting me all my life?"

"You must be thinking of someone else," I said. "Your grandmother, probably." For I had been laying great stress on the age difference between us.

"No, not my grandmother," he answered, a querulous note in his voice. "At least, I don't think so." His talk became disconnected, and I could see he was losing control. Moving his head in a tortured way, he said, "You were cruel to me. You hurt me in there."

Then he began to talk in a flirtatious manner, completely at variance with the deference he had recently shown. When I said firmly, "The time has come for you to go," and stood up, he too got to his feet. He apologized again, told me it had helped a great deal to talk, and asked me to kiss him good-by. He made a move toward me, and I stepped back.

Now, as he stood there swaying a little, a foolish uncertain grin on his face, the full horror of the situation swept over me. I doubted I could fight or talk my way out a second time. I saw only one desperate hope—to get him out of the house.

I grasped him by the arms and resolutely marched him toward the door. Surprisingly, he let me. His body under my hands felt rigid, poker-stiff: he walked with the jerky step of a robot. I reached around him, turned the doorknob, opened the door wide. Just then he turned and faced me. His arms clamped tightly around me with the mechanical motion of a trap. For an instant that expressionless face, with the round black holes for eyes, again looked into mine.

But we were at the door, and it was open. I caught hold of the doorjamb and somehow pulled myself away. I ran out to the road, faster than I'd ever run before, and up the hill, crying, "Help, help!" I did not slacken my pace until I reached my nearest neighbors' house. They telephoned the state police.

The police were at my door within 20 minutes. When the troopers presented me with a large selection of photographs of men who had criminal or sex-offense records, I easily identified my assailant, whom I shall call Jack Smith. He had been in three mental institutions and was an escapee from the third. One week later he was arrested, charged with housebreaking and attempted rape.

While we were awaiting the trial, I had a conversation with Jack Smith's mother, a pleasant looking woman slightly younger than myself. She told me that Jack had been an honor student at a well-known military academy until he voluntarily entered military service during World War II—before he was 18. His trouble began to show up after his release. It had been diagnosed as schizophrenia, but he never admitted that he was sick.

The grand jury returned an indictment, and Jack Smith was arraigned. He was given a psychiatric examination and pronounced a paranoid schizophrenic, unfit to stand trial. He was sent to the state prison for the criminally insane.

Would it be possible for him to get special treatment? "Not a chance," I was told. "The prison is overcrowded and understaffed. He'll probably stay there the rest of his life."

Yet men sometimes escape or are released from these prisons, and return to society less able than ever to cope with their compulsions. Might Jack Smith one day return to terrorize another victim? I asked myself this question many times. The answer leaves me deeply concerned.

"Let Not This Sparrow Fall!"

by Rex Alan Smith

Whenever I recall that day, the memory starts in the middle, and I am once again flying a Piper Super Cruiser—tiny, ancient, noisy—somewhere over the mountains east of Fayetteville, Arkansas. Through the frayed and faded bucket seat, I feel the tremble of the clattering engine, and the sun-flooded cockpit has that familiar old-airplane smell—hot oil, hot radios, gasoline. A thousand feet below, a gleaming cloud layer stretches trackless as an arctic snowfield.

Ordinarily, a cockpit is a friendly place. And ordinarily there is a tangy beauty in the lonely spaces above the clouds. But not now. Now I am in the middle of what is politely called "a situation." The cockpit has turned hostile. The gleaming cloud layer has become my enemy. The earth—that solid earth upon which I stood so securely only an hour ago—is gone.

Old pilots used to say, "When you are in 'a situation,' figure out your assets and liabilities." So I do, knowing I will be embarrassed by the accounting.

My assets are quickly counted. Plenty of fuel. Smooth-running engine. Radio contact with a flight service station.

My liability list is much longer. The cloud layer is unbroken, and thickening. The sun, now glaring in my face, will soon set. The needle of the Omni-navigator twitches aimlessly. The compass was disturbed even before take-off; now the truth is no longer in it. Worst of all, I somehow have to get down through those clouds. I *will* get down: gravity is one law from which there is no appeal. But the oft-proven fact is that, to fly in solid clouds, a pilot needs special instruments to tell him which way is up and whether he is turning. Without them he soon loses control, and may dispatch himself to the graveyard. I have no such instruments, and this is my largest liability. It completes the balance sheet. I add it up, and sense bankruptcy ahead—insolvency from carelessness.

I still wonder how I could have put myself into such a box. How had it begun?

I had an important business appointment in the east-central part of the state at Batesville. Pilots who think they have to keep appointments "no matter what" are usually remembered only by their pictures. I *knew* that. Nonetheless . . .

Driving to the airport that afternoon, I saw the clouds were low, but not *too* low, and were well broken. Moreover, according to the weather reports, the Batesville area had only a high overcast with widely scattered lower clouds, and even that was expected to improve. I disregarded the fact that the forecast was several hours old, and thus the first liability was entered in my ledger.

While warming up my plane's engine, I checked the radio. The Omni-navigator was feeble and confused. But voice reception and transmission were fair. *Good enough,* I thought, *for such a simple flight.* There's an unwritten rule that says no flight can be considered "simple." I broke it. Another liability.

Taxiing to the runway, I checked the troublesome compass. It committed perjury on every heading. Still, by adding a massive correction, I seemed to be able to make some sense out of it. Liability No. 3.

When conditions are right, flying yields a deeply satisfying pleasure. This trip started like that. The airplane that had been lumbering so awkwardly grew light and graceful as it gathered speed. I pressed back the stick and soared up into air that was as soft and smooth as old wine. Ahead, the Ozark hills rose blue-green through veils of silver mist.

But, as the approaching hills grew higher, the contrary clouds grew thicker and pressed lower. Before long, my ceiling and floor had drawn disturbingly close together. *Probably just local,* I thought. *I'll head north and fly around it.*

Fifteen minutes passed. Clouds and mountains still walled off the east. Then, suddenly, I flew under a long rip in the clouds. Above it blue sky beckoned, tempting me to cruise in the sunshine on top. And I bit. I tugged at the stick and sailed up through the mist-walled canyon. Climbing, and then leveling out to skim over sun-bright fleece, I realized I had flown off the north edge of my chart. No matter; I'd soon be back on.

My debit entries were now complete. I was no longer a pilot; I was an accident in incubation.

Twenty minutes later, I came to the higher overcast mentioned in the weather report. The space between it and the clouds below was thin and dark—an ominous slate-gray cavern that I obviously had no business entering. And so I made my first intelligent decision of the day: Go home. Rolling into a tight turn, I picked up the microphone.

A faint faraway voice responded to my call. Fayetteville radio. I asked for weather.

"Fayetteville, 800 feet, overcast."

Overcast! I felt a chill.

I asked about Fort Smith. Then Little Rock, Tulsa, even Springfield, Missouri. The answer was always the same: "Overcast!" A freak weather shift was packing the entire area with a thickening cover, and all airports within my fuel range were solidly clouded over.

I had to face it. The sins of the day had overtaken me, and I was caught. I felt a sudden frantic urge to break out of the trap *now!* To dive into the clouds toward the hidden world, only a mile or so below, and take my chances. Then out of somewhere came a memory of the barn sparrows I had observed as a boy. I had wondered why, when they were frightened, they would dash themselves against the closed barn windows; if they had only kept their heads, they could easily have escaped through an open one. I would not dash *myself* against the closed window. I'd keep my head and figure out an escape.

There's a childlike instinct in all of us that makes us want to run home when we are in trouble. That's where I wanted to be now—back over Fayetteville, over home. But what was the course? Then I thought of the sun. That was it! Fayetteville must lie just to the left of the setting sun. I headed for it.

My waiting time begins, and I sweat out each creeping minute. Five . . . ten . . . fifteen. No holes. Fayetteville radio is broadcasting an alert to all pilots flying in the area. It's good to know they are out there watching for openings for me. But it will take more than watching to make the clouds part. What I need is a miracle.

Suddenly, as my eyes sweep the instrument panel for the hundredth time, I notice a change in the Omni. The needle has ceased its wandering and is hard-over against the pin. I roll the course-indicator knob. When I do, the needle follows. Although it still flutters, I can center it well enough to get a rough reading: 300 degrees to Fayetteville radio. I roll into the new heading.

As I fly the course, the needle grows firmer and the sound signal louder. It *is* leading me home. But when I get there, the sparrow will still need an open window. Why do I keep thinking of sparrows? Then it comes to me . . . a Biblical quote: "And one of them shall not fall on the ground without your Father. . . . Fear ye not therefore, ye are of more value than many sparrows."

I think an unvoiced prayer, *Let not this sparrow fall!*

Soon the needle quivers, flips hard right, then left. Fayetteville radio must be directly below. I call in.

"Fayetteville, cruiser niner-six-four now over transmitter. Will maintain holding pattern while you advise. Over."

"Roger, niner-six-four. Have you over transmitter. Stand by."

I wait. Fly a long orbit. And another. Then it comes: "Niner-six-four, Central Airlines pilot reports large break on Fayetteville radial one-eight-zero at 25 miles. Over."

A hole! I whip into a turn that stands the wings on end. I've got to get there before it closes. Turning the Omni-indicator to 180 degrees "from station," I come to a course that centers the needle. Again slow minutes pass, and the clouds turn rose and purple in the fading sunset.

Suddenly, there is darkness beneath. Far below, car lights wink in the dusk. I'm over the break! Already it has closed to a rift—a mere crack in the floor—1 1/2 miles long, perhaps a half-mile deep. A dive through would build speed that could tear the aircraft apart in the pullout. My only choice is a straight-line descent, and I must take precious moments to fly past and make it on the return, from south to north toward lights and an open valley rather than toward an ambush of dark mountains.

Throttle closed, I flicker through mist into the very tip of the rift. It's going to be awfully close, but now that I'm down in the hole, I'm committed. There's no turning back.

The descent indicator shows an altitude loss of 700 feet per minute. Not good enough. Crossing the controls, I force the airplane into a hard sideslip. Now it is flying forward and falling sideways at the same time. The plane's fabric drums an angry protest as the ground lights rise swiftly toward me. Then all goes black. I've lost the hole and flown into the overcast! But only for an instant. Almost before I can react, I've broken out over sudden scattered jewelry—the lights of West Fork village, just minutes from the Fayetteville airport!

I feel a quick shock of transition—of instant adjustment from the insubstantial world of fleece-floored space to the solid world of people, houses, ground to stand on.

Twin lines of runway lights appear in the distance. As I line up and approach, I review all the things which, despite grave liabilities, have brought this sparrow home: the hole which appeared when there were no holes, and stayed open just long enough; the pilot who flew in exactly the right place at the right time to report it; the Omni-navigator that was dead but came to life when needed, and without which I couldn't have found the hole....

The airplane floats down between the lights. The wheels touch, and roll. The books have been balanced—but not by me. By coincidences? By miracles? No one can really know. But, as the old pilots used to say, "There are no atheists among fliers."

Could You Have Loved as Much?

by Bob Considine

The story begins in the Taylors' small apartment in Waltham, Mass. Edith Taylor was sure she was "the luckiest woman on the block." She and Karl had been married 23 years, and her heart still skipped a beat when he walked into the room. As for Karl, he gave every appearance of a man in love with his wife. If his job as government-warehouse worker took him out of town, he would write Edith each night and send small gifts from every place he visited.

In February 1950, Karl was sent to Okinawa for a few months to work in a new government warehouse. It was a long time to be away, and so far! This time no little gifts came. Edith understood. He was saving his money for the house they had long dreamed of owning someday.

The lonesome months dragged on. Each time Edith expected Karl home he'd write that he must stay "another three weeks." "Another month." "Just two months longer." He'd been gone a year now, and his letters were coming less and less often. No gifts she understood. But a few pennies for a postage stamp?

Then, after weeks of silence, came a letter: "Dear Edith. I wish there were a kinder way to tell you that we are no longer married. . . ."

Edith walked to the sofa and sat down. He had written to Mexico for a mail-order divorce. He had married Aiko, a Japanese maid-of-all-work assigned to his quarters; she was 19. Edith was 48.

Now, if I were making up this story, the rejected wife would fight that quick paper-divorce. She would hate her husband and the woman. She would want vengeance for her own shattered life. But I am describing here simply what *did* happen. Edith Taylor did not hate Karl. Perhaps she had loved him so long that she was unable to stop.

She could picture the situation. A lonely man. Constant closeness. But even so Karl had not done the easy, shameful thing. He had chosen divorce, rather than taking advantage of a young servant girl. The only thing Edith could not believe was that he had stopped loving her. Someday, somehow, Karl would come home.

Edith now built her life around this thought. She wrote Karl, asking him to keep her in touch with his life. In time he wrote that he and Aiko were expecting a baby. Maria was born in 1951; then, in 1953, Helen. Edith sent gifts to the little girls. She still wrote to Karl and he wrote back: Helen had a tooth, Aiko's English was improving, Karl had lost weight.

And then the terrible letter. Karl was dying of lung cancer. His last letters were filled with fear. Not for himself, but for Aiko and his two little girls. He had been saving to send them to school in America, but his hospital bills were taking everything. What would become of them?

Then Edith knew that her last gift to Karl could be peace of mind. She wrote that, if Aiko was willing, she would take Maria and Helen and bring them up in Waltham. For many months after Karl's death, Aiko would not let the children go. They were all she had ever known. Yet what could she offer them except a life of poverty, servitude and despair? In November 1956, she sent them to her "Dear Aunt Edith."

Edith had known it would be hard at 54 to be mother to a three-year-old and a five-year-old. She hadn't realized that, in the time since Karl's death, they would forget the little English they knew. But Maria and Helen learned fast. The fear left their eyes; their faces grew plump. And Edith, for the first time in six years, was hurrying home from work. Even getting meals was fun again!

Sadder were the times when letters came from Aiko. "Aunt. Tell me now what they do. If Maria or Helen cry or not." In the broken English, Edith read the loneliness, and she knew what loneliness was. She knew she must bring the girls' mother here, too.

She had made the decision, but Aiko was still a Japanese citizen, and the immigration quota had a waiting list many years long. So Edith Taylor wrote me asking if I could help. I described the situation in my newspaper column. Others did more. Petitions were started, and, in August 1957, Aiko Taylor was permitted to enter the country.

As the plane came in at New York's Kennedy Airport, Edith had a moment of fear. What if she should hate this woman? The last person off the plane was a girl so thin and small that Edith thought at first it was a child. She stood there, clutching the railing, and Edith knew that, if *she* had been afraid, Aiko was near panic.

She called Aiko's name, and the girl rushed down the steps and into Edith's arms. As they held each other, Edith had an extraordinary thought. "I prayed for Karl to come back. Now he has—in his two little daughters and in this gentle girl he loved. Help me, God, to love her too."

Postscript: *Nine years later, when this article was published, Edith and Aiko Taylor were still together in the apartment in Waltham—"Aunt Edith" as the proud "other mother" of two happy, growing teen-agers. Aiko, who had learned to speak fluent English, was planning to visit her family in Japan. "Though God has taken one life I loved dearly," said Edith, "he has given me three others to love. I am so thankful."*

The Courage of Terry Jesko

by Wanda Evans

When eight-year-old Terry Jesko wasn't in school, playing baseball or at a 4-H Club meeting, he was with his father, Lee Jesko, helping feed the cattle or riding on one of the tractors. Ever since he could walk, he'd gone to the field with his dad, watching, asking questions, listening as Lee patiently explained the hundred-and-one tasks of a farmer.

On that Friday afternoon of May 4, 1973, Terry arrived home from school in Lazbuddie, Texas, at about 3:30. Brenda Jesko gave her son a snack, then took him to the field where her husband was planting grain sorghum. Lee was driving the huge six-row tractor equipped with planter boxes and a rod weeder, a knife-like device attached in front of the planter to cut down weeds and tall grass. Terry hoped his dad would begin teaching him how to drive the tractor. For the next few hours he rode in the cab, and after a while Lee let him sit on the seat and steer.

The sun hung low in the west when Lee throttled the tractor down until it was barely moving. "I'm going to get down and check the seed boxes," he told Terry. "You just take it easy and keep this thing pointed in the right direction."

Perched in the cab high atop the mammoth machine, Terry watched his father climb down and go behind the tractor. Lee Jesko finished checking the seed and started back toward the cab. Out of the corner of his eye, Terry saw him start up the steps. Then something hit the door and, when Terry glanced around, no one was there.

Suddenly frightened, the boy stared at the unfamiliar control panel. His first thought was to stop the tractor. Sliding forward, he put his full weight on both clutch and brake, then reached for the ignition key and switched it off. The tractor shuddered to a stop. Terry plunged out of the cab and down the steps.

His father lay unconscious on the ground, his right arm under the rod weeder, blood soaking his shirt, his legs twisted at an impossible angle. Terry glanced up at the rear wheel of the tractor, as tall again as he was. Somehow his dad must have fallen under that huge wheel and been drawn into the blade of the rod weeder.

Fighting panic, Terry tried to think what to do. The first thing was to get his dad out from under the rod weeder. The tractor was equipped with a power lift to raise and lower the planter boxes and the rod weeder. Maybe he could free his dad by lifting the equipment off the ground.

He scrambled back onto the tractor and grasped the power-lift lever, slowly raising the equipment into the air. Now he hurried back to his father and grabbed his torn and bloody legs, pulling as hard as he could. Nothing happened. The slight, eight-year-old boy was no match for the unconscious, 200-pound man, but at least the rod weeder no longer pinned his father to the ground.

Terry knew he had to get help, and fast. The lowering sun glinted off the Ford pickup sitting at the end of the plowed row, 100 yards away. If only he could get his mother, she would know what to do.

He ran toward the pickup and climbed in. The key was in the ignition, but his hand was shaking so much he could hardly turn it on at first. When the engine started, the boy slid to the edge of the seat, half standing, so his foot would reach the accelerator. The Jesko house was a mile and a half away—in the opposite direction. He would have to turn the pickup around in the narrow dirt road. He could almost hear his father's voice, as he had instructed him so many times when showing him how to do chores around the farm: *Don't get in a hurry. Do it right the first time.*

Terry put the pickup in gear, turned the steering wheel and pushed the accelerator. The pickup jerked, coughed and turned, but not sharply enough. Its snub nose lurched downward into a shallow ditch. Putting it in reverse, Terry backed across the road. Now the rear wheels slid into the opposite ditch. Frantically, he put it in "drive" again and straightened it out, this time headed in the right direction.

He drove east a few hundred yards and, without slowing down, turned north, taking the corner on two wheels. Pressing the accelerator, he kept his eyes glued to the road ahead. It seemed to take hours to go the mile to the next corner, where he would turn east toward home.

Suddenly, at the corner, he yanked the wheel—too late. The pickup careened across the barrow ditch, then headed straight into a four-strand barbed-wire fence. Terry braced himself against the seat and plowed through the fence into a neighbor's pasture. The pickup lurched and bumped across the pasture. A tire blew out, but all he could do was keep going. He was still traveling at an angle away from home.

A few yards ahead he spotted a deep gash in the earth. An irrigation ditch! He jerked the wheel with all his strength. The front tires narrowly missed the lip of the ditch.

That last sharp turn had finally pointed him toward home. He jolted across the rough pasture until he was directly across the road from his house. He braked standing up, turned off the ignition and tumbled out of the cab, yelling for his mother.

The kitchen was empty. He called again and again, running from room to room. The house was empty. He'd forgotten that his mother had gone to a meeting at church. He went to the telephone and dialed with trembling fingers. In a moment, an operator came on the line.

"Help me!" the boy begged. "My daddy's hurt!"

"Who are you? Where is your daddy?" the operator asked.

"I'm Terry Jesko. My daddy's in the field, and he's hurt."

"Where?" the operator asked again. "Tell me where your daddy is."

"In the field," Terry repeated, finding it impossible to tell her just where the accident had happened. Then he had an idea. "Call Pete Jesko!" he cried. "He's my daddy's cousin, and he lives close to us."

Soon Pete Jesko's pickup roared into the driveway. Terry climbed into the cab, and they tore out of the yard.

* * *

Not long after his son had started home, Lee Jesko regained consciousness. Memory returned with a rush. As he had started to climb into the cab, his foot slipped off the step. He was sucked under the wheel and drawn into the sharp edge of the rod weeder.

Strangely, he wasn't in pain, although he could see there was blood, and he must surely have broken bones. He called Terry. No answer. Raising his head, he looked toward the road. The pickup was gone. *Good boy. He's gone to get his mother.*

Then a disturbing thought occurred to him: he was a large man, and when Terry and Brenda came back, they wouldn't be able to get him into the car. It would be better if he could get in the tractor and drive it to the road.

Slowly he rolled over and, holding on to the planter, he pulled himself to his feet. His chest hurt so bad he could hardly breathe. *If I could only get on the tractor, into the air-conditioned cab, I'd be all right.*

It took all the strength and determination he had to struggle up the steps and into the cab. Streaks of pain began in his right hip and surged upward. *I was wrong. It isn't better up in the cab; it's worse. Something is terribly wrong with my right side. I'd better lie down. But first I must get to the road.* Fighting off unconsciousness, he started the engine and drove the tractor to the end of the row. Then he crawled out and crumpled to the ground.

Terry grinned with relief when he saw the tractor at the road. His dad was alive! By now it was dark. Pete Jesko directed the pickup's headlights toward the figure sprawled on the ground. He climbed out and looked closely at his cousin. "You hurt bad?"

Lee nodded weakly. "I think so. You better get me to the hospital."

"No, I can't move you. An ambulance is coming from Muleshoe. You just take it easy."

While they waited, Terry sat on the ground and held on to his dad's big hand. It was enough to know his dad was alive.

Headlights and a revolving red light appeared in the distance. Silently, Terry watched the ambulance attendants ease his father onto the stretcher. Then he insisted on climbing in after the stretcher. On his knees in the back of the ambulance, he found his dad's hand and held it throughout the jolting, high-speed trip over the 17 miles to the hospital.

The staff had been alerted, and was prepared for the injured man. A nurse led Terry to the waiting room. Each time Terry heard footsteps in the hall, he glanced anxiously toward the door, expecting his mother. He refused Pete's offer to take him home.

At last his mother came into the waiting room, and Terry ran into her arms. "Will Daddy be all right?"

His mother tried to smile. "The doctors don't know yet. He's hurt—terribly." She told him of the diagnosis. His father had a broken collarbone and some broken ribs, one of which had pierced a lung. His pelvis was crushed, and he had multiple lacerations and other internal injuries.

"I want to see Daddy," Terry begged. "Please, Mom..."

The small hospital didn't adhere to strict rules for visitors. Even so, the doctor hesitated; Lee Jesko needed rest and quiet. However, he understood Terry's desperate need to see his father. A minute's visit was arranged.

A shaded lamp over the bed revealed Lee lying, eyes closed, white as the sheet beneath him. There were tubes in his arm and in his nose. The boy stood by the bed, wordless, then reached out and gently touched his father's hand. The eyes flickered, then opened.

"Son..." Lee Jesko's voice was husky from pain and sedatives. Slowly, he turned his head the merest fraction, until his eyes met Terry's.

"I was so scared..." Terry's voice broke.

"You...did...exactly the right thing, son," Lee whispered. "You saved my life."

With tears streaming down his cheeks, Terry let his mother lead him from the room. Now he could go home.

Lee Jesko, after a four-month recuperation, was able to return to farming—in time to harvest that summer's crops.

The Best Investment I Ever Made

by A. J. Cronin

On the liner's second day out from New York, while making the round of the promenade deck, I suddenly became aware that one of the other passengers was watching me closely, following me with his gaze every time I passed, his eyes filled with a queer intensity.

I had crossed the Atlantic many times. And on this occasion, tired, I wanted to rest, to avoid the tedium of casual and importunate shipboard contacts. I gave no sign of having noticed the man.

Yet there was nothing importunate about him. On the contrary, he seemed affected by a troubled, rather touching diffidence. He was in his early 40's, I judged—out of the corner of my eye—rather short in build, with a fair complexion, a good forehead from which his thin hair had begun to recede, and clear blue eyes. His dark suit, sober tie and rimless spectacles gave evidence of a serious and reserved disposition.

At this point the bugle sounded for dinner and I went below. On the following forenoon, I again observed my fellow voyager watching me earnestly from his deck chair.

Now a lady was with him, obviously his wife. She was about his age, quiet and restrained, with brown eyes and slightly faded brown hair, dressed in a gray skirt and gray woolen cardigan.

The situation by this time had begun to intrigue me and from my steward I discovered they were Mr. And Mrs. John S———, from a small suburb of London. Yet when another

197

day passed without event, I began to feel certain that Mr.
S—— would remain too shy to carry out his obvious desire
to approach me. However, on our final evening at sea Mrs.
S—— decided the matter. With a firm pressure on his arm
and a whispered word in his ear, she urged her husband toward
me as I passed along the deck.

"Excuse me, Doctor. I wonder if I might introduce myself.
If you could spare a few minutes . . . my wife and I would so
like to have a word with you."

A moment later I was occupying the vacant chair beside
them. Haltingly he told me this had been their first visit to
America. It was not entirely a holiday trip. They had been
making a tour of the New England states, inspecting many of
the summer camps for young people there. Afterward, they
had visited settlement houses in New York and other cities.

There was in his voice and manner, indeed in his whole
personality, a genuine enthusiasm which was disarming. I
found myself liking him instinctively. Questioning him further,
I learned that he and his wife had been active for 15 years in
the field of youth welfare. He was by profession a solicitor
but, in addition, found time to act as director of an organization
devoted to the care of boys and girls, mostly from city slums,
who had fallen under the ban of the law.

As he spoke with real feeling, I got a vivid picture of the
work these two people were doing—how they took derelict
adolescents from the juvenile courts and, placing them in a
healthy environment, healed them in mind and body, sent them
back into the world trained in a useful craft and fit to take their
place as worthy members of the community.

It was a work of redemption which stirred the heart, and
I asked what had directed his life into this channel. He took
a sharp breath and exclaimed: "So you still do not remember
me?"

I shook my head: to the best of my belief I had never in my
life seen him before.

"I've wanted to get in touch with you for many years," he
went on, under increasing stress. "But I was never able to bring
myself to do so." Then, bending near, he spoke a few words,
tensely, in my ear. At that, slowly the veils parted, my thoughts
sped back a quarter of a century, and I remembered the sole
occasion when I had seen this man before.

* * *

I was a young doctor and had just set up in practice in a working-class district of London. On a foggy November night, toward one o'clock, I was awakened by a loud banging at the door. In those days of economic necessity any call, even at this unearthly hour, was a welcome one. Hurriedly I threw on some clothes, went downstairs. It was a sergeant of police, in dripping helmet and cape, mistily outlined on the doorstep. A suicide case, he told me abruptly, in the lodgings round the corner—I had better come at once.

Outside it was raw and damp, the traffic stilled, the street deserted, quiet as the tomb. We walked the short distance in silence, even our footsteps muffled by the fog, and turned into the narrow entrance of an old building.

As we mounted the creaking staircase, my nostrils were stung by the sick-sweet odor of illuminating gas. On the upper story the agitated landlady showed us to a bare little attic where, stretched on a narrow bed, lay the body of a young man.

Although apparently lifeless, there remained the barest chance that the youth was not quite beyond recall. With the sergeant's help, I began the work of resuscitation. For an hour we labored without success. A further 15 minutes: it appeared useless. Then, as we were about to give up, completely exhausted, there broke from the patient a shallow, convulsive gasp. It was like a resurrection from the grave, a miracle, this stirring of life under our hands. Half an hour of redoubled efforts and we had the youth sitting up, gazing at us dazedly and, alas, slowly realizing the horror of his situation.

He was a round-cheeked lad with a simple countrified air, and the story he told us as he slowly regained strength in the bleak morning hours was simple, too. His parents were dead. An uncle in the provinces, anxious no doubt to be rid of an unwanted responsibility, had found him a position as clerk in a London solicitor's office. He had been in the city only six months. Utterly friendless, he made bad companions, and like a young fool began to bet on horses. Soon he had lost all his small savings, pledged his belongings, and owed the bookmaker a disastrous amount. In an effort to recoup, he took a sum of money from the office safe for a final gamble which, he was assured, was certain to win. But this last resort failed.

Terrified of the prosecution which must follow, sick at heart, sunk in despair, he shut himself in his room and turned on the gas.

A long bar of silence throbbed in the little attic when he concluded this halting confession. Then, gruffly, the sergeant asked how much he had stolen. Pitifully, almost, the answer came: seven pounds ten shillings. Yes, incredible though it seemed, for this paltry sum this poor misguided lad had almost thrown away his life.

Again there came a pause in which, plainly, the same unspoken thought was uppermost in the minds of the three of us who were the sole witnesses of this near tragedy. Almost of one accord, we voiced our desire to give the youth—whose defenseless nature rather than any vicious tendencies had brought him to this extremity—a fresh start. The sergeant, at considerable risk to his job, resolved to make no report upon the case, so no court proceedings would result. The landlady offered a month's free board until he got up on his feet again. While I, making perhaps the least contribution, came forward with seven pounds ten shillings for him to put back in the office safe.

The ship moved on through the still darkness of the night. There was no need of speech. With a tender gesture Mrs. S—— had taken her husband's hand. And as we sat in silence, hearing the sounding of the sea, and the sighing of the breeze, a singular emotion overcame me. I could not but reflect that, against all the bad investments I had made throughout the years—foolish speculations for material gain—here at last was one I need not regret, one that had paid no dividends in worldly goods, yet which might stand, nevertheless, on the profit side in the final reckoning.

Glenda's Long Lonely Swim

by Frank Sargeant

In the storm-racked blackness of the Gulf of Mexico, the pretty 23-year-old woman trod water, alone. Lightning snapped through the night, and the wind-whipped waves pummeled her ceaselessly. Land was more than ten miles off, in what direction she had no idea. Fourteen hours in the water had brought her close to exhaustion. And now the conviction was rising that she could not last out the night.

There had been no hint of danger when Glenda Lennon slipped into the calm, beautifully clear water to spearfish, that sunny August afternoon in 1970. Her husband, Robert, kept watch from their 21-foot T-Craft cruiser, anchored near the last of the channel markers five miles off Homosassa, Fla. But at the head of the Homosassa River, where they had launched their boat, springs spew out 120 million gallons of gin-clear water each day, and on an ebb tide currents surge along this channel. About 15 minutes after Glenda entered the water, she felt the current sweeping her away. Concerned but unafraid, she called out.

Robert dived off the boat to help her, and a few swift strokes brought them together. Glenda's small poodle, Spunky, leaped overboard to join them, only to be swept quickly down current. At his wife's plea, Robert left her side to rescue the little animal. When he turned back toward his wife, however, he found he could scarcely hold his own against the current. Only by swimming very hard was he able to tow Spunky back to Glenda. The fierce August sun had driven most boaters off the water; there were none in sight. Moment by moment their cruiser grew smaller in the distance.

An expert swimmer and water-safety instructor who had swum competitively for 14 years, Robert knew he could not possibly pull his wife against this current. With her diving mask, snorkel breathing tube and swim fins, she was in no immediate danger. He decided to try for the boat on his own. Once aboard, he could quickly rescue his wife. He reminded her of survival techniques: remain calm, don't fight the water, raise your head only to breathe. He also warned her that she might not be able to hold Spunky for long. Then he struck off toward the boat, by then only a dot in the distance.

For more than an hour, as Lennon fought against the out-going tide, he continued to drift steadily seaward. Well out of sight of land, he had only the sun, now arcing toward the western horizon, to guide him. He kept it at his back and swam on.

At last the ebbing tide ceased its flow, and he began to make progress. But would he be able to locate the boat in that vast expanse of unmarked sea? The chances seemed astronomically small. But he toiled on, repeatedly switching strokes to rest his weary muscles.

Suddenly he saw a flash in the east—it was the rays of the dying sun catching the boat's radio antenna! Confident now, Lennon pushed himself to the limit and finally clambered aboard his boat, six long hours after leaving it.

For a few precious moments he lay still, too weak to move. But then he forced himself to get the boat under way. The wheel supported his tired body as he raced westward toward where he had left Glenda, and where, all too rapidly, the sun was now sinking in the jade-colored water. The outbound shrimp-fishing fleet from Homosassa heard his repeated radio calls for help and joined the search, relaying the message ashore on their powerful radios.

Within a few hours, the area was ablaze with searchlights from private boats, law-enforcement vessels and the shrimp fleet. Coast Guard aircraft from St. Petersburg roared overhead. But Glenda was nowhere to be found.

When Robert swam away in midafternoon, his wife fully believed he would soon return in the cruiser. But as the hours passed and darkness drew near, she became increasingly frightened. Perhaps he had not been able to reach the boat. Perhaps both of them would perish.

For a while Spunky had rested quietly, but eventually Glenda's anxiety communicated itself to him. He began to claw at her and try to climb on her shoulders, pushing his mistress under with his frantic efforts. She tried to calm him by holding him afloat at arm's-length; then she attempted to cradle him against her chest. But his wild struggles continued and at last the effort became too much for the tired girl. "Spunky, I'm sorry," she murmured. "Good luck." She released her hold, and in a moment they were separated. Glenda could not bring herself to look after him.

As the sun went down, she remembered stories of shark attacks in the outer Gulf. "Not that, dear God!" she prayed. Her swim fins were cutting into her heels from her constant kicking to stay afloat. Fatigue was beginning to weaken her. Dehydration built a powerful thirst, but she knew she could not drink the salt seawater.

The squall that had been building up broke with a vengeance, and icy rain came down in sheets. The fresh water relieved her salt-burned lips, but rolling seas made it difficult to keep the snorkel clear. And although Gulf waters are relatively warm, Glenda's body temperature was beginning to drop. With the chill, drowsiness crept up on her—despite the jagged streaks of lightning and blasts of thunder.

When the storm ended, Glenda simply could stay awake no longer. She cradled her face on the sea as though it were a pillow and drifted off. Her snorkel remained above water, providing air as she dozed.

She had no way of knowing how long she slept, but when she woke up the sky had cleared. The stars were brighter than she had ever seen them ashore. Phosphorus glowed in the water, and schools of fish made trails of light as they flashed past.

For the first time she heard a plane. Flares began to dot the darkness, far off, then nearer. When one of the glowing parachutes drifted down only 100 yards away, she swam for it frantically, waving her arms and shouting. But the plane droned off into the night without slowing; no one had seen her. Her heart sank.

Now, with little hope, Glenda's thoughts turned to details

of the life she had left ashore. She had saved for months to buy Robert an expensive watch for Christmas. It was to be a surprise; she had placed it on lay-away. If she did not survive, would he ever receive it?

Thinking of Robert made her feel for her wedding ring, and she realized the slim band was working loose as her fingers contracted in the water. She slipped it off and placed it on her thumb, locking her hand into a fist with the thumb inside. It was hard not to think of the things she would miss: the children they had wanted, the handsome old home they had planned to renovate. She prayed only to be alive for the sunrise.

In the pre-dawn hours, tiny, needle-teethed fish nipped at her like swarms of mosquitoes; the salt water irritated the raw abrasions on her heels. She wondered if her blood would attract the sharks, or if she would simply drown from fatigue.

At last the sun came up on a calm but empty sea. As it rose higher, thirst returned with a vengeance. Her lips burned, her tongue felt too large for her throat. Salt had crusted her hair into a solid mat. Her thighs were rubbed sore from brushing against each other every time she kicked to raise her head for air. She judged she had been swimming for at least 18 hours. "This can't go on forever," she thought. "Perhaps it would be better to end it now."

Twenty miles to the east, the searchers collected at Homosassa. All were determined to continue, although most felt there was little hope left of finding Glenda alive. A partner in an ambulance service, Robert had often experienced the tragedy of others. Now he said to his father, "I've learned not to believe in miracles."

But one among them believed that he still might be able to find Glenda—"with the grace of God and a little mathematics." Duncan MacRae, a taciturn, ruddy-faced Homosassa marina operator, had spent most of his 50 years studying the Gulf. He knew its moods, its currents, its inhabitants and terrain perhaps better than any man on the entire coast. Knowing there was little chance of finding Glenda during darkness, MacRae had agreed to join the search at daybreak.

The long gentle slope of these shallow flats, he figured, holds out the big sharks that roam the deeper water of the west. If Glenda had miraculously found the strength to keep on swimming, she might still be alive.

In the morning's first light MacRae put out from his marina

in a small, fast runabout. Two volunteer searchers accompanied him to the channel marker where the Lennons' boat had been anchored.

Once there, MacRae let his little boat drift as he studied the restless surface. He knew that the Gulf current had run out at about eight knots the day before, but its flow had been nearly half gone when the girl left the boat. The incoming tide that night would have brought her back toward shore, and the present outgoing tide would again be carrying her seaward. The drift would be to the northwest: a wind averaging ten knots had been blowing consistently in that direction. After a brief mental calculation, he opened the throttle and sent the boat careering west northwest.

As they raced out to sea, MacRae instructed his two passengers: "Watch for a flash in the water. If you spot something, don't take your eyes off it even for a second." (Without a point of reference, sightings at sea are often impossible to relocate after being lost.)

By MacRae's estimate, most of the search had taken place too far inshore. His calculations were at best an educated guess, but his guesses had often proved out in the past. Yet he had also been humbled many times by the unpredictable Gulf, and even if his piloting was exact, finding a single swimmer in so much water would be largely a matter of luck.

In the next half hour, they repeatedly rushed down on shining objects, only to find discarded cans, bottles, crab-trap floats. MacRae began to believe they might have by-passed Glenda in the growing chop. Or perhaps she was no longer floating. He was thinking of turning back when one of the spotters pointed to a gleam ahead.

At the same instant, something in another direction caught MacRae's eye. The silvery flash could have been a mackerel. But mackerel are uncommon in this part of the Gulf in August. MacRae decided to head for his own sighting.

A moment later, a thin white arm rose above a rising wave. "My God, she's alive," one of the men murmured.

"We'll have to get her out quick," MacRae said. "Sometimes when they see help coming they think they're safe and relax too soon."

As the boat neared Glenda, MacRae cut the motor. The forward momentum of the craft carried it directly to the girl. As they slid by, MacRae caught one of her wrists in his powerful right hand, and with one motion rolled her over the low gunnel. Glenda Lennon's long swim was ended.

"Thank God," she breathed. "Thank God." Too weak to move, she began to cry, and there were tears on the faces of all three men. They wrapped her in blankets. Her left hand was still tightly clenched around her wedding band. "I want to go to my husband," she whispered through salt-swollen lips.

At full throttle, the runabout headed east. The first boat they sighted inshore was the Lennons' cruiser with Robert at the helm, still searching desperately. As MacRae pulled alongside, Robert suddenly saw his wife lying on the deck. In one mighty lunge he leaped from his boat and landed beside Glenda, nearly capsizing the smaller craft. The Lennons were reunited at last.

Glenda had swum more than 20 hours without any artificial flotation, kept up only by her desire to live, one more moment at a time. She had lost 20 pounds through dehydration, and her feet were permanently scarred from the friction of her swim fins. But after a week in the hospital, she was herself again. Friends brought her a tiny black poodle to take Spunky's place. And a year later, in September 1971, she bore the first of the children that, on that long night alone, she had thought she never would see.

Robert wears his Christmas watch every day. It is a reminder of his wife's courage, of the skill of a fine seaman, and of a miracle that did happen.

Teen-Agers' Rendezvous With Death

by George Mills

Eighteen-year-old Francis Elwood plowed all day on the Heilskov farm where he worked near Hampton, Iowa. After supper he went up to his room to write some letters. He planned to go to bed early.

In northeast Hampton, big George Kibsgaard, 18, had helped his electrician father move a meter that day. After supper he took his 13-year-old Oldsmobile and went downtown. It was so routine that he didn't even say good-by to his parents.

In west Hampton, little Russell Jensen, 19 and young-looking for his age, washed up in the back-lot house where he lived. Russ had polished cars that day in the Ford garage. Now he was going to the Skelly lunchroom where the teen-agers hung out.

Lloyd Casey, 18, a big, likable redhead, went home from the Hampton *Chronicle* where he was working as a printer's apprentice. He and his brother Leon, 16, thought they too would drop over to the Skelly lunch after the evening meal.

In three other homes—the Muhlenbrucks', the Bonjours', the Numelins'—boys ate at the family tables, looked at comic books, talked on the telephone, got ready to go out for a while.

As the minutes ticked away that Tuesday night, the cast slowly gathered for the tragedy in which four were to die.

Little Jane Maneely, 16, might well have been among them. She had been along at other times when Lawrence ("Sleepy") Muhlenbruck, 18, and George Kibsgaard laughingly darted out of the grasp of death in their cars. This evening, however, she had a job taking care of children. Bonnie Jones and Bonnie Martin might have been along, too. They promised, instead, to meet the boys afterward.

The usual crowd gathered at the Skelly lunchroom. Parked outside were Sleepy Muhlenbruck's 13-year-old Ford and George Kibsgaard's Olds. Neither of these boys—nor any of the others for that matter—indulged in liquor. But George had been fined three times for reckless driving and Sleepy had been haled into court too. The two had been in a near crash several nights before. Their idea of a good time was to play "swerve" with cars going 60 or 70 miles an hour.

Inside, several boys clustered around the pinball machine. Somebody broke a salt shaker. Elsie Woodley, the lunchroom waitress, didn't like that. To punish the boys, she pulled the plug on the pinball machine so nobody could play it. "The fellows all sat quietly on the stools for a minute," said Elsie, "just to show me they knew how to act."

Along toward eight o'clock the crowd began to break up. Where the youths went and what they did for the next half hour, nobody has told. All that is known is this: About 8:30 Kibsgaard, with two passengers, was westbound on Highway 3, his 1936 Olds wide-open at 73 (the speedometer jammed there). Speeding east was Sleepy's Ford, with five aboard. At least one car had its headlights turned off.

Death waited near a stone farmhouse six and a half miles from town.

The highway patrol says one car was 18 inches beyond the middle of the road, the other 14 inches over. That's the story the marks tell on the concrete. Whether the drivers didn't see each other or were testing each other's nerve is uncertain.

With a tearing impact of metal on metal, the two cars met. Kibsgaard's bluish-green Oldsmobile literally climbed up on the left side of the Muhlenbruck car. Bodies hurtled from the seats. The Olds landed with a crunch on the shoulder of the road, its rear wheels down in the ditch.

It also landed on top of Francis Elwood, the boy who was going to write some letters that night and go to bed early.

George Kibsgaard, too, died quickly, perhaps immediately. His face and head were crushed beyond recognition.

Russell Jensen lived until seven o'clock the next morning. He had a fractured skull, and a scalp wound that bled interminably.

Lloyd Casey had a badly cut throat, cuts on his face, internal injuries, a shattered left leg. He died Friday night.

Sleepy Muhlenbruck had four fractures of the pelvis, a broken left arm, a right-shoulder-blade fracture and severe cuts and abrasions. He wouldn't be driving a car for some time, even if the authorities let him.

Russell Bonjour, 22, had his left arm and leg broken, and severe facial cuts and bruises. Leon Casey had a tear in his face from his mouth to his ear, lost all his upper and lower front teeth, suffered a crushed nose and a broken right wrist. Merlin Numelin, 16, had a skull fracture.

The accident toll of four dead and four injured shook the town of Hampton to its foundations. M. J. Greenfield, the undertaker, said afterward: "If all the teen-agers in town could have been out there picking up those boys, it would have been the best lesson in driving they ever could have." The accident also uncovered some startling things about teen-age driving which are not peculiar to Hampton or to Iowa. Jane Maneely, whose life may have been saved because she had to take care of children that night, said some things in an interview that should open the eyes of law-enforcement officers and safety officials.

"I like reckless driving and I like speed," she said frankly, in telling of "rat racing" and "swerve." "Rat racing," she explained, "is one car racing to pass another. In swerve you just swerve the car down the road, back and forth, back and forth, just enough to give it a gentle rock."

Muhlenbruck, from his hospital bed, said he and Kibsgaard had gone "ditching" before. Ditching, he explained, is "where one car tries to ditch the cars that are chasing him. It is like hide-and-seek, only it is played with cars." He denied that the boys were playing "chicken" when the crash occurred. In chicken, two cars head toward each other at top speed, and the driver who swerves first is "chicken."

Merlin Numelin told of being out riding one night with Muhlenbruck. "George Kibsgaard was going like the devil with no lights on and Sleepy had to turn so George wouldn't hit him," Numelin said. "George had to swerve, too."

Mayor Joe Liebendorfer of Hampton, who handled many traffic-violation cases in his court, knew George Kibsgaard and some of the other boys well. "Kibsgaard contended the authorities were 'picking on him,'" said Liebendorfer. "Last time

I made the mistake of taking George's promise that he would start from the ground and learn to drive. My first thought was to have his driver's license suspended. That's what I should have done."

A number of Hampton teen-agers had had trouble with the law over their driving. These youths believed the adults of Hampton were partly to blame for what happened. Said one boy: "We ain't got nothing to do in this town. Why don't they start a recreation center here? All there is to do is run around in cars and chase each other."

"Please Don't Hurt My Baby!"

by Joseph P. Blank

It was a horror that Frances Lauver had never imagined. As the 22-year-old mother lowered her only child, 11-month-old Tommy, into his car seat, then slid behind the wheel of her old station wagon, the door suddenly flew open and a man touched her side with a knife. "Move over," he ordered. "No," she answered in astonishment. He pushed the knife against her and she felt a trickle of blood. "Okay, okay!" she gasped.

He got in. "Give me the keys. Stay cool and nothing will happen." Her heart pounded with fear. *Who is he? What does he want?* As he drove out of the Modesto, Calif., supermarket parking lot, her mind automatically registered his description: slim, in his early 30s, large nose, reddish-brown hair, pale complexion, small eyes and several days' growth of beard. He wore blue jeans and a dark turtleneck sweater. "How much money do you have?" he asked.

She checked her bag. "Forty-five cents."

"Keep it. I need a lot more than that. Give me your address."

She wrote it with a lipstick on the back of her shopping list. He pulled up at a roadside bar and ordered Frances, "Get out." She reached for Tommy and he said, "No."

She broke into tears. "Please, I want to take my baby with me."

"No. I'll leave a note in your mailbox telling you where you can find the baby and the car. Don't call the police."

"Please don't hurt my baby!"

"I wouldn't hurt him," he said, and squeezed Tommy's foot in seeming affection. Frances numbly got out of the car and the kidnapper quickly drove away. The slim, black-haired mother rushed into the bar and tearfully said, "Somebody just took my baby!" While the bartender dialed the sheriff's office, Frances asked the waitress to telephone her husband.

It was Saturday afternoon, January 20, 1973, and within a few minutes sheriff's deputies were questioning Frances. Her husband, Tom, a 26-year-old serviceman in a mobile-home company, sat by in confused shock. It made no sense. Why would anyone want to steal his son? He didn't have any money to pay ransom.

An hour later, deputies discovered the Lauver car, empty, near another bar. It contained no fingerprints or other evidence of the kidnapper.

The law officers began by probing Frances's own story and concluded she was telling the truth. An alarm, a composite drawing of the kidnapper and a photograph of Tommy now went out across the country. During the first week the sheriff's office received more than 500 tips and leads by mail, telephone and telegram. There was, however, no word from the kidnapper himself.

Three weeks after the kidnapping, when the great bulk of leads had been investigated and found worthless, Detective Wesley Williams of the sheriff's department was assigned to work full time on the case. Williams is a big, burly man, intelligent, determined and patient. Several times a week he visited Frances and showed her stacks of mug shots, which eventually totaled well over 1200. FBI agents also dropped in with photographs. None checked out.

Doggedly the detective pursued every lead and tip. One man was absolutely certain he had seen the child in a gray Plymouth. Williams checked out every gray Plymouth in three counties—to no avail. Adoption agencies were queried. From Louisiana, Georgia, Illinois, Ohio, and Alberta, Canada, police sent reports and photographs of abandoned children. Once the detective received an early-morning call about "freshly turned earth that looks like a small grave." He quickly dressed, grabbed a shovel and drove to the site. He dug up a shoe box containing a dead squirrel and a plastic flower. In the course of his search he found one baby who had been purchased for $250 in Mexico, and another child, apparently abandoned, who was being kept by a carnival worker. But not Tommy.

By summer the leads had dwindled to a few a week, and Williams was painfully aware he had accomplished nothing. "Somewhere there's a couple with a baby that doesn't belong to them," he told his wife. "*Somebody* knows about it. How can I find that somebody?"

At about this time, some four miles from the Lauver house, Marjorie Coffey, 30, wrote a letter to her onetime neighbor Margaret Rains, who was living in Texas. She told Mrs. Rains that she and her husband, Bob, a machinist, had adopted a little boy. Mrs. Rains knew that her friend had two girls by a previous marriage and had since undergone a hysterectomy. She asked for details about the adoption. Marjorie Coffey replied tersely: "It is a boy and his name is Shawn."

In September the Rains family moved back to Modesto and took a house a short distance from the Coffeys. When Mrs. Rains inquired further about the adoption, the Coffeys refused to tell her anything and she assumed the baby had been born to a friend of theirs who did not want him. She never saw the baby being walked or wheeled in a carriage along the street. When she visited the Coffeys, the child was usually kept alone in a room with a closed door, though she was allowed to see him. But the adoption and the couple's treatment of the baby puzzled Mrs. Rains.

By now Detective Williams was more than puzzled. He began to wonder about his own abilities as an investigator. He discussed every aspect of the case with fellow detectives, questioned Frances over and over about every detail. During the year he had eagerly coöperated with newspaper, radio and television reporters on stories about the kidnapping. Each mention of the crime invariably brought new leads. As the months passed, however, publicity virtually stopped. There was nothing new to report.

Frances never lost hope. "It's just going to take one lead," she told him, during one of his visits to the Lauver home. "Maybe it'll come tomorrow. Maybe next month." As Williams left the house he glanced into the baby's room. The crib was made up and the toys were laid out as if Tommy would be returning within the hour.

In January 1974, Williams talked with Steve Ringhoff, a reporter on the Modesto *Bee,* and suggested a first-anniversary feature about the kidnapping. The detective knew the story would be picked up by the wire services and the kidnapping would once again get national as well as local attention. And there always existed the possibility this could be the story that would make one reader somewhere provide the tip that would lead to Tommy Lauver.

On the evening of January 19, Marjorie Coffey visited Mrs. Rains. After some small talk she asked, "Do you know how I can get a birth certificate for Shawn?"

Mrs. Rains was surprised. "Didn't they give you one when you adopted him?"

Her friend hesitated, then said, "Don't tell anyone, not even your husband. The baby is stolen."

Mrs. Rains didn't give the statement immediate credence. Her friend had been drinking. In such condition she often spun fantasies about her past—her nightclub work as a go-go dancer, her career as an undercover narcotics agent, her singing with a nationally known country-music group. But a few days later Mrs. Rains read Ringhoff's article about the kidnapping in the Modesto *Bee*. She had known about the crime, but the photograph of Tommy Lauver stopped her. He looked like Shawn Coffey. Marjorie Coffey's confession suddenly became alarmingly significant.

Mrs. Rains worried. Was Shawn Coffey really Tommy Lauver? Should she call the Detective Williams mentioned in the article? Suppose Shawn Coffey was obtained illegally, but was *not* Tommy Lauver? And what about the Lauvers and their suffering?

She lost sleep, was distracted at her job. When her employer criticized her work, she confided in him. His reaction was immediate. "Call the sheriff," he told her. "You're a mother. How would you feel if *your* baby had been stolen?"

She telephoned Williams. At first the information didn't impress the detective. The woman sounded hesitant and unsure of herself. But his attitude changed dramatically when she got to Mrs. Coffey's question about a phony birth certificate. Excitedly he telephoned the local FBI agent and the pair visited the Coffey house.

Mrs. Coffey denied that she had a baby. She said she had been taking care of her sister-in-law's baby, but the mother had taken the child back three months previously. The officers left temporarily to compare impressions. They agreed the woman was lying. A telephone call to Mrs. Rains confirmed it. She insisted she had seen the baby two weeks ago.

There was no time to obtain a search warrant. The Coffeys had been alerted. If the baby was Tommy, they might try to escape with him or, worse, try to conceal or dispose of the "evidence" of kidnapping.

While the FBI agent took off to find Coffey, Williams and a fellow deputy, Sgt. Charles Curtis, returned to the house. Mrs. Coffey asked if they had a search warrant. "If you have no baby here," Williams said, "why should you object to a search?"

After long moments of silence the woman said she had a baby in the house and agreed to get him. During her brief absence Sergeant Curtis impulsively opened a closet door. Coffey was standing inside. He stepped out without a word.

His wife brought out a baby boy. The officers bundled him and Coffey to headquarters. There the child's footprints were taken to be matched against Tommy Lauver's hospital prints.

Williams waited and sweated. Finally the identification deputy returned and said, "I've charted 15 matching points." (Under FBI standards 12 matching points represent a positive identification.) "That's the baby. No doubt about it." Williams went from sweating to chills.

Frances and Tom were given no explanation for being called to the sheriff's office. Tom assumed the worst, that he would have to identify his son's remains; he wondered what he could do to help his wife survive the shock. But when they arrived, Williams greeted them with a big grin "We think we have Tommy," he said.

Frances broke into tears and asked, "Are you *sure?*"

"I won't be sure until you're sure."

Then Tommy was carried into the room. Frances stared, her eyes widening and her face turning white. "Well, take him," Williams said.

She reached for Tommy and the child began crying. Frances, between sobs, said, "That's his cry. That's my baby!" Suddenly, mother and baby hugged each other, and their tears mingled as she kissed his forehead and cheek. Now everybody in the room was crying. Williams felt the adrenalin drain out of his body; he had to stiffen his legs to prevent himself from sagging.

On the following day Frances immediately picked Coffey out of a line-up. He readily admitted the kidnapping. His wife was depressed because she could not have another baby, he said, so he had stolen Tommy to save his marriage; his wife knew nothing about the kidnapping. Mrs. Coffey also disclaimed knowledge. But Mrs. Rains' sworn testimony made a lie of this statement. Coffey was sentenced to five-to-twenty-five years in prison; his wife, one-to-five.

Tommy was in fair condition. He had bruises on his chest and arms. Bruises around his ankles and poor circulation in his feet indicated that a restraint had been used on him. During his year and 16 days with the Coffeys his physical and mental progress had been impeded.

"But now he's fine," Frances said to me a few months later as she looked lovingly at her son. "I know that a baby is a gift from God. I've been given the same gift twice. It makes me aware of every minute with my child—and I'm thankful for every minute."

A Will
of Her Own

by Fulton Oursler

The fragile old lady was wet and tired. One of the first in a line that curled half a block from the box office of a New York cinema palace, she was waiting in the rain for the doors to open.

Under one arm she carried a bag of sandwiches; with the other she held an umbrella. She had been standing there for hours, when suddenly she pitched forward in a faint.

The resplendent doorman in blue and gold picked up the old lady and carried her into the empty theater. There a doctor brought her back to consciousness. Soon, seated in a gilded chair, she was looking into the kindly Irish-blue eyes of the theater's assistant manager.

"Are you strong enough for me to take you home in a cab?"

"Weak enough, you mean," grinned the old lady. "I came here to see the picture. For mercy sake, does this mean I've lost my place in line?"

She had a gallant smile, and a positive way of shaking her head as she talked while adjusting her preposterous hat with its faded green feathers. She was like a print out of the past, with her leg-of-mutton sleeves, a feather boa around her neck, and full skirts with—oh, there was no doubt about it—many petticoats beneath.

"Tell me about yourself," said the manager. "Is your husband living?"

"No. Gone. My son's gone, too. That's why I came to see

this Gary Cooper picture. He looks like my son. If you let me get back in my place in line now—"

"You come with me. They're rehearsing the stage show and you can sit and watch that. I'll send you some hot coffee and you can just sit there right on through the show."

"I always see the picture twice," she said. "Can I sit through two shows?"

"As many as you like."

Thus began a friendship. Whenever there was a new picture, the old lady arrived, sandwiches, feather boa and all, and invariably she rapped on the manager's door and, as she expressed it, "had a yarn with him."

One day she invited him to come to her place for tea. He could not leave the theater that long, but they did break bread together at a drugstore counter around the corner. Neither of them knew that they were never to see each other again. There was depression in the world those days. The theater closed its doors and the assistant manager went elsewhere to work.

Then one day the police were told that an old lady who lived all by herself in a three-story brownstone dwelling at 146 West 88th Street had not been seen going in or coming out for several days. Officers forced the front door of that gloomy gas-lit house. Through silent, empty downstairs rooms they hurried; then they climbed a dusty staircase to the door of the bedroom. It was locked.

They could hear faint groans now. But when they tried to break in, the door was too strong for all their united strength. They had to put up ladders from the sidewalk to the front bedroom windows. There she was, delirious with a complication of paralysis and pneumonia. Taken to a hospital, she died that night.

This fragile old lady left a will. At the Chase National Bank it was found, signed with her name—Edna Morss Allin Elliott. Among other charitable bequests, she had remembered the assistant manager of the theater: "I make this gift to him because through him I received numerous privileges at the theater which have helped to make recent years of my life more pleasant. He contributed a great deal to my happiness by kindly and courteous acts. And he never expected anything from me."

Where was the manager? They found the man with the Irish-blue eyes working as an attendant in a hospital at $52 a month.

The news they came to tell him was that his old lady friend had left him nearly a million dollars.

That was the original estimate. With taxes and other shrinkages the amount he finally collected was nearly $150,000—which was still a very large sum of money at that time.

Don't misunderstand me. Such things happen very seldom in this world. But this I can tell you: there is often a million dollars' worth of happiness that comes into the heart when we spread a little kindness in this world.

Angel Dust—A Family's Nightmare

by Ursula Etons

Ten o'clock on an autumn Sunday morning, still in bed. The phone rings. Vincent, my husband, answers in the kitchen. "Owen?" he is saying. "Where? When?"

I sit up and reach for the extension phone. "What is it?" I ask.

"Owen is ill," a strange voice informs me. "Your son was found running through the dormitory halls with a fire extinguisher in his hands. He's quite incoherent. He's going to need treatment—in a hospital."

"We'll come up for him," Vince says on the other phone.

"No, that won't be necessary," says the caller, who explains that he is the psychologist at my son's university. "He's asked to have his brother drive him home. We called and he's on his way here now." (Marc was at a neighboring university in upstate New York; we live on Long Island.)

I hang up the phone and look out, numbly, at the now-too-bright sky. Three psychiatrists are called. Each is too busy to take on new patients. But the third doctor asks questions. Frightening questions.

"Does your son take drugs?"

Owen? What was he talking about?

"Well, Mrs. Etons, drugs are a fact of life on campus. You tell me your son has always been happy and well adjusted—that he's always been an excellent student. So I can think of only one explanation—drugs."

Later—much later—we learn that he was right. My son was a victim of angel dust. . . .

On Monday, Owen and I are alone. His eyes stare but do not see. Rosemary's Baby's eyes. Gleaming silver. He is talking, incessantly, incoherently. He points to our Siamese kitten. "The eyes, Mother, check out the eyes." They gleam. Like his own.

And then he asks for a notebook, a pen. All is abstract. Reality has been replaced by symbols. So I attempt to communicate with him through these same symbols. During the long day, the legal pad fills up:

> Religion is key
> R - P (Rel-P)
> 1
> Key to the Future
> G.G.G.G.G.
> W.W.
> G.P.

General

Practitioner

When my younger son and daughter come home from school, Owen is pacing, ranting. *Guilt*. The word has been announced all afternoon. "I'm going to kill you, Mother." At one point he grabs my hand, squeezing hard.

The hours before the six o'clock appointment with the psychiatrist drag by. The doctor talks with Owen only a few moments, then decides to send him to the Long Island Medical Center.

The center's psychiatric emergency room is a lower level of hell. We wait. And wait. Finally, it is Owen's turn. The interview goes on for half an hour. My husband and I are then called in. Owen waits outside.

"We must assume that your son has been on drugs," the doctor says. "What kind of drugs I don't know."

"I can't believe it!" I protest. "Not Owen."

We are told that Owen must be placed in a locked ward, for his own safety and that of others. We stand silently as he is led away, my young, gentle college boy, by two burly, uniformed guards to a strange secret place called Ward 10.

> The sky speckled in white
> becomes blend to early
> morning viewers

Owen had written that. It is part of a poem that has been published. Now, when I go through his papers, I find that the poems have changed. Like his mind.

> Turn it on and off but
> not with the door open spec
> tators see what
> the cut did to you theres
> a cut over my eye and its
> killing my brain

I approach Ward 10 with caution. The door is tightly locked. Visiting is limited to a single hour in a waiting room outside. Locked and complete with nurses and security guard.

Owen is not given any medication at first. The doctors are waiting for whatever is in his system to get out. Then, on Wednesday, he is put on a tranquilizer, Haldol (haloperidol).

He seems to get worse. The overt agitation has ceased, but he is like a zombie. He walks peculiarly. He will not communicate. He wears hospital clothes because he doesn't remember how to get dressed.

After six days of struggle, the haze lifts.

"How are you doing?"

"I'm okay."

Very matter-of-factly. *I'm okay*. And now, finally, we get some answers. Owen tells the doctor that he has been heavily into marijuana, has tried speed, but the thing that literally blew his mind was angel dust. All his brain cells have been altered, the chemical balance has been outrageously upset.

Phencyclidine (PCP) is a chemical used experimentally some years ago as an anesthetic for humans, but discontinued because of adverse reactions. At the present time the FDA allows it to be used as a tranquilizer for animals only. Yet somehow the chemical, which is cheap to manufacture, has got into the hands of pushers and users alike, and they have christened the light, powdery substance "angel dust."

* * *

I cried
when I knew
I'd been asleep all these years
I shivered
my eyes were wet . . .
Relax, insane
I'm going insane
relax, insane
I'm skimming the drain
relax . . .

Owen is now himself once more: coherent, in touch with the real world. He is moved to an "open" floor, where patients considered well enough may wander around freely.

Yet his physical condition seems to worsen. He walks stiffly, tilted forward. His hands shake. Left alone in his room, he tries to walk, becomes dizzy and falls. My husband finds him lying in a pool of blood, from a nosebleed caused by the fall.

Now Cogentin is injected intra-muscularly to counteract the side effects of the Haldol. Owen lies in bed, frightened, his hands still shaking. He stares up at the ceiling. Why, I wonder, must one take one step forward and two steps backward?

Then, for some reason, Owen begins to make slow but continual progress—although we later find out he had been taken off the Haldol after his fall. When I arrive for my visits he wears street clothes; he needs no assistance dressing. And one day I find him playing ping-pong with another young male patient.

After 17 days, Owen is released from the hospital. As we leave I want to celebrate. I stop the car in the park. Gleefully, I flit from flowerbed to flowerbed, like a busy bee, plucking the fat marigolds, zinnias and shasta daisies. Owen watches. Silent. I offer him the fresh bouquet.

"Shall I get some more?"

"I want to go home."

Owen is restless. I am concerned. Is the angel dust still lurking in the crevices of his brain?

After a week at home, on no medication, Owen's restlessness increases. On the seventh afternoon he stalks into my bedroom, his face contorted in anger.

"I warned you—I may become violent!" His eyes are wide, shining too brightly.

On the seventh night, at midnight, we take Owen back to the psychiatric emergency room. The young doctor on duty says he's okay. She smiles at my skepticism and gives us a choice: Dalmane (a sleeping pill) or Thorazine (a major tranquilizer). Let it be Thorazine.

That night Owen sleeps well. I do not. Why is he getting sick again? And why doesn't anyone else notice it?

The next night, he goes to bed early with two Thorazine tablets. Vincent and I, both exhausted, fall off to sleep before ten o'clock.

Hours later we both awake to strange, maniacal laughter. Voices. Owen is having a lively conversation in the living room. But who would be visiting at 1 a.m.?

Owen's visitor is a young man who worked with my son at the local supermarket the previous summer. The young man whispers something to my husband. When our "guest" leaves, I come out. Vince shows me a razor and a bottle of Librium that Owen had in his pocket. My unused Librium. I shake my head in disbelief as Vince informs me that Owen had just wandered out into the cold night in his pajamas and bare feet, crossed Main Street and entered a local pub. His friend found him there and brought him home.

"He was high on something, Mr. Etons," the young man had said. High on something? Still? Was there no end to this high?

Numbly, we enter the bathroom. Owen is seated on the tub. A previously unopened bottle of syrup of ipecac (a drug that induces vomiting) stands on the sink. Empty. Can it be that Owen drank it all?

Owen stares at us. Silent. Eyes glimmering. Silver. We help him dress and get him out to the car. At the Long Island Medical Center, doctors determine that Owen has indeed ingested the ipecac. And the Librium. Mixed, of course, with the Thorazine. He is questioned and watched for over an hour.

We wait. And wait. It is nearly dawn. Owen goes into one of the small rooms to lie down. His ordeal has fatigued him. When I check on him, I find him lying there, staring at the ceiling. In tears.

At 5 a.m., two security guards lead Owen back to the open ward. He has been officially readmitted.

For close to a week the nightmare continues. Then, after heavy doses of Thorazine, rationality gradually returns. Owen smiles when we visit. Once more he socializes with the other patients, plays ping-pong and cards, watches TV.

But he has delusions. He worries constantly about the Russians, about atomic warfare. On December 7, alarmed that he has been off medication for several days, we transfer him to a private hospital. Although he is rational, I notice an increasing irritability when I speak. At one point he tells me to "shut up."

Owen's new psychiatrist, Dr. Glenn, is shocked to find that Owen has been off medication. Since I express my concern about side effects, the doctor puts him on a different drug, Taractan.

Owen gets worse.

The doctor tries a different medication, or combination of medications, every day.

Owen gets worse. By the weekend, he is once more in the throes of a full-blown psychosis.

Different medications continue: Serentil, Cogentin, Tranxene and God knows what else in what combination. The doctor appears to be playing with Owen's body chemistry.

I visit my son. He asks me if I've come on the SST.

He becomes more difficult to handle. He is isolated in a small room that has a bed and a lock on the door.

Dr. Glenn has a long talk with Vincent and me about the chemistry of the brain, about one of the biogenic amines, dopamine, and how Owen's dopamine level was altered by use of the drugs he was taking. He suggests a super bombardment of Haldol injections, along with Cogentin, every hour for six hours, and then a reduced dosage starting the next day. If that doesn't work, he suggests shock therapy. We object to shock treatment, but, in desperation, go along with the medication plans.

For several days Owen is out of touch with reality. He wanders about the hall, aimlessly taking Christmas trinkets off the tree. And yet there is a glimmer of rationality. Owen can remember telephone numbers. He glances through newspapers.

After a week, Owen appears to be much better. After three weeks he is discharged. As we leave he notes that he has spent three holidays in hospitals: Halloween, Thanksgiving and Christmas.

Five months pass. Owen is a day patient at the Long Island

Medical Center for the first three months, then is released when
he gets his old summer job back. I can say he is almost perfect
again. He now drives and is working, although he still needs
small doses of Thorazine. He will start classes in the fall at
a college on Long Island.

And now I know it will not be long before Owen can again
write like this:

> The sky speckled in white
> becomes blend to early morning viewers,
> and a tranquilizer to men of other times.

*Editor's Note: Owen was attending college again in early
1979, when this article was published. He had been off medication, with no recurrence of problems, for one year.*

The Midnight Ride of No. 602

by Michael Strauss

It was 3:37 a.m. when Lt. John Terry of the Essex Junction, Vt., police noticed a diesel locomotive moving at about six miles an hour along the railroad tracks where they intersected the village's West Street cutoff.

"Mighty strange," he thought. "Who would send a locomotive up here all by itself in the middle of the night?"

Terry drove to Pearl Street, which runs alongside the tracks, and peered through the darkness at the locomotive's cab. "That cab looks empty," he said to himself.

Terry continued to follow the engine, which he now realized was traveling in reverse. It did not stop or sound a whistle at the Summit Street crossing—as was customary—but, in fact, seemed to pick up speed. The lettering on the engine's side identified it as a Vermont Railroad diesel—No. 602—not an engine of the Central Vermont Railroad, along whose tracks it was rolling.

"Could the engineer be lying on the floor—dead?" Terry wondered.

When the locomotive continued past two main crossings without offering so much as a warning "beep," Terry decided to act. Using his patrol-car radio, he instructed two policemen on the village's force, Wayne Bither and Rodney Mills, who were finishing a strenuous 16-hour shift, to pursue the engine. He also told them to watch the remaining crossings in Essex Junction to protect unsuspecting motorists. Then Terry himself hightailed it to the police station to call the State Police and

227

the St. Albans office of the Central Vermont Railroad.

"He must be crazy," commented Bither on receiving the radio call. "Missing engineer? Sounds as if he's been watching too many reruns of 'Twilight Zone.'"

Bither and Mills had no trouble keeping up with the locomotive and guarding the town's remaining crossings. They, too, were not able to spot any engineer—only a jacket and cap hanging inside the cab.

"Maybe we'd better hop aboard," suggested Bither. Mills agreed.

"We pulled ahead of that locomotive three times, stopped our car, and tried to climb aboard," Bither said later. "Each time, however, it was moving too fast—maybe 30 miles an hour. We couldn't chance it."

Boarding the lumbering giant proved extremely difficult because both men had to use their flashlights to spot the engine's boarding rail and find its bottom step as it drew abreast. Then they had to quickly stuff their 16-inch flashlights into their back pockets, make a grab for the handrail and leap onto the boarding rail. It called for exact timing. About eight miles north of Essex Junction, the two officers finally made their big leaps.

Mills got aboard on his first try. The heavier Bither succeeded in grabbing the handrail, but failed to gain a footing on the lowest step. His legs thrashed. Finally, he got a toehold. It was now about 4:10 a.m. on Sunday, October 21, 1973.

"We shouldn't have any problems now," said Mills. "And Lieutenant Terry was right," he added as he poked his head through the cab's window. "There's no engineer."

Mills' burst of optimism about having "no problems" stemmed from a conversation with headquarters on the police radio. Lieutenant Terry had said a railroad official in St. Albans told him how the engine could be stopped: "All you do once you get inside the cab is reach for that big lever over the engineer's seat and yank it."

"Here I go," said Mills in a jaunty tone as he climbed through the cab window after finding the door locked. "I'm going to—" He never finished the sentence. His flashlight's beam showed there was no big lever over the seat. The railroad official, it developed later, had guessed incorrectly about the type of engine in flight. Mills' closer inspection of the cab revealed a collection of levers and switches that he found baffling. "I might as well be in a space capsule," he moaned.

Now the two men found themselves wondering how they might best get off the engine, which had reached a downgrade and was picking up speed. "Just keep pulling on those switches and see what happens," Bither advised Mills. "I'll see if I can spot a clearing we can jump into."

Mills was lucky. By manipulating one of the levers, which turned out to be the throttle, he brought the engine to a stop halfway up an upgrade. But it didn't stay stopped. It started to roll back toward another upgrade. Manipulating the throttle once more caused the engine to roll forward again.

For the next ten minutes the two men found themselves involved in a backward-forward operation, lodged between two upgrades. Mills continued to work the throttle, which brought the engine to a near stand-still, but he was unable to stop it completely. "It's no use," he finally said in despair.

Help came at last. A policeman from neighboring Colchester arrived and climbed aboard while the engine was barely moving. He turned the handbrake at the front of the locomotive. By that time there were police cars from Milton, Colchester and Essex Junction, three state troopers' cruisers and cars belonging to railroad officials.

During the deliberations about where to send the locomotive, a natural question arose. Where had the engine come from?

Investigation over the next few hours showed the 120-ton No. 602 must have started its journey from the Vermont Railroad's yards in Rutland.

Rutland! That seemed inconceivable. Rutland is 74 miles south of Essex Junction. To complete the trip from Rutland, the unmanned engine would have had to go through more than 100 highway crossings. It seemed incredible that no accidents had been reported.

Now came the task of determining what had caused the engine's flight through the quiet of the Vermont night over hills and valleys, across trestles and roadways.

Charles Bischoff, the railroad's chief engineer, provided a logical explanation. "Our engine house in Rutland has room for only two locomotives," he said. "We were keeping our third one outside with its engines idling so they wouldn't freeze. The culprit, whoever he was, first broke the lock—it was found hammered beyond repair—to a switch which provided entry for the engine onto the main track. Then he entered the locked engine's cab by sliding open one of its big windows.

"And since the locomotive was facing away from the main track, he had to start in reverse. Only someone familiar with such a locomotive could have known how to do this without using the reverse lever, which was locked in our engine house."

Once under way, the locomotive apparently encountered no problems. It wound its way through such quiet Vermont communities as Pittsford, Brandon, Middlebury, Vergennes and Shelburne. It had no difficulty switching onto the Central Vermont Railroad's trackage once it got into Burlington's busy freight yards. Although there is a maze of tracks, the switches happened to be perfectly set for the changeover to Essex Junction.

A year later, the villain still had not been caught. There were few leads, not even fingerprints. Patrolman Mills, in his desperate attempt to stop the locomotive, obliterated them when he handled all the levers and switches in the cab. The consensus among railroad men was that the culprit may have been a train buff who learned about engines from railroad magazines.

In any event, it's a good thing Lieutenant Terry spotted the engine at Essex Junction. If he hadn't, old 602 conceivably could have triggered an international incident by continuing right into Canada just a few miles away. It had enough fuel to take it as far as Montreal.

Summer of the Broken Calf

by Dorothy Rood Stewart

The summer of my seventh year I grew almost three inches—shot up like a stalk of tipton weed, my father said. And it was that summer, too, that the calf was born, the first baby animal on our new farm.

"Just you wait, Dorsie," Papa told me. "Before you know it we'll have a whole herd of cattle. And running water in the bathroom for Mama. And a piano so you can take lessons." He swung me high in the air, so I kicked and screamed and waved my arms. But I wasn't frightened—not with Papa holding me. He was so big and strong, I knew he wouldn't let me fall.

Anything he did or said was always right. I would rather have been with him than play with my dolls or even listen to Mama read "Cinderella." His mustache tickled when he blew in my neck, and he always smelled like tobacco smoke. I loved him very much. Back in the city he had been gone all day at the office; here on the farm I could tag after him from morning until night.

The calf was born on the last day of school that June. I came home and there in the barnyard stood the cunning new calf, wobbly legs wide, butting at its mother. I gave a cry of pleasure and rushed toward it, but Papa held me back.

"Stand here and just look," he said. "Isn't she a honey?"

"Can I name her, Papa?"

"I don't see why not." He took off his wide straw farmer

231

hat and rubbed the red line on his forehead. "She has a mighty pretty white star between her eyes, doesn't she?"

"Then I'll name her Star."

Naming an animal seems to make it your very own. Every morning after breakfast I'd run down the little hill to the barnyard to watch Star nuzzling her mother. Soon she knew me and would snuffle her wet rubbery nose against my hand. At first, when she was small, I tried to lift her. But by the time her mother weaned her she had grown so much that, when I fed her her mixture of milk and bran, it was all I could do to keep her from butting the pail from my hands.

Star was almost three months old when her leg was broken. I was the one who found her, half lying on her side, one foot caught in a crack between two rough stones. After Papa got her free, he asked our neighbor to come and look at her.

"Always with a broken leg they die," Mr. Hansen said. "Better to butcher now for veal."

My father shook his head. "I'm going to try to save her."

At his words my heart gave a jump of relief. Of course he could mend Star's leg; he could fix anything that was broken. Hadn't he made my doll's buggy as good as new even after the wheels came off? So now Papa rigged up a sort of hammock out of a gunnysack, with a rope pulley that hoisted Star up until her hoofs barely touched the floor. He bound her broken leg between two thin slats of wood. Then he offered her bran mash; but she wouldn't touch it.

"She's frightened and in pain," he said. "You try her again after a while, Dorsie."

She wouldn't even take it from me. "Oh, Star, Star," I told her. "Papa's going to fix you. You'll be all right." But when I flung my arms about her neck she pulled away.

Many times that day, and the next, and the next, I went to the barn. But Star only drank a little water. She hung in the dusty air of the stable, her soft rubbery nose becoming hot and dry, the moist light in her dark eyes growing dim.

Then one night I heard my mother and father talking in low voices in the kitchen. I was in bed, supposedly asleep.

"It's no use, dear," I heard Mama say. "Put the poor thing out of her misery."

Papa's voice sounded tired. "Yes," he mumbled. "I guess I'll have to."

"Then do it now," Mama whispered. "While Dorsie is asleep."

I had watched Papa load his revolver at other times, so I knew the clicking sound the cartridges made sliding into the cylinder. I remembered, too, the time he'd shot a weasel that was after the chickens. He'd fired his shotgun twice, telling Mama and me afterward. "I was afraid I'd only wounded him the first time. I wanted to be sure and put the poor little devil out of his misery." Then he'd smiled at me. "Animals don't mind being dead, Dorsie, if you kill them quickly."

When I heard the screen door close softly, I slipped out of bed. In the bright moonlight I saw Papa walk slowly down the hill toward the barn. I waited until he had opened the barnyard gate before I followed, holding my white nightie up with both hands to keep it from the dusty ground. I had no clear thought about what was going to happen; I only knew I wanted to be there with Papa.

When I looked through the doorway, he had lighted a lantern and had set it on a barrel top near where Star hung suspended in her sling. The revolver was in his right hand. *No, Papa!* But I only thought the words; they made no sound. I felt stiff and frozen like a statue.

Papa pointed the gun directly at Star's head and fired. She made a quick shivering motion as though she had shrugged away a fly. I heard my father gasp. He fired again. Star flicked her tail and moved one leg a little.

"My God!" Papa cried out. "What's wrong!" In desperation, he blazed the last four bullets so fast the whole barn seemed to explode with the noise. Dust sifted down from the rafters into the lantern light—and then I saw the thin dark trickle of Star's blood.

My father stumbled to the open door before he saw me and called out. "Dorsie!" His voice sounded hoarse as though he had a cold. Then he clung to the doorpost and was very sick.

I did not think about the loss of Star, not then; I was trying to understand my father. I had never seen him like this before, and I thought: When *I* feel bad about something he always comforts me. So I leaned to him, put my arms around him up as far as I could reach. "There, there, Papa," I said. "I'm right here."

I heard the breath in his chest catch like a sob. And I knew that never again would I see him quite as I had before, so invincible, so almost godlike.

But never would I love him any more than I did at that moment.

Awake Through a Brain Operation

by Annette Anselmo

For 30 years, ever since age four, the author had suffered epileptic seizures with devastating frequency. Anti-convulsant drugs and a brain operation performed by a local Salt Lake City surgeon had banished the severest seizures. But she still suffered smaller convulsions, sometimes as many as 65 an hour.

In the fall of 1953, Annette Anselmo traveled to a well-known neurological institute, where a renowned brain surgeon—call him Dr. Jones—studied her case history, made exhaustive tests, took brain Xrays and EEGs. "We believe an operation will help you," he said finally. "But I do not promise a complete cure. And you realize the risk: you may be paralysed."

For Ms. Anselmo, the possibility was worth the risk. She decided to go ahead with it.

Early that morning a barber came into my hospital room and shaved my head so it resembled a large billiard ball. Then my bed was wheeled into the hall, where Dad and my sister kissed me, trying hard not to cry. "Don't worry," I said. "I'll be back." My feeling was, "Today is the beginning of the end of my 30-year war against epilepsy."

In the X-ray room, a doctor said to me with a smile, "This is a big day for you." In one hand he had two wires, each about a yard long; in the other a glass of water. "I'm going to insert a wire in each of your nostrils," he said. "I want you to take a drink and swallow when I tell you to." The wires were to go down into my stomach. Each time the doctor said, "Swallow," a few more inches would disappear, until only about a foot and a half remained in view. Then the doctor took an X ray to see if the wires were in proper position. Three times they were not, and he would say, "Let's start over."

Finally the wires were in place. As he taped the ends to my chest, he explained that these electrodes would provide a reading of stomach movement—the sensation I had often experienced with the onset of an attack. When electrical stimulation of the brain came close to the point from which my attacks originated, the stomach sensation would be produced.

Now my bed was wheeled into the anesthesia room. I knew I was to remain fully conscious throughout the operation so Dr. Jones could be guided by my reactions. The anesthetist was to give me injections to deaden the feeling in my face and scalp.

He asked me to open my mouth and, with his thumb, located the hinge bone connecting the upper and lower jaw. Into it he inserted a needle—so far upward it seemed to reach my skull bone! I felt a searing pain. But these injections were the only way to deaden the feeling in my scalp and facial skin. Each time he picked up another needle, I glanced at the remaining pile. It seemed to grow larger instead of smaller.

Dr. Jones now entered, and I could feel him tracing a design on my scalp. "This is the skull opening I want," he said to the doctors with him. One replied, "Yes, a full butterfly flap."

The anesthetist said, "She is about ready for the operating room."

"I'm not afraid," I said, "but do me a favor. When my skull is about to be opened, will one of you tell me a joke?" I thought it would help to mask the moment of intense pain I anticipated.

Out in the hall the doors of the operating room opened to allow my bed to pass through. I had reached the point of no retreat.

Inside, I looked at the wall clock: 8:05. I could see the glassed-in gallery where doctors, nurses and students were waiting to observe. Each of the six doctors who were to take part in the operation wore special glasses, for the room had ultraviolet lighting instead of glaring overhead bulbs. I heard one doctor say, "We'll be lucky if we get out of here by suppertime."

A doctor behind my head said, "This will sting. I'm going

to paint your head with iodine." The anesthetist told me to lie flat on my back and turn my head to the left. Towels were placed around my neck to hold my head in place. They held it firmly but not uncomfortably. In fact, I hardly noticed them after a few minutes.

Now Dr. Jones was standing at my head, a tray of instruments beside him. With foot or hand controls he raised my head to the proper position. It was up to me not to move; no sandbags or straps restrained me, except one to keep me from falling off the table. He asked if I was comfortable. I said, "Yes, but I'm freezing." A blanket was tucked around me. doubtless the impact of what was about to happen had given me chills.

"I'm going to inject several needles at the base of your skull, Annette," Dr. Jones said. "This will eliminate as much pain as possible, but you know I can't deaden it entirely."

He began inserting the needles, As he worked, Dr. Jones occasionally consulted his associates, and sometimes dictated notes to a secretary in the gallery, through an intercom. I thought: "Imagine doing a delicate operation like this—and dictating at the same time." He told the type and amount of medication in each injection, reviewed my case history, and explained what he believed to be the cause of my seizures: a birth injury, damage resulting from an interference with the circulation of oxygen-carrying blood to one side of my brain at the time of my birth.

Each needle felt as if it would come through my mouth. I finally lost count of the needles. "How many more?" I kept asking. "Not many. Try and bear it a bit longer," the doctor would answer.

I glanced at the clock. It seemed impossible but it was already 11:30.

Now I felt the pressure of what I was certain was a scalpel against my scalp. No pain; just the sudden warmth of liquid trickling down my cheek. When I realized it was my own blood, I said, "I'm going to throw up." A pan was held close to my face. My mouth felt parched. A piece of ice was placed between my lips.

Dr. Jones said, "Annette, we are about to make a few holes in your skull." The drilling began. There was a period of dull pain, and a dull grinding sound. There were to be, I knew, five to seven fairly large burr holes.

After an interminable interval, everything was still, almost morbidly so. Then I heard the sawing of bone. I waited for the pain I so vividly remembered when the skull had been opened in my other operation 2 1/2 years before. I finally asked how much longer it would be before they would break through my skull. Someone patted my hand and said, "It's already done, Annette."

The clock showed 12 noon. A nurse held a cup of something steaming—soup perhaps—and Dr. Jones drank it through a straw.

I heard, more than felt, the awful sensation of liquid being squirted over my brain. When the brain is exposed, the air dries its surface quickly, and it must be continuously moistened.

At 1:30, Dr. Jones said, "Turn the machine at this angle." I knew he was referring to the machine he would use to stimulate the electrical activity of my brain cells.

Pictures were taken, both in black-and-white and in color. Then Dr. Jones spoke to me quietly. "Annette, from here on I will need your full coöperation. We are going to stimulate your brain, and I want you to tell me exactly what you feel and where." Was I ready? I said I was.

A few seconds later I felt a light current go through my body. I said, "I feel as though I am about to fall off the table to my left." He answered, "That's fine. We'll try it again." This time the current was stronger. I said, "My left leg feels as though it is about to fall off the table." Moments later I felt someone lift my leg back onto the table. Then I heard the doctor say, "I want a few more color pictures, please."

More brain stimulation. "Doctor, that felt as though my left forefinger pointed inward." Dr. Jones repeated the experiment, then said, "Let me hear what Annette said during the stimulation." I heard my own voice and realized my words were being recorded. Immediately after, Dr. Jones said, "Annette, I am going to remove a small section of your brain which is causing some of your trouble."

Then I heard words which I shall never forget: "Annette, remember, just so much is in my hands."

A few minutes later came the clicking sound of metal as he put down the instrument he had used, and I knew the excision had taken place. I looked at the clock. It was 2:30. How much longer?

Dr. Jones said, "Annette, I'm going to stimulate again. Please tell me what you feel." I felt the current, and at that instant I felt my left eye turn inward. It was repeated. Then Dr. Jones said, "I am going to remove another small piece of brain."

At that crucial point I said, "Doctor, I have a funny feeling I've never had before. I'm afraid I'm going to have a seizure." Metal clicked as he laid aside his instrument. A few moments later I had the seizure, a small one.

"What kind of reading did you record?" Dr. Jones asked an assistant. The answer came, in medical terms.

Once more I felt the stimulating current go through my body. And this time I had a familiar, sickish feeling in the pit of my stomach.

Once again the doctor said, "Annette, I'm going to remove another affected bit of brain." And, speaking to his assistants, he explained how far into the brain he was going. He said that the Salt Lake City surgeon had excised at precisely the right spot, but had not gone this deep, fearing he would leave me paralyzed.

For the first time I felt true cutting pain momentarily. When it ceased I said, "If anybody ever says again there is no feeling inside the brain, Dr. Jones, don't believe him. I know better."

I kept saying, "I'm tired, Doctor. Please put me to sleep." He answered, "I'll bet you a quarter you'll fall asleep within the hour, Annette."

Then he said that he was about to make his third excision, and now he would touch the section of the brain that controls vision. For the first time, I said a silent prayer, asking God to steady Dr. Jones' hand. Then I heard him put down his scalpel. I could still see the anesthetist clearly—and I thanked God!

Dr. Jones said, "Still awake? I guess I owe you a quarter." The recording shows that I replied weakly, "Deduct it from my bill."

I was so tired I could hardly hear the voices around me. After a while the doctors began testing the reflexes of my arms and legs. Dimly I heard them say, "All four extremities have good reflex actions. No paralysis."

The anesthetist spoke: "Hold your arm steady, Annette, while we locate a vein." It meant the operation was over. Now they would put me to sleep to close my skull.

Exhausted, I glanced at the clock as I felt the needle going into my arm: 4:30 p.m. "No paralysis." All was well.

* * *

The kind of surgery performed on Miss Anselmo was quite unusual, undertaken only in certain rare, specific cases. For more than 99 percent of all epileptics it would be neither applicable nor beneficial. It should also be noted that the techniques described have changed, with progress in neurosurgery over subsequent years.

In Annette Anselmo's case, the operation was successful. On mild medication, she was now able to lead a full, active life with no restrictions on her activities. She still had seizures, usually mild and brief; but they came always at night, and only two or three times a year. The memory of her extraordinary experience was one not likely to fade.

"Good-By, Stephen"

by Abbie Blair

I am a social worker. Part of my work is with unwed mothers. Yesterday one of my girls surrendered her baby for adoption.

The day I first saw her she was standing in the doorway of the shelter saying good-by to her parents. They were about to return to their home in a well-to-do suburb in another state. Still fragile, though obviously pregnant, with dark auburn hair tumbling down her back, she looked even younger than her 16 years. She watched forlornly as the big car pulled away.

"Three months isn't forever," I said. "You'll be back in the world again."

For a moment she didn't answer. "It seems so far away— school, church, parties, dances. . . ." She sat down heavily, and was silent. Then, "I thought I loved him."

"I know."

We sat there for a few minutes.

"Now," I said, "we have a lot of talking to do. And you have a lot of thinking to do. You have a big decision to make."

"Yes," she said. "The baby." I nodded. "My mother says my aunt will take the baby, pretend she adopted it from an agency. That way I could still see him."

I looked at her.

She hurried on. "But I'm not going to do that. I'm going to give him up. It's not going to be easy—but I've already decided."

Every week when I came to see her we would talk it over,

241

but she did not change her mind. "It's the only thing to do," she would say, and she would put her hand on her stomach. "I can't do much for him, but at least I can do this."

I had taken down her social and medical history and forwarded it to the adoption agency so they'd know as much as possible about the baby's background. When we visited the agency, she came out shaken but calm. They had shown her the papers she would have to sign. She saw those words "final" and "irrevocable." She was very quiet all the way back to the shelter. But she did not change her mind.

"When the time comes, I will be able to do it."

And yesterday the day had come.

She walked slowly down the hall with her ten-day-old-son in her arms. "I've put on his best things," she said. "Blue is his color. Doesn't he look nice?"

He looked very nice. Sleepy, and contented as a kitten.

She said her good-bys at the shelter and we got into the car with the baby. She pulled the blanket closer about him and I started the motor.

We drove in silence for a while, I looking at the road, she looking down at her baby. "Stephen is such a nice name," she said. "Do you think they'll let him keep it?"

"No, dear. His new mother and father will want to choose their own name for him."

"Well," she said fiercely, "Stephen's his first name. He will always be Stephen to me."

She cuddled him for a while. "He's a real snuggler," she confided. "He just loves being held. See how he's smiling."

I looked. Stephen appeared to be regarding the world with myopic satisfaction.

She studied him carefully. "Stephen is a very pretty baby, isn't he? I mean—he really is, isn't he?"

I assured her I thought Stephen was one of the most appealing babies I had seen in a long time.

"You think his new parents will like him, don't you?" she asked suddenly. Then she answered. "Well, if they don't, they're just out of their minds. He's a real winner."

"Stephen is an absolutely darling baby," I said. "All you have to do is look at him to know that."

"You know, it makes me feel good to know my other babies will probably . . ."

She stopped abruptly and leaned toward me.

"Suppose, after I'm married, I can't have any children. Do you suppose I could adopt some?"

"I don't know why not," I said.

"I almost called you night before last," she announced.

"Oh?"

"Yes. But then I worked it out for myself. I heard about a wealthy couple who were looking for a baby. For a while I was awfully tempted. But then I thought, if these people are so anxious, why don't they go to an agency? I mean, suppose they just aren't the right people for my baby?"

"I think you were very wise," I said.

"And anyway," she said, hugging the baby to her, "money can't buy Stephen. He's not for sale."

At the agency we were shown into a pretty room with a beautifully decorated bassinet. She put the baby in the bassinet and took off his sweater, cap and booties. Stephen kicked his feet and waved his arms.

The agency worker came in with coffee. "The doctor is here to examine Stephen," she said. "Shall I take him now or would you like a little visit first?"

The girl put her hand to her son's face and caressed his cheek. "Could I have a few minutes?"

"Of course," said the worker, and went out again.

Time ticked away. I offered to leave Stephen's mother alone with him, but she asked me to stay.

The door opened again. "I think I had better take him now," the worker said. "Don't go. As soon as the doctor okays Stephen, we'll need your signature." The worker picked up the baby and walked briskly out of the room.

I looked at the girl. She was staring at the empty bassinet. For a few minutes neither of us said anything.

Then she said in a low voice, "If I could only cry. I've tried to. It would help a lot if I could cry."

"It will come when it will come," I reassured her.

"Do you think . . ." she said, and was silent. Then, "Do you think his new parents will tell him about me?"

"They won't know very much."

"But when he asks about me—why I gave him up. Will they tell him I loved him?"

"I'm sure they will tell him you did," I said.

And then the worker was back—without the baby. It was time to sign the papers. The worker put them on the table, with a pen. There were the words the girl knew: "I do hereby voluntarily, unconditionally, absolutely and irrevocably surrender the said child." And, "I expressly pledge not to interfere with the care of said child in any way, or allow or encourage anyone else to do so." The girl signed with a hand that was not too steady. The document was witnessed and notarized, and we were ready to leave.

"You'll let me know when Stephen goes into his permanent home, won't you?" the girl said.

"Don't worry," the agency worker replied. "I'll drop you a note as soon as he's placed. You won't know much more than that. We think it's the best way."

The girl nodded. "I just want to know he's all right. I want to know that for sure."

We went out to the street. Her parents were there, ready to take her home.

Her mother took my hand, her eyes full of tears. "You've all been so kind."

I looked from the mother to the girl. Her head was bowed and all the life seemed drained right out of her.

"Good-by dear," I said. "Good luck!"

The girl touched my arm and looked into my eyes for a minute without saying anything. Then they all got into their car and it pulled away.

I watched until it was out of sight. Then I started my own car and headed home.

Good-by, Stephen!

No Time for Fear

by Philip Yancey

The two young Canadians huddled close to the rusty steel heater. Malcolm Aspeslet, 19, and Barb Beck, 18, were on their longest date yet— a hike to Balu Pass, 6700 feet up in British Columbia's Glacier National Park. Yesterday the climb had seemed a pleasantly uncomplicated way to celebrate a day off from their hot, noisy kitchen work in the park lodge. The hike had gone smoothly until they reached the top. But there they had been unexpectedly caught in a freak snow flurry and forced to spend the night in one of the park's alpine cabins.

Now, next morning, the two sat yoga-style on the floor, talking and laughing. They had met two months before, and had spent many hours together. Both loved the mountains enough to spend their vacations doing kitchen work just to be near the Canadian peaks. It was the first day of October, 1971, and the summer season had just ended. There were no un-shuttered windows in the cabin, so periodically Malcolm would open the door and check weather conditions. About midmorning the snow had stopped, and the young couple began their descent hike. Barb, wearing slick-soled, knee-high fashion boots, kept slipping and falling on the ice.

The three-mile trail, marked with frequent switchbacks, followed a creek bed down the mountain. It took the couple only an hour to reach the halfway point. They stopped to rest for a minute, leaning against a bank of piled-up snow. The sun, out now, had warmed them, and both were wearing only sweaters, their coats tied around their waists. A nearby waterfall gurgled with newly melted snow; they dipped their hands in the cold water and playfully splashed each other. Then they started off again, Malcolm in the lead.

A hundred yards farther along the trail, Malcolm stopped short. Two bear cubs were playing in the creek gully, 20 yards to their right. The day before, they had seen a mother grizzly and two cubs. They had yelled and waved and watched through binoculars as the mother reared up and roared at them. That had been more funny than frightening, with a safe mile of distance separating them. But now a mother bear—maybe the same grizzly—could be just over the ridge, obscured by alder bushes.

Malcolm stood stiffly, trying to decide what to do. Perhaps they could sneak by quietly. But as he lifted his boot for the first step, the mother bear suddenly came charging over the ridge with a half-growl, half-scream of rage. Barb saw immediately that it was a grizzly—the silvertip fur glistened in the sunlight, and there was the characteristic hump on its back. *How can something that huge move so fast?* she thought, then felt herself being flung into a snowbank by Malcolm.

Malcolm saw the charging grizzly's open mouth. The bear was drooling flecks of foam and making short grunting sounds. A second before the bear was on him, he ducked. But one swat of the grizzly's paw knocked him senseless.

For a moment he went blank. When he raised his head he saw that he'd been thrown ten feet. The grizzly had found Barb. The girl was face down and motionless in the snow, and the giant beast was standing on her leg, gnawing near the back of her neck. Malcolm did not hesitate—there was no time for fear. Instinctively he grabbed a hunting knife from his belt and ran toward the bear, yelling. The mother bear stood over seven feet tall and probably outweighed him by 600 pounds. When he leaped on her back, she didn't even quiver.

Malcolm could hear the gnawing sound of teeth against bone. Crazed with anger and desperation, he plunged the knife clear to the handle into the grizzly's neck fur. He pulled himself higher on the thick hump back and slashed at her neck. Warm blood spurted. The grizzly let out a deafening roar and snapped her head backward. That quick head motion sent Malcolm's knife flying and broke his wrist.

Now the snarling grizzly turned full attention to Malcolm. She grabbed him with both paws and squeezed him against her chest. The smell of blood and bear nauseated him. The grizzly swatted at him with her huge claws. The first blow took off his hair in one piece like a wig, most of his scalp going with it. Then he was rolling over, clutched by the bear. The dizzying motions stopped when they reached the gully bottom. The bear raked his face repeatedly. As she bent to rip into his neck and shoulder with her teeth, Malcolm feebly jabbed with his fist at her sensitive nose. His jabs had no effect.

Malcolm closed his eyes. *It's all over,* he thought, and stopped struggling. Incredibly, almost as soon as he stopped moving, the grizzly let go. She swatted him once more, then scraped dirt and twigs over him and lumbered away.

At first Malcolm wasn't sure he was even alive. He was lying half in and half out of the creek. He felt no pain except a throbbing in his wrist. Slowly he wriggled out of the creek and called weakly, "Barb, are you okay?"

Barb, afraid the grizzly was still around, didn't answer. She crawled to the edge of the gully and saw a bloody clump of hair. Then she saw Malcolm, half-buried. His face had been split with a wicked slash, and the right side of it was peeled back to reveal muscle and sinew—and a nearly severed eye. She yelled, "Malcolm, hold on—I'm going for help." Tossing her coat to him, she started running toward the lodge.

Malcolm lay still for a while, trying to take inventory of his injuries. His wrist wouldn't move and must be broken. One kneecap had been torn off, and he couldn't feel any front teeth with his tongue. He could partially see out of one eye, but was afraid to turn his head because he saw loose facial skin hanging down. He felt no revulsion, just an aching hope that it hadn't happened, that it was all a nightmare.

Spotting his knapsack up toward the trail, he determined to reach it and use it as a bandage. Tediously, he dragged himself up backward. His one good eye kept sticking shut, and periodically he'd have to stop and open it with his good hand. Finally, he reached the knapsack and lay back, physically drained from the exertion. He prayed, and wondered whether he would live, and what he'd look like if he did.

Meanwhile, Barb, her arm slashed and her hair flecked with blood, had run along the winding, switchback trail to the lodge.

Staggering into the lobby, she cried, "A grizzly got Malcolm! He can't walk! Help. . . ." And then she burst into sobs. People appeared from nowhere—wardens, fellow workers, lodge guests.

The first that Malcolm heard of his rescuers was the static of a walkie-talkie. He had sat propped against a stump for an hour and a half, and was still conscious. Warden Gordy Peyto, Malcolm's good friend, ran to him. "Well, pal," he said. "I always end up looking after you. How you doin', man?"

"I'm okay, but kinda hungry," Malcolm replied gamely. "Guess I really did it this time, Gordy. I think my wrist is broken." Gordy sucked in his breath. He saw a bloodless white head. The bear's swipe had cleanly lifted off the scalp and blood vessels, exposing a layer of tissue next to the skull.

Ned Clough, a first-aid attendant, wrapped Malcolm's face and the chewed gashes on his legs in gauze, then strapped him in a stretcher. They radioed for a rescue helicopter to pick him up at a clearing down the trail and take him to Queen Victoria Hospital in Revelstoke.

Surgery began with a seven-hour emergency operation. The surgeon put in more than 1000 stitches. "Restoring Malcolm's face was like putting a jigsaw puzzle together," one attending doctor later said.

Malcolm was then moved to a hospital in his hometown, Edmonton. He remembers little of the first weeks. He was under heavy sedation, and his mind wandered endlessly, drifting between dreams and semiconsciousness. He underwent 41 skin-graft operations.

In time, life began to look up. Doctors assured Malcolm that he would soon look fine, after the grafts were finished and the rolls of gauze came off. But one day close to Christmas, when the nurse was changing his bandages and was called away momentarily, Malcolm edged over to the bathroom mirror for the first look at himself. It almost made him sick. The doctors had tried to repair damage by constructing a nose from arm muscle and by grafting skin from his leg across his face. He had no hair, and thick scars crisscrossed one side of his face. The skin was still puffy and an ugly shiny-red.

That one incident started a rejection period lasting weeks. Malcolm refused to see his parents or friends, hating the world and himself. He couldn't bear the thought of people's stares. He ignored the growing stack of letters from Barb. How could anyone love a freak?

But Barb wouldn't give up. She wrote Malcolm faithfully—five to seven letters a week—even though he never responded. Malcolm's friends who knew Barb wrote her about his self-pity. "He simply can't believe you care about him, looking the way he does," they told her.

One day, shortly after his Christmastime despondency, Barb surprised Malcolm by walking into his hospital room after a journey of 775 miles. The two spent long hours together, talking across the barriers of bandages. Malcolm was stubbornly aloof. But her presence forced him to reminisce about the good times he had shared with her. *Maybe she does love me*, he thought. *After all, I'm the same person she said she loved last summer.*

Whatever doubts Malcolm had were dispelled in January, when he received a marriage proposal in the mail. "It's a leap year," Barb explained demurely.

Her persistence began to pay off. Though Malcolm would not answer her proposal, he did promise to visit her. In February 1972, five months after the accident, an unsteady, slim figure with a badly scarred face and one arm in a cast stepped off a train at Fort Langley, near Vancouver. Malcolm was promptly smothered by a delighted Barb.

And a few days later she had her answer. Malcolm drove her to the town of Langley and stopped at a jewelry store so they could choose an engagement ring. Barb, smiling and crying simultaneously, was overwhelmed. On July 21, 1973, they were married.

Meanwhile, Malcolm discovered that word of his exploit had spread all across Canada. (To his surprise: it had never occurred to him that he could have run and left Barb with the grizzly, and he had never seen his actions as heroic.) The Royal Humane Society, London, awarded him the Stanhope Gold Medal for performing the bravest deed reported that year in the entire Commonwealth; he received the Gold Medal for bravery from the Royal Canadian Humane Association, and the Carnegie Medal for heroism from the Carnegie Hero Fund Commission. He was also chosen for the Canadian government's Star of Courage, and was asked to go to Ottawa to receive that medal from Queen Elizabeth during her state visit to Canada.

So it was that Malcolm and Barb Aspeslet spent their honeymoon, at government expense, in Canada's capital. In an elaborate ceremony, Malcolm received his Star of Courage from the hand of the Queen of England.

In 1976, Malcolm and Barb were living in Surrey, near Vancouver, where he ran the kitchen at the Newton Inn and she had an office job. Except for scars and harrowing memories, they seemed little different from any of Vancouver's other young couples. Malcolm's twisted facial features were being improved by surgery each year (doctors restored his eye, but he still had difficulty using it), and he had recently received an unusual appropriation of $2035 from the British Columbia Department of Health for his first permanently attached hairpiece.

Sometimes people ask Barb if she married Malcolm out of a sense of obligation. She says, "I loved Malcolm before the accident, and I always will love him. Handicaps should be accepted in life. Scars don't change the person."

"There Is Nothing in This World He Cannot Do"

by Frances Runner

It is a picture that haunted us for months. Jolting our spirits. Chilling our spines. Dreaming it, we moaned suddenly in our sleep. The picture is of a tall ponderosa pine. Lying in it, precariously supported by its sloping branches, 20 feet above ground, is the body of a boy. Several feet above him are two black wires. The child is Chuck. Age 11. Our son.

The air rings with the shrieks of Chuck's friend, Tom, clinging among the branches of another tree nearby. Tom has just seen smoke curl up from Chuck's blue jeans toward the Colorado sky. He has just watched Chuck crumple over backward, free of the wires.

That is the picture. But it is no longer a terrifying image. For now we can see it as one of many pictures in a series, a small part of a growing story—a life story.

Immediately, in response to Tom's screams, his parents and his brothers came dashing out of their house. A big brother looked up where Tom was pointing, and ran to the tree. His mother implored him as he ran: "My God! There are *wires* in the tree! Don't touch them!"

But the boy was already climbing the tree, shouting as he climbed: "Be ready to catch him! He's slipping off the branch! He's falling . . ."

And so the little body fell, crackling through the branches.

And into the arms of Tom's father, braced for the catch beneath the tree.

It was snatched, then, the limp body, and laid face-down among the rocks and pine needles. Tom's mother started pumping on the back ribs in a terrible urgency: "Out goes the bad air, in comes the good . . ."

Shouts carried through the woods. "Get Charlie and Fran!" "Call an ambulance!" "Call for oxygen!"

Seconds passed. Minutes. And then the body stirred. "He's alive! Thank God, he's alive!"

Those were the precious words we heard as we ran up through the woods to the little group clustered there beneath the tall ponderosa.

He was alive. But he kept lapsing back into a sort of sleep. Or was it death? His eyes would open. His gray face would twist with pain. And then again—oh, God!—his eyes would close, his face would slip quietly into repose. So still! Immediately, then, his back would be pumped again. "Out goes the bad air, in comes the good . . ."

As we heard the distant sirens heralding the arrival of the doctor, the boy was able to get some words out. "Why can't I let go of the wire? Why *can't* I let go?"

These things he kept muttering as the doctor medicated and probed.

The boy's charred right hand looked like a burnt, clenched eagle's claw. The doctor was gently encasing it in a sort of chicken-wire cage. (Do doctors always carry chicken wire in their little black bags?)

The left leg of his jeans was now cut off with long, shiny shears. There, high on his thigh, was a ghastly charcoal-black gash. It was as if it had been cauterized with a blowtorch—at its base we saw a glimmer of white bone.

Several hours later, we walked slowly beside Chuck's cart as it was wheeled from the operating room. "I'm sure we can save the leg," the doctor said. "But the hand—I don't know." He was shaking his head. "There's nothing more to do about it tonight. We have to wait."

The ring of the telephone sliced through our sleep. The clock said 1:10. Dark. Cold. I listened, heart pounding, to

Charlie's voice. "But the hemorrhage is stopped? Yes, doctor. If you say it has to be done, we'll sign the papers."

Charlie hung up. I waited. But the word was not spoken. That terrible word. It hung, ugly and unsaid.

It *had* to be said. I began to grope among the clothes in our closet. I took a deep breath. And then I made myself ask out loud: "What does one wear to an amputation?"

It was now five o'clock. Pale dawn. We were at home again. Charlie went immediately to bed. I paced. I sobbed like a child. When the eastern sky began to glow with color, I telephoned Tom's mother. Tom's mother—who had pumped life and heartbeats and breathing back into Chuck's lifeless body the week before. "It's happened, Ev! It's happened," I wailed.

Her jeep roared up the hill in minutes. We embraced in a torrent of tears. Five minutes of anguish. No other awareness. Pure grieving.

Then, suddenly, Ev stood up. "All right!" She said it sharply. "No more! This is your last tear. Your last sob. The very last shred of pity you are going to feel! I am going to tell you something. And what I'm going to say to you I want you to *think* all day. I want you to say it out loud. Over and over. As often as you can. I want you to say it to Charlie as soon as he wakes up. I want you to say it to Chuck when he comes out of the anesthesia. I want you to think it, and say it, and think it, and say it, until you *feel* it! *Because it is true!*"

She said it slowly, knowingly: *"There is nothing in this world he cannot do!"* Then she said it again. "There is nothing in this world he cannot do." And again.

So. Those were the words Charlie heard when his alarm went off at seven. "There is nothing in this world he cannot do, Charlie! Nothing he cannot do! It's true, Charlie."

And those were the words we repeated again and again to Chuck—lying asleep—pale and moist and white-gowned. *"There is nothing in this world you cannot do, Chuck! There is nothing in this world you cannot do!"*

Charlie said it quietly, again and again, as I did. And every time we said it we believed it a little more. More and more and more.

And then Chuck was fully awake at last, and looked with wonder and dismay at the pitiful little white-bandaged stump of his right arm. Those were the words he heard as he looked at it, and touched it and moved it around, experimenting.

The words released a flood of inquiry. As the day flicked by, he asked a thousand crucial questions. You mean I will learn to tie my own shoes? I can learn to write with my left hand? He asked the nurses, the interns, the orderlies, the doctors. He asked us, again and again. You mean they play *golf?* You mean there really is a *watchmaker* with *two* artificial hands?

And the answers to all his questions allowed him to believe. He came to believe those words. And they are true.

It took us a while to get used to it, the artificial arm. Pink plastic, shiny steel, nylon cords, leather and plastic around-the-shoulders-in-a-figure-eight harness. A veritable miracle of technological compensation.

Often he hung it on something—the doorknob in the bathroom, the pencil sharpener in the hall, the stair railing, or the post of his top-bunk bed. But frequently it would come to rest on the can opener in the kitchen, or the fireplace mantel, or in the middle of the couch. Eventually, of course, we all got used to it. It was part of the household—like everybody's spectacles, and the bikes that leaned up against the house outside the front door.

One night, as dinner was about to be dished up, I put some bread in the oven to toast. Charlie was leaning against the refrigerator, a cocktail in hand. Juni was setting the table. Tim and Chuck sat at the kitchen counter, legs crooked around the rungs of their stools, ravenously hungry, impatient.

Suddenly, black smoke billowed out of the oven door. I dashed for hot pads. Charlie ran to the drawer in the cupboard where we keep our tea towels. Tim leaped from his stool to the towel rack. Juni came running at us with paper napkins. Then Chuck vaulted over the counter, snake-hipped around the interference, and arrived, skidding, at the oven. He reached in with his hook and clamped it over the grill. He carried the smoking thing, unruffled and unhurried, and dumped it in the dishpan. Zzzzzzzzzzz . . .

Perhaps two whole seconds passed. We all stood stock-still, our frantic motions arrested—no, frozen—by the surprise of this mock-heroic feat. And then Tim expressed our collective relief: "Show-off!"

Chuck himself used to take a sort of perverse delight in people's questions and evident curiosity. One day, after leaving the arm at the prosthetist's for some minor adjustments, we went to a supermarket. As almost always happened, a group of little kids straggled up and down the aisles behind us, gazing at Chuck's empty sleeve—curious, interested. One of them finally ventured, shyly, "What happened to your arm?"

Chuck stopped. He looked at the empty shirt-sleeve, then directly at the questioner, then back at his sleeve. And called out in a loud voice, "Hey, Mom! I musta lost my *arm!*" And he began to make a big thing out of looking for it—down in the aisle on his knees, digging in the shopping basket, searching the shelves. The kids, scared to death, hightailed it back to their mothers.

Chuck had been a dry-fly fisherman, fully bitten by the sport. Now, for hours at a time, he would stand out in the middle of our dirt road and cast with his left hand into an automobile tire 50 feet uphill. It was a new game. Deadly serious. But challenging and fun, too, for a lad who had learned to stick out his chin and begin on things.

Tim helped him a lot. Pitching balls for batting practice was a neverending function of the older brother. The help was neither graciously nor grudgingly offered: it was just there. And Chuck worked with a dogged and increasingly rewarding determination to perform well.

We were zooming along up Berthoud Pass. It was our first ski excursion since the accident.

As usual, the kids were making a terrific racket—shouting, bickering, screeching with laughter. I was working hard at their not discovering that something was wrong. I was trying terribly hard not to weep out loud. Charlie was silent, looking straight ahead. Our conflict: rope-tow versus chair-lift.

I hadn't even thought of the matter until a few miles back. Then it had come over me in a great despairing wave. "Charlie!" I whispered. "We'll have to spend a lot of money today. Did you bring enough?"

"How come?" he asked, obviously unaware of the problem.

"Our rope-tow days are over. We'll have to buy chair-lift tickets. For Chuck! And we must not treat him differently from the others."

"Nonsense!" said Charlie, eyes straight on the road.

"But, *Charlie!*" It was essential to keep our voices to murmurs. "He can't handle a rope tow with *one arm!*"

"Oh, yes, he can."

"But, Charlie!"

"Stop worrying." I was dismissed.

The noise in the back seat grew louder and louder. The boys were now daring each other to feats of wild speed and reckless courage. Down the Slalom Run they were going to race.

Tears were now streaming down my face. I groped about for words.

Finally, the words came to me. "Charlie," I whispered. "Charlie, we *can't* subject the kid to failure!"

I was certain that the statement comprised the whole argument for the chair-lift. Absolutely convincing.

"Yeah," he said. "But..." And I knew that now *he* was seeking the right words.

We rounded a horseshoe curve and began the steep ascent up the pass. He shifted gears. The engine sound crescendoed in the climb.

He found them.

"It's even *more* important," he said, "it is most important of *all* that we don't deprive him of any chances for... victory!"

Those were the shining-proud, father-instinct words.

Of course!

For a moment I had forgotten that there is nothing in this world he cannot do.

Okay.

So!

Feeling like myself again, I turned around and told the kids to cut the racket.

Clear the Road for Nancy!

by Jim Bishop

Everything was right for Nick. He had a house (with a mortgage); a tall, blond wife named Nancy who thought he was the greatest man in the world; he had Vicky, age 12, growing up as stately as her mother. Then there was that healthy, running, jumping terror of the school yard, James Robert Nickerson, eight years old. Nick himself was a sergeant of police in the Dade County Public Safety Department, working out of the Perrine, Fla., substation, earning a good salary.

Nick was 35, six-feet-two-inches lean, with ruddy face and black hair. He was easy-moving, modest, a sweet-talking cop who couldn't be tough unless he was goaded. Everything was right for Sergeant Nickerson. The right job; the right woman; the right children.

Under the tall modesty of the man he not only loved the serene blondness of Nancy; he admired her for having the things he didn't. She was outgoing. She bowled with him and sometimes beat him. She worked as a volunteer at the John Knight Children's Center for Retarded Children. She contributed extra money each week working as a barmaid at a local club.

Maybe it was too good. Some couples become alarmed when the road is smooth over a long period of time. Nick felt no alarm, Nancy felt no elation—this is the way it was meant to be.

One March evening in 1969 she was behind the bar at the club and she picked up a can full of empties and fainted. A friend of Nick's ran around to lift her. Nancy said she was sorry. It was nothing. The perspiration on her forehead and upper lip was cold. The friend had to argue to drive her home.

Nick said he would call the family physician. No, Nancy said. It was just one long lousy headache.

A week later, she was in the kitchen at 2 a.m. and fell. Nick no longer listened to Nancy. He phoned an internist, who thought the symptoms seemed akin to polio and said to take her to the hospital. He'd meet them there.

The big attractive girl—just 29—said that everyone was making a fuss about nothing. Two doctors worked up an assortment of tests. It wasn't polio. It wasn't a cerebral hemorrhage. It wasn't a brain growth. It wasn't heart. What was it? Nancy was sent on to Baptist Hospital for a brain tracing. Both arms were punctured and the doctors watched the flight of the injected fluid through the arteries, up behind the shoulders and, climbing the neck, into the brain, and then the rapid crisscross of the lighted substance through the road map of the mind. The arteries, illuminated by the white substance, looked like strands of spaghetti. Suddenly both lights seemed to fall into a lake.

The doctors tried the test again. Nancy had an artery with a weakened wall which, like a blister on the inner tube of a tire, was stretching.

"She has an aneurysm, Nick," a doctor said. "We've got to go in now."

"What's an aneurysm?" Nick asked. The doctor drew a diagram. "We're going into the brain and we're going to clamp off that weakened artery." No one had to tell Sgt. James Nickerson that it was going to be a delicate job for several doctors and God.

He insisted that he be the one to explain it to Nancy. Her blond hair was a long pale flame on a white pillow. He told her. She told him, holding his big hand in hers, that she was in such pain that the doctors could start right away. But first Nick brought in the children to see her, and Nancy came up off the pillow and hugged them tight.

The children were waxen with fright. She smothered them to her breast and said, "It's nothing. Be good until I get home." They promised. Nick took them home and then visited a church. He prayed in a whisper.

There was a team of five doctors. At Baptist Hospital on March 17, Nancy, softly sedated, was wrapped in a cooling

blanket to lower her temperature to 80 degrees, then taken into
the operating room. The beautiful long blond hair had been
taken off, and the face was bland as the masked men began
to drill holes in the skull and to saw through the bone between
them.

A big piece of skull was lifted out and the dome of diffused
light overhead showed the pulsing aneurysm on the brain. The
doctors worked silently and carefully as if they were defusing
a time bomb.

But the aneurysm burst. Blood began to pulse out. Trans-
fusions had been made ready and two doctors with sponges
began to sop up the blood to find the rupture. From noon until
9 p.m. the doctors worked on Nancy and put 12 pints of blood
into her to replace losses. They found the rupture and sealed
it, and two neurosurgeons wheeled her to intensive care.

One of the doctors saw the police sergeant. "Nick," he said,
"she hasn't got much of a chance. Everything went wrong."

Nick trotted alongside the cart as though love itself could
restore consciousness. "Nancy!" he said. The tired girl surprised everybody. She opened her eyes and said, "Hi, honey!"
Then she lapsed into a coma.

For 18 days Nick came to sit beside his sleeping Nancy
three times a day. She had bandages around her head and green
plastic tubes everywhere. On April 4, Good Friday, he thought
her eyes followed him around the room. "Honey," he said,
"do you know me?" She had a tracheotomy tube in her throat,
and talking was a chore. "Yes," she said, and smiled real big.
"You're my Nickerson." Then she lapsed back into the deep
sleep.

Nick began to hope. He drove to the Church of the Little
Flower and began to make all the promises no man can keep.
God kept putting a thought into his mind that Nick didn't want
to remember. A year ago Nancy had said, "I've been reading
about these heart transplants. Nick, if anything happens to me,
let me help somebody else." He shut it out.

Nancy went into cardiac arrest. An oscillating machine with
a greenish wavy line began to order her heart to beat. At 5:30
a.m. a doctor phoned. "Nick," he said. "Get over here quick."
The big man hurried to his wife's side and her eyes were open
and unblinking.

"The damage is irreversible," a doctor told him. "Would
you agree to a heart transplant?"

Nick stayed with the question until 4:30 p.m., then he said

yes and his head fell between his knees. He was giving his wife away.

The oscillating machine kept Nancy's heart going on the 20-mile ambulance ride to the Miami Heart Institute. She was taken to a big squarish room with little curtained booths. In one was a 55-year-old man, dying for want of a heart. "Your wife," the doctors said, "is clinically dead." Nick looked at the green face of the heart machine and saw no wavy lines, just a straight one. Sixteen doctors waited to give a man her heart. Another patient, in another curtained booth, was dying for want of a kidney. A blind woman, age 65, needed one eye. So did another, 35.

The man dying of heart disease could not wait. He died. Another man got Nancy's heart, and it functioned for a while in his chest. A second patient got a kidney from Nancy. The two women each received an eye. Sergeant Nickerson had given his Nancy away, and now the salt tears came. They had loved together and laughed, and now she was a cold shell without eyes or heart or kidney.

At the funeral, 60 policemen showed up in uniform. There were 12 motorcycles. One of the men said, "Sergeant, what can we do for you?" He asked them the same thing he had asked God: "Just clear the road for my Nancy."